WHERE I LAST SAW YOU

WHERE I LAST SAW YOU

GRACE SMOKOWSKI

Bloomington, IN   authorHOUSE™   Milton Keynes, UK

AuthorHouse™
1663 Liberty Drive, Suite 200
Bloomington, IN 47403
www.authorhouse.com
Phone: 1-800-839-8640

AuthorHouse™ UK Ltd.
500 Avebury Boulevard
Central Milton Keynes, MK9 2BE
www.authorhouse.co.uk
Phone: 08001974150

First published by AuthorHouse 9/5/2006

ISBN: 1-4259-4278-4 (sc)

Printed in the United States of America
Bloomington, Indiana

This book is printed on acid-free paper.

For My Parents
who taught me how
to live the dream.

CONTENTS

"Truth is revealed in time; lies fade away to nothing."
—Marie

LACKAWANNA, NEW YORK

Truncated afternoon shadows of Saint Barbara's Church bell tower and dome shielded lawns from early autumn heat. We were standing on scorching blacktop in the parking lot behind church, Mom, Dad and I, waiting to meet the tour group with which we would be spending the next two weeks, for better or worse, traveling Europe.

Nerves ruled the departure as we were ready an hour early to soothe them. From being ready at home to being ready while waiting on the bus in the church parking lot designated for assembly, Dad, and residually Mom, was in a state of nervous readiness. The two-hour ride from Lackawanna, just south of Buffalo, to Toronto was just enough time for Dad's nebulous worries of customs and airplanes to turn into muscle twinging physical maladies. The destination is the experience in Dad's mind, not the journey. The journey is the frustrating, bothersome, exorbitant price of the experience of the destination.

The tour bus approached the Peace Bridge, the bridge connecting Buffalo, New York with Fort Erie, Ontario, Canada. Its arches heralded

1

the way. A perky young blonde lady entered the bus for customs and inspection. After a few moments of chatting with the driver, she wished the group to have a great time and with a general wave of hand was gone, off to the next bus or truck behind. Peacefully, cheerfully we crossed the bridge.

ABOVE THE ATLANTIC, FLIGHT FROM TORONTO TO WARSAW

Once in the Toronto airport, I had the wherewithal to check all bags for all of us-Dad, Mom, Marie and I. That saved quite a bit of hassle for Dad, as each maneuver in the process of traveling is a mountain of anxiety for him. Matthew, our light-hearted tour coordinator, passed in front of us with a wheelchair full of luggage, pushing it as if it were cart or dolly. I asked him of it to which he responded that it might come in necessary one day. Unfortunately going through the metal detectors was not as easy. Dad kept buzzing the machine alarms, although his pockets were emptied on first pass. With each rush through the gate he became more and more agitated. At the third pass he had his belt off and his boxer tops exposed; all to discover a forgotten tic-tac container in his vest pocket was the culprit. Curse those foil labels on tic tacs! He almost had to take a nitro pill over it, let alone reorganize his drawers.

Even though there was almost an hour before flight, Dad would only sit at the gate, ready for boarding as soon as announced. Others from our loose group went to eat at a café or shop in one of the many stores along the concourse. Mom and I chose to stay and sit with Dad, calming him slightly with mild, benign conversation.

Across from the rows of seats were a coffee shop and a souvenir shop. Between the stores was a cramped, dim access hallway. Crouched down against the right wall was a tall young man. He was barely perceptible in the shadows. What was he doing bent and hunched? I stared at him for several minutes like a dog staring at a door it wants to open. His back must have bothered him; he straightened it along the wall, revealing notebook on lap and pen in hand. Writing was good use of vacuous airport time. However, I was not brave enough to pull out my journal in large crowds, clever of him to find such a perfect spot of solitude amongst the masses. Where was he going and where did he come from? What needed to be written in that moment? I wanted to creep near him and look over his shoulder, but settled for staring at his light brown hair hovering over angled head and book. His hand strode fast over the clean page, blue ideas in gray light.

Marie approached us after having a beer with others from the group. The lady sitting next to me was knitting, another good use of airport time. The faded red scarf on her head hid her gray hair, yet nothing could hide her grin as Marie complimented her work: a hibiscus-colored square of taut needlework in interlocking circular pattern. She spoke some English but preferred Polish. Marie and Dad began to speak in Polish with her. She was from Warsaw and had visited relatives in Canada. Now it was time to go home. As they conversed, she continued to knit a square that would one day be an afghan, uniting with other loose time-filling squares in the bag at her feet. Dad understood her and had a pleasant time with the talkative, friendly lady. I looked to my secret hallway to discover the writing man had gone. His moment now past, I missed him.

Boarding the plane, we settled in seats but not in disposition. Dad wriggled in his seat. Mom reclined and shut her eyes. I slipped a page from my travel journal sleeve. It was a Polish encyclopedia page from nineteen hundred, a photocopy. On it was an entry highlighting the accomplishments of my ancestor, Wincenty Smokowski. Four generations could not separate me from his riveting portrait, inquisitive stare through glossy finish. On an attached page, there was a translation of the entry: Wincenty was an artist, professor and doctor of medicine who pioneered woodcutting technique as book illustration. Born in Wilne, Poland (presently in Lithuania), educated in St. Petersburg, Russia, resided in Warsaw, Wincenty wrote biographies of famous Polish figures in the nineteenth century as well as painted their portraits. The most astonishing fact reeled in my mind throughout the flight: he was the first Polish naturalist to sketch in nature, a Polish John Jay Audubon or possibly a Polish Thoreau, his contemporary. I ached to view one of these sketchbooks. However, the encyclopedia page did not reference where any of his works where located. And I did not have the time to research at home before the trip or to write to any libraries to inquire of their possible holdings.

The page came to me by chance, by miracle, as Mom would say. My Dad's cousin, Zenia, fancied genealogy and studied the Smokowski family line. Proclaiming Wincenty and his wife, a poet, the most interesting of her research, she perpetuated family rumor and myth that we descended from great artists. As children, this idea of artistic ascendants guided our creative endeavors, elementary school through college. My sister wrote a book report in high school on our genealogy, where Zenia supplied her with this encyclopedia page and translation. The report was enthusiastically received and then, as most childhood schoolwork, lost. Being very young at the time, I did not remember the details.

For a month before this trip, I contacted everyone in the family to track down the school report. No one had any idea where the report would be; most thought it long discarded. I contacted Zenia for the original document, only to find her ailing and physically unable to help. Three days ago my other sister Frances, who had just moved from Arlington, Virginia to Silver Spring, Maryland, found a copy of the encyclopedia page, not the full report, in a box of college painting supplies she had not opened for years. Yesterday I received a rush delivery of the page in hand. So begins my unplanned quest to learn more, to learn the truth. My faced beamed with possibility as I replaced the folded page in its protective sleeve before slipping the journal into backpack.

Jean and Charlotte sat in the row ahead of us. Through cushion and crevice we could hear their conversation, peering with slit vision. With permed hair dyed blonde, Jean had the demeanor of a refined businessperson, blouse and pants pressed to suit the attitude. Always polite, Jean smiled at me as she moved for more comfortable seating position. Charlotte was the more relaxed and flamboyant sister of the two, still proper, however, in every way. She wore her gray hair down and styled as if she were a famous news anchor on television. Charlotte, in her mid-seventies, broached the topic, although Jean was the older: you are getting old, honey, what if you die on this trip?

With objective tone, Jean explained that her family was instructed not to incur the expense of transporting her body for services at home. Simply, they were to bury her where she died, in the least expensive cemetery, with no formal service. Being a traveler at seventy-nine-years-old, Jean thought seriously about the matter. Charlotte agreed that that was the most practical course of action. If it came to it, Charlotte disclaimed, she would follow the same course of action. For they have both seen life and were not afraid to live it. These enlightened travelers would pursue sensible adventures, taking every event with a practical grain of salt. The eventuality of death was only one more possible event on the roster. I closed my eyes and hoped that Dad could not hear them speak. He did not flinch nor mention a word of their conversation. Dad was silent, blankly staring forward. That was not a good sign.

Luckily, nerves subsided with a comfortable glass of red wine for Dad and juice for Mom and for me. Dad was able to find the humor in the metal detector fiasco.

"When was the last time they had those machines calibrated?" he wondered, a witty joke for a scientist.

We had a calming sleep, although short. In eight short hours we had crossed the same ocean it took Piotr, Zenia's father, and Jan, Dad's grandfather, Polish teenagers moving to a new world, eight weeks to transmigrate by boat. A century and three generations apart, we are together in the spirit of discovery of something more of our selves and our world. Dreams mounted as tidal waves to new shores for Piotr, a boy of fifteen. His older brother Jan was not as fanciful; the voyage was necessary to escape trouble with the government, which was never explained to family or otherwise. The vices of the past were extinguished in waves of hope. I flew backward for the first time, the same jet stream of dreams propelling to know more of our past to understand my future. And now, the plane prepared for landing where the foreign adventures, new and awakening to the senses, will begin.

WARSAW, POLAND

After we settled into the hotel, Metropol, in Warsaw, the group rallied onto the bus for a tour of Old Town. Once in Old Town a guided walking tour began. A memorial of the last struggle of the people of Warsaw against Hitler, The Warsaw Uprising, started the tour. Large bronze statues, army green from oxidation, of men depicted the flight of desperate citizens into sewers to save their lives. Some men armed with makeshift weapons, some soldiers were storming out of the sewers, a valiant attempt to save country and city. Jozef Mazurkiewicz, a World War II veteran himself, stood pondering the sculptures for a long moment; the figures five times as big as himself. He stepped back; he walked forward, lurching. He got up close as if studying each figure individually, face-to-face. What could he be thinking? Was there a face of a lost friend recalled in bronze? Theresa allowed him this space.

Jozef Mazurkiewicz planned his retirement as an opportunity to relive ideal childhood: he could say exactly what he wanted to say, do what he wished to do; freedom suited him. When he was happy, he was ecstatic; when he was quiet, something big was brewing. His wife, Theresa, espoused the same philosophy and demeanor only manifested it in more subtle ways. They were true playmates in love with life and each other.

He continued the tête-à-tête with the uprising soldiers. Memories of being a young officer during the war must have been ignited. Flowers and candles at the base of the rising statues flickered and shimmied in the wind. Somber and steadfast bronze faces stared at Jozef Mazurkiewicz unapologetically. He rejoined the group, strangely glowing with private thoughts and recollections. I could not pry; I did not know him well enough, yet.

Warsaw is still recovering psychologically from the war. Remembrances are everywhere—in the foundation of a royal palace there are bullet marks from Nazi soldiers lining people for targeted slaughter. The Raczynski Palace was a hospital during the war. Antoni, the tour guide, told of Nazi soldiers killing all patients, first ones who could walk to their deaths at the wall; then ones bedridden were murdered where they lay. This palace wall, this small strip of bleached foundation was the most troubling and affecting of the tour. How could you continue to live and work with signs all around of former horrors? Isn't it painful to remember genocide? Memorials like that of the valiant soldiers soothe the mind, but don't bullet holes pock the face of rejuvenating Warsaw? Or is each mark a sacred remembrance of a stolen life, a family ripped? Each mark is a life extinguished, each hole originating from a well of prejudice. Yet the foundation did not falter, surface marred but structure resilient.

Most, if not all, of the buildings in Old Town were restorations of buildings destroyed in World War II. Old Town, the medieval section of town, essentially consisted of castle and town center encompassed by retaining wall and airy chasm. This retaining wall and parts of buildings were salvaged from war rubble and rebuilt. Steeples towered over the small square, creating a cozy sense of intimate space. Shops and restaurants occupied the ground floors of most of these buildings. Unfortunately the windy, cold autumn in late afternoon, early evening closed most of the stores before we could explore them.

Except for Kathy Jo and Doris, they could force open the door of any commerce center. They dove into an amber store while the rest of us toured a church. Naturally, Kathy Jo bought a stunning, outrageously expensive bracelet. Best friends and neighbors, Kathy Jo and Doris were merry widows traveling throughout the world on a perpetual shopping spree. Dressing as if they were half their age, in leopard prints and rhinestones, they tackled every metropolitan area with vivacity; or so they extolled on our first introduction in Warsaw.

Mist and wind sped through the streets. The dark brickwork of buildings capturing the last rays from cumulous clouds left little impression when shivering in thin clothes. The street continued but we channeled into a Gothic portal flanked by buttresses. A gypsy in many more layers than I stood beside the portal, head bowed, hand extended. I looked askance upon entering; Mom gave him a swata. The interior of the cathedral warmed, not from heated furnace but shelter from the elements.

And in St. John's Cathedral, my mind was first enraptured with medieval representation of stained glass windows. Dark, rich fragments of magenta, azure, and green lit upon my eyes like jewels held in a dusty cabinet. The only electric light in the cathedral was aimed at the copy of a Black Madonna, Our Lady of Czestochowa, gold encrusted. Colors of the waning natural light hovered over the Madonna's head, a moody impressionistic rainbow. Then, I knew that I was going to see and learn more than I ever expected, more than I could have ever imagined. The colors of awe crown experience.

We withdrew from the cavernous heat of the cathedral into the clammy streets once more. The avenue emptied into the courtyard of the Royal Palace where an obelisk stood guard. The group huddled at the obelisk, waiting for the bus to come and fetch us. The vista was spellbinding: the palace rolled down hill to river where a new spider webbed suspension bridge drew the rest of the city to it, like insects to web. The bridge entranced, a post-modern sculpture amidst medieval relics and communist blocks.

In my peripheral vision I could faintly see Dorothy and Norm to the left of the group. They were an unassuming quiet couple: he tall and robust; she small and mild, both were gray and sensible. Norm was the traveler; Dorothy was around the world dragged. While leaning on an aluminum cane with a tripod claw, Norm grew tired of the view and anxious for the return of the bus. He flipped an odd plastic plate hinged onto the side of the cane and sat on it. It was a cane-chair from some strange geriatric mail order catalogue. As much as the apparatus repulsed me, I was amused by it as well. Norm gloated as he sat on an aluminum tree staring at the vista of steel spider web.

The bus returned to the hotel to give us time to rest before the evening meal. Although tired, Marie and I could not rest. We were on a new continent waiting to be explored. There was no time to rest, too much needed to be experienced. Dad wanted the rest. Mom met Marie and I in the lobby and we ventured out to see what we could on foot.

I was pink, Pepto-Bismol pink, cotton candy pink. Wearing a pink cotton oxford with kaki cropped pants and walking shoes was like being dressed for Mardi Gras on Ash Wednesday. I stood out as a tourist, someone different. Among the masses of tasteful gray and brown suits, and subdued black dresses I was a carnival of color. It was a chilly afternoon; I could have used a sweater or jacket that I did not think to pack. The breeze with a crisp, cold sting in it felt like driving wind on skin. We aimed for the busy intersection where tunnels, as if connected for subways, channeled pedestrians underground to cross the roads.

Under the street we ambled, interrupting the hurried pace of the crowds rushing to catch bus and train. The pedestrian circle under the street was lined with shops and fast food counters. Slowly with no intentions besides viewing everything, we browsed shoe shop and candy kiosk, newsstand and Polish McDonald's. We sallied into a clothing store the size of a closet. It had a variety of gray and black coats and capes. I considered buying one. I was that cold. Mom convinced me that we were heading into the sunshine of Rome, where heavy jackets were not necessary. If the weather remained cold when we return to Warsaw, then contemplate buying a jacket. She was right. We thanked the clerk for showing us several different capes and departed. Marie was already nosing the pastry at a small lunch counter two shops down.

As Mom and I proceeded to Marie's side, many people passed in opposite direction. One middle-aged lady in a black suit and gray cape brushed by me, looking into my eyes while wagging her right index finger, saying forcefully, "Too bright. Too bright!"

I was shocked, wide-eyed, mouth agape. A sophisticated stranger reprimanded me for my external appearances. This was the first English statement I heard from a native Pole, other than our guide or hotel personnel. Mom thought it was amusing, free critique from a fashionable lady. My after-shock led to laughter. With no intention I was already causing a stir. With no intension, I usually cause stirs.

We emerged from the pedestrian underpass and walked past a large clothing shop, the size of a department store. The windows were dressed with the latest fashion: beige scarves draped over gray suits, black wool capes over sleek black dresses, and the most avant garde, navy blazer over beige linen suit. This is the new old, the historical modern, the communist history meshed with new capitalism. I indeed am too bright today, by these standards. Turning back, we retraced our steps to land in the Metropol Hotel lobby with a short time to dress for dinner. An olive green shirt, black pants and black shoes seemed appropriate.

Marie and I sat in the lobby, entertaining ourselves with idle chatter and brochures advertising events, exhibits, and other attractions of Warsaw until the group met for dinner. On second thought, Marie wanted a jacket and ambled to the room to retrieve one. I sat on a lobby sofa alone, observing through a picture window the locals rushing to and from train station and bus stop. A lanky, debonair man entered the building. His unpretentious demeanor reinforced the sincerity of his brown-eyed glance. I greeted him; he smiled and bowed his head. This was Piotr, the twenty-three-year-old native cousin of Joe and Harry Porok. They had been acquainted through the Internet on a genealogical search and were scheduled to reunite with family long departed, starting with Piotr in Warsaw. Piotr would travel with the group through Gdańsk, fraternizing with his newfound American cousins.

We gathered for a bus ride through Warsaw at night on the way to the restaurant: lamplight strewn historic light onto cobblestone sidewalks and medieval streets. I could imagine ancient carts pulling wares to market. I could imagine regal ladies strolling with suited gentlemen in top hat. Shadowed allies beaconed secret rendezvous of filtered rays. All was as exciting as living in a dream without the threat of daylight squelching it.

The group ate dinner at a traditional Polish restaurant called Restauracja Polska. Long candlelit banquet tables nestled comfortably under dark wood columns and exposed beams. Crests decorated the walls, catching the romantic lighting from the massive chandelier in the middle of the room. Dancers dressed in traditional folk costume paraded from the side room into the main room and entertained the banquet hall filled with tourists—some from Ukraine, some from Germany, a small group of ladies from Brazil, most from the States.

The first course was white borscht, excellent. The main entree was fine: pork roast with a cured plum at the center of each cut with a plum sauce, buttered redskin potatoes, and braised cabbage. Dad enjoyed both our servings of pork while I enjoyed an extra slice of homemade rye bread still warm. And for dessert, a beautiful cheesecake with raisins in it and a crumb crust. Although raisins in cheesecake first seemed strange, the supple textures and flavors complimented each other well.

Marie exchanged her cheesecake for four perogi: two cheese perogi and two pork perogi. With the appreciation of a newly released prisoner's first meal, Marie gobbled those perogi without frill. The carefully crimped edges of perogi recalled Nana's touch: aged fingers with bulging knuckles painstakingly pinching edges of newly filled perogi closed. After many where made and tire set into hands, a fork was used instead of fingertips. Potato, cheese, and, Nana's favorite, prune perogi would fry with butter and onions into a caramelized glaze of traditional happiness. And right now that is what we felt: the handmade traditional happiness of being in the land of family legend.

If this meal were a sign of dinners to come, Dad would be in heaven for the next couple weeks. Jozef Mazurkiewicz relished every morsel.

Peg and Don, across from me, were like honeymooners exchanging whispers of succulent pleasures, although married for thirty-five years. The reedy couple was particular and refined, highly selective in what they praised or valued. Don was a retired city councilman and Peg was a real estate agent for pleasure. Doris and Jo Ann loudly pronounced it the best meal of their lives.

When the dancers resumed after a short break, they again sang folk songs while each dancer exhibited one's finest steps: the ladies slapped heals and were swung rapidly by their partners, then the men formed a circle and performed low Russian-style kicks. For the next song, each dancer chose a partner from the dining visitors. Doris, at the head of the table, was grabbed to dance with the leading man. Tucked in a corner I could not be reached; thankfully I participated as observer only. Doris loved it though, jubilant through the entire song although she did not know the words or the steps. It was a folk courting song. Jozef Mazurkiewicz knew the words and sang along in Polish, crooning to his fair Theresa. Dad and Don were interpreting for those of us who did not know Polish well enough to understand.

In jovial spirit, I relayed the subway story of being called "too bright." Mom added too much. When I was a child, Dad would take us to visit his work friend, Stan, and his family respectively. Stan had twins, a boy and girl, my age. We liked to play, but by the end of the game one of them would say, "your eyes are too big." I was a small girl with big brown eyes, still am, but now have glasses to conceal them. My brothers picked up on this saying one visit and extrapolated, calling me the "too much girl." Not only were my eyes too big, I used too much soap to wash the dishes, or I piled too much frosting on the cake. What ever I did, my proportions were incongruous. This familial concept of myself has followed me into adulthood. For once I wished to be in a place, a state of being, where too much was just enough, eyes just the right size. Yet, then, I would be as everyone else and what fun would that be?

At the table behind us sat two couples from New Jersey. It was their last day before flying home. They had spent a month touring Russia, Ukraine, and Poland on their own. Their tour group of four maneuvered with no set plan, no reservations. Recalling all their adventures, they agreed unanimously that Poland was the best part of the trip. Poland has the culture and history of Eastern Europe with the comforts of Western Europe, they explained. An early morning flight would not wring this happy group from their banquet seats. There were many people to meet and more food in which to indulge. With an exchange of good wishes and farewells, we parted.

Light dripped like honey from streetlamp to wet pavement. This golden glow intoxicated as much as food and wine. Everything was new. At every corner a new experience awaited, something different to be seen.

Back at the hotel, Marie and I congregated in Kathy Jo and Doris's room to debate the authenticity of the bracelet. Doris made an off comment about her daughter mistakenly buying a necklace of plastic amber, a fake marketed as real. This agitated Jo Ann to the point where no amount of reassurance would console her doubting mind. Doris regretted her comment, too late.

Then an idea struck me. I telephoned Dad to come down into the fray because we were rambling through briars of authentication. Dad reassured Jo Ann that from his standpoint as a chemist and physicist it was real and rare. The hotel room did not provide a space to conduct an experiment. If the amber floated in a tank of chemically treated salt water, then it is real. Fake amber sinks, plastic heavier than amber. By the eye of a scientist, it was authentic, Dad proclaimed. His professional opinion assuaged. Our consensus was that it was indeed real, if not expensive in any country, most likely real. Our reassurances then augmented its significance. She willingly paid the toll of dreams, of connection to an illusive homeland as she begged admittance with expensive baubles. She would enjoy the bracelet regardless of unverifiable quality, as a lovely piece of jewelry.

Overtired, we all went back to our respective rooms to sleep, finally.

ptember 11,

"The weather patterns of the States effect Europe within days."

—Mom

ABOVE ITALY

THE HEAVY CLOUD cover of the morning did not effect the temperature, pleasantly mild. The smaller group of nineteen tourists heading to
Rome ate a late breakfast in the hotel restaurant. The Prorok Brothers
and cousin Piotr were finishing their breakfast when we entered. Piotr
spoke little English, however ventured to communicate his emotions
through dramatic facial expressions. Now he smiled grandly as we
wished them a wonderful trip. Piotr would be their dapper personal
tour guide, showing the brothers Poland. A group of six flew to L'Wów,
Ukraine; this group included our trip coordinator, Matthew. Two other
couples wandered Poland on their own: David and Brendon, Alma and
Steven. David and Brendon were good friends, both professionals in
their mid-thirties to early forties, both sharing an intense interest in
genealogy. David, the president of the Polish Genealogical Society of
New York State, was traveling to research his family history as well as
obtain resources for the society's library. Brendon, a brusque research

17

librarian, was traveling to research family history as well as step foot in his family's legendary homeland, Kashubia. Alma and Steven, a married couple accustomed to world travel, where searching for Alma's family in church records, villages of origin.

Just before David and Brendon ventured forth, Dad and I caught them on the way to our breakfast. Eager for a professional opinion of his search, Dad requested that I show them our information, our quest. I did not produce the copy of the encyclopedia page, but reiterated the scant detail Dad already explained to them on the plane: we have a relative four generations removed from Dad, that was an artist in the nineteenth century. David had walked into the parking lot, meeting his guides to make plans and organize luggage. Dad asked advice on how to research effectively while in Poland. Brendon answered that most people have no idea what they are doing and think they will stumble into information easily; he explained that we should begin as all proper research should: in death notices, marriage licenses, and gravestones; those facts are most concrete. Then, he continued smugly, if the connection is indeed valid, you might proceed. Thanking him vaguely, we turned to enter the restaurant. Dad was disappointed only for a moment, until the aroma of a Polish breakfast buffet tantalized his senses awakening the need of herring and horseradish, kielbasa (Polish sausage) and hard-boiled eggs, hard rolls and glazed fruit.

After breakfast, we had an hour to walk the town before loading the bus for the airport. Our flight to Rome was not until noon; arriving at the airport at eleven o'clock was certainly enough time, Antoni prepared us last night at dinner. Mom, Marie and I decided to stroll around the block. Heading north, we could see the Palace of Culture, a gift to the people of Poland from Stalin. It was a symbolic gesture to preserve and protect the culture of Poland. The steeple, clock tower and parapets jutted insolently into the sky, demanding attention. A banner advertising Newsweek Magazine hung between parapets, covering the entire side of the building. Is that a gift from America? Is that a welcome into the global community of information and commerce?

The hectic boulevard stretched for miles, we turned after only one thoroughfare. Heading west down a compressed alleyway, skyscrapers blocked sunlight. Storefronts lined the street, a salon on the right and a Cantor currency exchange kiosk on the left. Some entrances seemed closed; some seemed dankly foreboding. Turning a sharp corner, we faced south. Walking the wrong way down a one-way street, we saw a small park on the right. Parked cars confined the sidewalk. Pedestrians shuffle close to buildings or almost in the street.

In the basement of a communist style brick building on the left, I had to stop and take a second look. The stark utilitarian edifice stood in direct contrast to the ornate window display of pastry and confections. Plates of delicate petite fours and miniature cookies with sculpted frosting were on display in the window. Inside was a bakery filled with lustrous pastries and breads: the wall to the right filled with breads, buttered and glazed with a sheen of pure gold, the glass case in front brimming with pastries. I forced Mom and Marie to step inside and smell the sweetness of Polish baking.

It was difficult to choose what to sample; I forced myself to pick just one as I had finished breakfast a short while ago. Miniature raisin cheesecakes struggled for attention with jewel-toned tarts. Placek, sweet bread with raisins and a butter crumb topping, and placzanka, potato bread also sweet, with or without raisins, and lightly glazed, filled a baker's rack behind the counter with the stately elegance of traditional celebration breads. Mom, led by my smiles and giddiness, was politely interested. Proudly she surveyed the breads with the critical eye of a traditional home baker. Her placek and placzanka were as grand as theirs. There is no need to buy when you can make it when you wish. Mom had that skill, and therefore, no need for a treat at the moment.

Mounds of the pungent spicy drop cookies, resembling ginger-snaps or amoretti, composed the glass display case under the cash register. What were they called, these gems of earthy sweetness? The selection was amazing, the decision difficult. The lovely cashier laughed loudly at me as I prattled in English over the beauty of her bakery. Not openly speaking or understanding English, she found amusement in my intonation, animation. Her wordless hospitality encouraged my dissertation. Marie asked the cashier about the ingredients in various cookies and cakes. Their Polish conversation I would have loved to understand, but I merely observed their pantomimes and tones of casual exchange. Marie did not care for raisins, so she discounted all desserts that contained them. The debate whether or not to indulge raged in Marie's dieting mind. At last, she decided she could not be enticed by any sweet confection—none suited her tastes at the moment. No cravings to eradicate or fixate. We left the bakery in cheer, waving to the grinning cashier.

Delighted with this spectacular find, I memorized its placement, sure to return to it after the sojourn to Rome. The white, wax bag in hand swung happily as we turn another corner to be in front of another long communist style gray building housing our Hotel Forum. We passed the neon-outlined casino on the corner and entered the hotel in a sugared daze.

In the hotel lobby, I ate the Polish chocolate éclair in front of the others, forcing them to ask directions to the bakery. Waiting until the delicate semisweet chocolate melted on tongue to respond, I swallowed the velvet goodness and then proceeded to describe the shop and directions to it. Within a minute four people (Kathy Jo and Doris, Peg and

Don) were running down the block to stuff their purses with treats for the plane ride to Rome.

"What a bad influence I am!" I playfully joked with Mom and Marie as we watched the others dart through doorway and by picture window.

CENTER ONE HOTEL, ROME, ITALY

The turbulence of storms in Central Europe made for a long and bumpy plane ride, never taking off the "fasten seat belt" sign. It was a nervous flight for all. Don would pester Peg for pastry treats stashed in purse. Peg would dole out one at a time, each with a warning that it was the last.

Finally at Da Vinci Airport, armed guards with police dogs greeted the disembarking passengers. An eerie stillness enveloped the concourse. There were no travelers with carry on bags hustling to meet their flights. There were no employees, no one but the people from our flight and militia. Don commented that Italian airports have more security than American ones; militia is normal here. We did not understand that the airport was closed. Most of us were oblivious or unalarmed. At customs no one checked our passports or questioned our arrival, just ushered us to collect luggage and meet the tour guide. I felt slighted that my passport did not get an Italian stamp.

There were two small bags in a discrete corner of the luggage claim: one a carpetbag and one a strange blue case sealed in duct tape. Mom began to approach the unclaimed luggage. I held her back. Annoyed, she thought she was being helpful, trying to reunite luggage with passenger. I insisted that our group's luggage was secure; I demanded she leave all unattended luggage alone. Perturbed, she obeyed. We funneled through the concourse to the main entrance where our guide was loitering. Don recalled one guard that said a plane landed on the White House lawn. Why would a plane on the White House lawn close the Rome airport? The group gathered on the bus and headed straight for the hotel.

We were stuck in traffic. Our local guide, Daniella, explained that a soccer match was held today between Italy and Poland. Masses of people were rushing to the game. The bus was instructed by a traffic officer to follow the train tracks, get out of the way of cars. Our driver was more than willing to jump on track and speed through lines of traffic. Don asked Daniella about the closed airport. She confirmed the story that a plane landed at the White House and all airports across the world were closed to ensure security. I thought it was a joke, like the boy who flew his makeshift jet into Red Square so many years ago. Some daredevil is flouting national security to be on television.

A warm greeting admitted us to Hotel Center. The desk clerk, Tony, was a picture of Italy: salt and pepper gray hair stylishly cut, defining the age of the otherwise eternal beauty of smooth olive complexion, slight build, shining chestnut eyes, hospitable nature, and impeccable suit. I signed into the hotel book and received my room key with a wink and a smile from Tony.

In the hotel lobby a tall, blonde American man tells us that two planes crashed into the Twin Towers causing them to collapse. "They attacked mainland America," he screeches; "they destroyed the towers; they hit the Pentagon too," he stammers; "what is the next target?"

I stared at him with a dumb, blank expression, trying to reconcile the scant information. The daredevil from the White House lawn flew into the Twin Towers in New York City. This makes no sense. I grimaced in confusion.

"Who are they?" I asked of the blonde who was already talking to someone else.

No…there is some mistake. He pointed into the sitting room where an Italian news station was turned on the television. The language barrier did not matter; the pictures told the horrifying story. One tower on fire, a plane smashed into midsection of the other tower. Smoke. Fire. Collapse. Crumbling buildings emitting a tumult. Chaos. People running. Plumes of smoke and debris spread.

Oh my god…no. This is not happening.

Hundreds, perhaps thousands—we are not being told—have lost their lives, the people on the planes. How many are dead in the buildings? How many are injured in the surrounding areas? Were the buildings evacuated before they fell? Incredulous we stand in front of that television, luggage still in hand, frozen. The vision is not penetrating. This is not real. What evil lurks that would willingly cause such a catastrophe, a malignancy of nature?

Some terrorists hijacked four planes in Boston, then used them as suicide bombers to annihilate the World Trade Center and do partial damage to the Pentagon. No information is being released on the Pentagon, as if America does not want the world to know the extent to which its heart is struck. Luckily, if it could be called so, a plane crashed outside of Pittsburgh or else another landmark would have been targeted. Now the group is realizing that we were in the air when this was happening. We were flying over central Europe when the planes hit the Twin Towers. We were in a plane when the plane crashed into the Pentagon. The fear and empathy for the passengers on those planes seeped into bone and nerve with a shiver. The airport, and all airports across the world, was closed because of the threat of terrorism.

Where is John, my cousin who works in the Trade Center, I thought but would not express to my shaking parents. Mom was already thinking the same, her face transparent with disgust and anxiety. Dad stands by her in stoic reassurance, the only way he knows to cope and soothe, while inside he trembles. His gaze projects the tremor of a worn soldier contemplating new war.

Where is Ellen, John's sister who works in the International Trade building across the street from the Pentagon? Is she all right, a witness to disaster? My sister, Frances, works in Washington on the other side of the district from the Pentagon. She is safe; she must be safe. My mind spins with crazy logistics my mouth would not express as to not further rattle my parents.

Kathy Jo was in a tearful frenzy to call her daughter in Boston. The young American man let her use his cell phone to call Boston. Her daughter was unharmed and mourning the loss of several business associates in the towers. Kathy Jo returns the cell phone with no ease of spirit, no comfort in her daughter's words. No phones in the hotel or on the streets were allowing calls to America.

"All lines are busy, please try again at a later time," the recorded operator would say.

Only cell phone lines were working. I left my cell phone at home. It could have been so useful now, allowing everyone to contact one's family. This would begin days of attempting to call home from any street corner or from hotel phones. Kathy Jo would be the only person to successfully contact home while we were in Italy, using this American's cell phone. All eager attempts at communication would be in vain.

Kathy Jo and Doris provide vocal outbursts for our stunned group. Jozef and Theresa, Norm and Dorothy, Dick and Lou are in their rooms, intimately reacting. Marie and I, Peg and Don, Mom and Dad remain in the lobby with few others, with few vocalizations of feeling. Kathy Jo and Doris shout at the television, wiping tears with tissue before make-up could be streaked.

The American blonde left to hunt for his brother, with whom he was traveling. The brother is a naval officer on three-day pass. The blonde called the naval base in Sicily. No answer. They would leave immediately to report to the base. Before running to find his brother, he offers Doris his phone to call home. It is strange that crisis dissolves the need to introduce oneself. Our American blonde informant and his naval officer brother would remain nameless; yet address us with the intimacy of family. Her relatives are nowhere near Washington D. C. or New York City, but she longs to talk with them to hear their reactions and to be reassured by them. Everyone is silent for a moment, courting the answer to her milling decision. Common courtesy prevails; Doris gratefully declines the invitation. Everyone would have liked a chance at that cell phone, just one call.

Marie, with her determined spirit, refuses to let any news get in the way of her plans. She keeps a schedule for a reason, and that reason is constant. Even though there is a warning for Americans abroad to take extra caution, Marie wants to amble through the streets this afternoon before dinner. Most of the group chose to settle into hotel rooms, watching television for news and processing the day's events. Even though Don has warned not to leave the hotel without at least four people, Marie could not be stopped. I would not allow her to go alone. She could not wrangle four to go with her, so she and I made our way south down the narrow avenue: Marie ready to take in the Roman scene and me feeling more like a protector than a tourist. The streets were empty; after all it was siesta (or, more appropriately, riposo pomerdiano—the afternoon rest). We followed the Arralian walls for a few blocks then turned to glance at a newsstand and walk up the block to a drug store. The brightly colored row houses curtsied with vitality, flowers and herbs growing in window boxes were nosegays to dreamy, shuttered windows and corrugated rooftops. A tree-lined avenue of row houses paved the way to few businesses open during riposo pomeridiano.

Instantly the world was different, reality severed. We were lost children, not ordinary tourists, being soothed and saved. Immediately we represented stunned America coping with the onset of a new era of fear. We were shocked New Yorkers astray, coddled by experienced and omniscient Europeans—they knew we were naïve, unprepared, mourning. This world was now volatile and deceiving. The adjustment to this world was difficult for some and impossible for others. Our group was orphaned teenagers forced into maturity by circumstance beyond control and imagination, fostered by tried relatives, emotions scattered and assuaged. There was no returning to the innocence of a deserted landing. All would be weary consciously or subconsciously.

Wherever we stopped, storekeepers asked if we heard the news. "The news" was all they said to imply the unthinkable events. It was all that was necessary. With a nod of the head we replied, and with a wink and a slight smile they greeted us. They empathized and consoled with kind words and expression, "You are American…I'm sorry. You are New Yorkers…very sad, so sorry for you. It is terrible; we are with you."

We bought postcards and candy and felt much better as we garnered kind interactions with Romans, and stowed away comments and condolences as a mental first aid kit, as if in some sort of protective haze. Meandering for a while longer through the resting streets of Rome, we wandered back to the hotel to get ready for dinner. But a drink would come first.

Marie and I sat in the lounge with Kathy Jo and Doris. Tony brought us beer and sat with us. No one knew where to begin talking about the day's events. Tony broke the tension with a personal story. His son and daughter-in-law were honeymooners in Los Angeles scheduled to fly home today. All airports closed, not knowing if more hijacked planes were meant for Los Angeles, Tony anxiously listened to news reports with us. He would not interpret the fear, the details and the speculation, only the facts that were already known. The news repeated only one, thirty-second film piece over and over, the falling of the towers. Later, Tony received a phone call from his son saying that they were safe yet delayed. They would accept any inconvenience for the first flight to Rome. At the end of the bottle of beer, we headed for our rooms with a few minutes to clean up for dinner.

Our little group met in the lobby to walk together to the restaurant. Mom and Dad chose to take the stairs instead of waiting for the confined elevator. The polished marble stairs glistened like newly encrusted snow on mountaintop. Mom did not see the short last step but rather the pure white field of icy marble. Falling, the deceptive stair hit her head, the last stair of the last flight. Immediately Dad held her up and guided her to a chair in the lounge. She would not complain, although in dizzied pain, and insisted on walking with the group to the restaurant.

The four blocks west it took to walk to the restaurant made everyone hungry. We passed through dim, quiet streets that poured into a piazza of neon and commerce. Every storefront from flower shops to clothing stores unleashed wears into the square. The restaurant was not far now, another block or so. Dad and I huddled on either side of Mom, who hobbled the distance head throbbing, knees locking, hip already bruised from the fall. Housed in a red brick villa, this traditional Italian restaurant, Rom Antica, captured the imagination and the appetite. Frescoes of Italian village seascapes filled the expanse of walls between the stained glass windows. Even on the dividing walls separating rooms and intimate niches, frescoes of windows and billowing curtains created an airy sense of space. Yet the dark wood of ceiling and floors cajoled the table candlelight into secret rendezvous. Smiling,

Mom was enchanted, along with most of us. She took an aspirin and said she felt much better.

The group was fed course after course: red wine, soup, antipasto, and pasta. The waiters were young, handsome, and eager to please. However, they forgot to serve me the pasta course. Embarrassed, the manager served me a plate full of rigatoni in a marinara sauce and a plate full of risotto with asparagus tips in a cream sauce. Since some people at the table complained of cold pasta, the waiter then brought to me a full plate of hot fettuccini in a light olive oil and crushed tomato sauce. All the dishes were marvelous. I passed around the fettucini, too much for me. I ate heartily only to quietly decline the main course of lamb, but indulging in the salad and French-fry potato side dishes. Eating vegetarian is tricky, trying not to offend the host. Finally I ate vegetarian and well with it being acceptable, no fuss.

Dorothy noticed my meatless plate and inquired. I am not a real vegetarian, but it is easier to profess to be than to pontificate my philosophy to every hostess and waiter. In truth I am just a picker eater: I do not eat red meat or seafood but will have chicken sporadically and turkey on Thanksgiving. While I live on pasta and vegetables, I enjoy ice cream regularly and an omelet occasionally. Being labeled vegetarian conjures ideals of Buddhist or of Bohemian existence. In truth my ideas are more Native American: if one chooses to be a carnivore appreciate and use every part of the animal that gives its life for yours. I prefer being an herbivore, wasting little, still appreciating what is sacrificed for my life. I cannot tell anyone what to believe or how to live; I am continually groping for understanding myself. Everyone at the table is very accepting of this explanation. Richard nods his head approvingly. Kathy Jo and Doris call me considerate.

A middle-aged guitar player serenaded the group all night. For one song, which I could not name, he sat beside me for a personal serenade. His baritone and rustic chords waft in my ear. I could not look at him. Richard sang along, knowing the Italian words. With a wild ovation from all tables in the restaurant, the suave musician passed his tambourine beginning with Richard sitting next to me. Everyone gave a bill, although others gave less than what seems complimentary. The tambourine roamed the entire floor; then came to me. Before I could add my contribution, the musician swiped his instrument, bowed to the crowd, smirked mischievously at me, and left for the evening.

For dessert, we ate an impeccable teramisu: subtle yet pungent with enough espresso on the bottom to create a balance of textures and flavors, smooth to spongy, solid sweetness to bitter liquid richness. You could never get this quality of tiramisu in America. The gods have securely left the divine recipe in Roman hands. Mangia. Dinner took over three hours to eat. By the end most of us were falling asleep in our dessert. We left before the dessert wine course, mildly offending the manager.

Mom was not well enough to walk back. Jozef and Theresa could not manage to walk either, so he called two taxis. Mom, Dad, Marie and I crawled into one, while Theresa and Jozef luxuriated in the other. The dexterity and precision of the taxi driver sped us to the hotel in what seemed under a minute. We paid the driver what he asked and disembarked to find Jozef and his driver arguing in the street. Jozef refused to pay more than 20,000 liras. The driver insisted that after midnight the minimum fee is 25,000. Theresa stood on the sidewalk, happy to be uninvolved. Jozef enlisted me to take his side, requiring me to pronounce what we just paid. 25,000 liras. Flattened, Jozef grumbled as he paid the driver his price. Elated, his driver bid us thanks, a happy stay and many returns. He sped into the night as if chased by unknown phantoms.

Reality greeted us at the threshold, our cozy room without comfort. I could not sleep. Marie is moving in her sleep, mumbling, unintelligible. I sit on the floor writing in line of the bathroom nightlight. My stomach and heart aches. How could I have the time of my life when my family and my country are going through such pain? Where is John, my cousin who works in the Trade Center? How is my cousin Ellen who works across the street from the Pentagon in the International Trade building? Dad is worried that we will be stuck in Rome due to security issues or stuck in Poland due to terrorist warnings or a sudden outbreak of war. He would really like to go back to Warsaw to be with the larger group. We do not know what tomorrow will bring. The tour will continue. But will we return home safely to our family intact?

Tomorrow the group will go to the Vatican for general audience with Pope John Paul II. He will know; he will have something inspiring to say, to assuage, and to heal. And we will find some sort of answer, some sort of peace of mind in his words.

Right now my mind is troubled. At least in Warsaw the palace still stands, with bullet marks and monument to honor the memory of those lost. What do you do with a pile of rubble, dust and ash incinerating all signs of humanity? We must learn from Poland and find the strength to renew ourselves, find the strength in society and culture to remember although painfully. Now well into the morning hours, I will try to sleep before sunrise. This mantra, this prayer is on lips always: Blessings, good wishes, and immortal peace bestow all victims who died in horror today. May their lives be cherished memories that live on forever.

SEPTEMBER 12, 2001

*"Do not allow pain and sadness to overtake you, but unite
and regain strength in friendship and the love of God."*
– POPE JOHN PAUL II TO THE GENERAL AUDIENCE

ROME

ROOFTOP BREAKFASTS REPLENISHED us each morning as Marie and I
would sit in the hotel café and survey the sleeping windows and empty
play spaces made from creative residents: hammocks hung between an-
tenna, hand-built storage sheds of mysterious contents, container gardens on tar roofs. Potted trees, manicured shrubs and busts of Roman
gods ensconced the perimeter of the rooftop café. While eating croissants, rolls, sweetbreads, or cereal, the gods greeted us good morning,
along with other members of the group. Only after the gods ruled our
breakfast were we ready for the new day and what discoveries lie within
it.

VATICAN CITY

The street leading to St. Peter's Basilica was lined with pilgrims and
tourists. Along the center of the closed street, a procession of invited

dignitaries solemnly walked toward the steps of the basilica going through St. Peter's Square. A stream of red, yellow and black robes wove through the crowds of anticipation, a ribbon of a present. For it was to be a solemn gift of wholeness to the mourning, to the broken spirit, a gift on the first day of a new age of awareness and sensibility. Slowly our group made way through the milling crowds to the designated seated area in the midpoint of the square. The obelisk commemorating St. Peter's death stood behind us imposing. Overflowing with visitors, an estimated eighty to ninety thousand people attended. Arms of the colonnade bowed wide to wrap pensive missionaries and bystanders searching for guidance. Looming marble Popes consoled from atop lofty arms. We were safe here. Undulating anticipation coursed through our group as we sat in awe of our surroundings. Bernini would have been proud to witness his square, his design succeeding in its intension: the Church as mother embracing her faithful children. The doubtful assembly murmured for signs of hope. St. Peter's dome resonated. Clear skies invited the sun to warm our backs.

Allowing for no pomp or applause, the Pope instructed the gathering to keep quiet, pensive state of being. No Pope mobile rides today. His black limousine drove in front of the square and up the altar to the red canopy, and attendants assisted him into his chair of red velvet and gold frame. Frailness, which has joined his countenance for several years, was now superseded by sorrow, empathy, and righteousness. Yesterday's events shook him, as it did everyone. A lifetime of service for global peace, now tried. A long moment of reticent anticipation introduced the spiritual figure, as he calculated the exact instant to begin. We stared fixedly, rapt in solace before an utterance spoken.

With words of reassurance and conviction, the Pope rallied courage and understanding. Calling a religious summit, Buddhist monks, Rabbis, and several Christian religious denominations were announced to support religious tolerance and peace. The Pope on large projection screens exuded the calm wisdom of love. Crested hand on forehead wrung of quelled sadness, augmenting love. His concentrated stare penetrated questioning spirits, our sprits now wrapped in peace, even if it were just for the moment. His speech was like a concerned, fatherly lecture to a grappling teenager being thrust into adulthood by tragedy, not readiness. The assembly was one mass in synchronicity as a school of fish undulating in currents of thought.

Overwhelmed by the events, the speech, the moment of solidarity, I cried. For the uncertainty of life in America, I cried. Tears of worry streaked down my face for the safety of my family. Words of comfort were rebuffed by thoughts of impending retaliation that may lead to war. And most of all, I felt guilty for being safe and happy while so much hardship was experienced at home.

With sidelong glance I noticed that others were touched as well. Mom was crying muffled tears, trying to go unnoticed. Dad took Mom's hand wordlessly, caressing. Everyone in the group was contemplative in one's own way. Joe and Theresa were also holding hands while peering at the pure white grain that was our vision of the Pope. Simultaneously they smiled, without looking at each other, only they knew why. Screens were not real enough. Kathy Jo and Doris were in repose. Marie was standing crouched, to the frustration of those sitting behind her, enthralled by the Pope's words and presence. She must view that spot where he sits. There was new kinship in our group; we were family abroad now. With pats on shoulders and hands, solidarity manifests itself.

The Pope read his speech first in Italian and then in English. Then, various cardinals read the speech in other languages: Spanish, French, Polish, and Greek. I only understood a few words in those recitations but the message was given time to saturate into the pores of spirit and mind. Eighty thousand people were in the square, within view, reachable, contemplating the same message in different tongues at the same time. I could see most of them: some contemplating, some in soulful meditation, some children gleeful despite everything, some bothered more by the heat of the day than by world events. A security helicopter flew overhead, quite low.

Tears were replaced with profound gladness to be there safely together. We were representatives of America united in purpose and circumstance. There was no better place on earth to be than in this international circle of friendship listening to a spiritual world leader extending a loving hand to all. I felt like embracing the world, and in some strange way already felt a return embrace, starting with the members of our small group and extending outward to all I encountered.

After the general audience, a couple from the State of Georgia realized that we were speaking English and walked over from across the aisle. Confused, they asked what had happened in America to prompt his speech. In straw hat and sundress, this plebeian couple in their mid-thirties had been driving through the Italian countryside on motor scooter the past few days. They had no knowledge of the news and were startled but not outwardly grieved upon hearing the information we had to share. Marie told them of the travel advisory for Americans abroad. President Bush had issued a statement for American international travelers to exercise extreme caution while abroad. They peered at each other in quixotic vision. They thanked us flatly for the information and continued across the square on their cloistered journey through byways northward bound. Our group was well aware of risks at home and abroad, yet no one mentioned going home. We would continue with spirits high. The journey had just begun.

The sky was ideal blue and cloudless. The sun began to oppress the more delicate in our group, burning Marie's neck and Lou's shoulders.

We waited along the reopened boulevard for the bus to retrieve us. Potted palm trees along the white stone boulevard provided enough shade for several people.

ROME

The noontime sun played with my freckles as we sat outdoors for lunch at Il Padellaccio café. A light lunch--light for Italy that is-- was served: salad consisting of three types of lettuce, beets, corn, and garbanzo beans; fettuccini in light tomato sauce, and fresh from the oven bread. The proprietors treated us with careful hospitality.

Our group engulfed the entire seating area in front of the café. Pedestrians glanced at our makeshift banquet table with alternating curiosity and hackneyed oversight. Each neighboring café marked its territory with decorative lures. On the far corner was a café of cloth awning and wrought-iron tables and chairs; next was an uncovered café with casual, circular wooden tables and folding chairs with white Chinese lanterns cording the space aloft; ours was also uncovered with square plastic tables in gingham tablecloths, ordinary white plastic chairs, and a rope of miniature flags festooned from tree to tree to café doorway. Our café was chosen since it was the first on the block to willingly accommodate a large group with no reservation. And so we sat under colorful flags and country blue gingham, enjoying the scene and the respite.

Marie teased the waiter from our first bite through the last. When she was impressed, she complimented profusely. The bread was the best she had ever tasted, crusty and brick oven fresh, allowing butter to melt from knife into porous cavities of heaven. The waiter was personable, the fettuccini perfect. She would relay all this between sassy comments to which the waiter responded evenly. As I collected the money to pay the bill, the amused waiter kissed Marie on both cheeks. Irene took gelato back to the hotel for Jozef, who did not feel up to the luncheon. The cook offered to make us special lasagna if we returned for lunch the next day. With a promise and a handshake, Don agreed to call him in the morning to confirm the reservation. We were getting up to leave and the waiter stopped us with a tray of complimentary mint sherbet. The Italian ice was a pure, white snowball of whimsy. It was a pleasure to return to our seats for the refreshing dessert, creamy and light as gelato yet an icy crisp crystal. Mom left an American twenty-dollar bill as a tip, pleasing the already congenial headwaiter.

The meal provided energy for a self-guided walking tour of Rome for half the group while the other half went back to the hotel for riposo pomeridiano. Mom and Dad sided with the half of the group going to the hotel for respite. Marie and I accompanied the half walking the streets. We darted west with no intention.

Earthy brick buildings lined the warm avenues behind parallel lines of trees, cobblestone paths and paved street. Cafes, grocery stores, shops and car dealerships occupied street level access while upper levels of buildings were apartments. Riposo pomeridiano must be for many types of rest, not sleeping only. In one block, a man in a white t-shirt leaned out the screenless window with a cigarette. In the next block, an old lady wrapped in a delicate, cream lace scarf for brief amusement watched me watch her. I briefly smiled; she steadily fixed her posture without mustering the energy to return the smile. I smiled to myself about her fickle regard. After all this is Rome; it conforms to no rules save those it created. Corner buildings curve to present a flowing sweep of brick rather than an angular intersection. Doorways arched or bore pillars. Windows mirrored the motif. Gates had gargoyles or proud lions guarding the entrance. Every avenue was distinct, radiant, traveling around, to or through ruins. There was no reason to rush and much to see.

Five blocks west we visited Hotel Presidente to exchange money and attempt to email home. Doris could not understand the email system; I helped her, but I could not get the system to accept her phone card as payment. Some grew tired of waiting for us; they left us to go hunting for any English newspaper. A group of ten now reduced to four, we slowly sauntered back to Hotel Center. We came upon a street pay phone. Doris tried to call her daughter, which was unsuccessful with her prepaid calling card. Frustrated, since neither email nor phone worked, the ladies bulleted to the hotel.

Doris had huge blisters on her feet from wearing impractical sandals all day. Even her corns had blisters. Kathy Jo ordered a large bowl of boiling water and a cup of Epson salt to her room for Doris to soak. This aided her feet but did nothing for her mood, which brooded for the rest of the day in partial ache of feet and in partial ache of heart. By four o'clock we all wanted siesta, in need of repose. Marie and I retreated to our room.

Rejuvenated after an hour's nap, Marie, Kathy Jo and I walked four blocks north to Piazza Emanuel: a small, walled playground where parents were watching children swing or slide or run. Many families found shade under sleek, willowy trees or spread blankets and picnic supplies across sunlit lawns fibrous grass. Stalls were set up around the perimeter wall as a market. Discarded crates once displaying fresh produce were strewn in the pathway. Old newspaper once used as packing material tumbled in the breeze along pavement. Kiosks were pushed against the wall. Unfortunately we were too late in the day, the stalls were empty, market closed already.

Shops lined the city blocks surrounding Piazza Emanuel, predominantly an Asian section of town. Into and out of several boutiques we wove, trying to find the perfect watch to replace Marie's broken one. A pawnshop with a glass cabinet full of watches drew our attention. Two clerks acknowledged us: an older Italian man, obviously wearing a toupee and otherwise unkempt winked at us, and a slightly younger Asian man in a plaid shirt with a gruff manner looked at us then turned to escape to an inner room. The older man unlocked the cabinet and allowed Marie to select and wear watches as she pleased. Diligently, Marie fitted watch after watch to her wrist. And as diligently, she found a particular reason why each was unsuitable. Finally, Marie found one that fit her taste and standards, and presented a traveler's check as payment. The clerk would not accept it, cash only. Marie promised the clerk she would return within the day to purchase the watch as we filed out of the shop. She would not return. It was not worth the trouble; the watch was fine, not perfect. In a critical mood from the watch quest, Marie investigated the street as we walked. Amazed by the amount of graffiti and market debris, Marie pronounced the street unclean.

We entered a clothing store with a display window of mannequins dressed in faux-leather jackets. Racks of clothing were bolted into the walls from floor to ceiling. Boxes of garments littered the floor, merchandise awaiting wall space. Two petite Oriental women were hanging shirts on the back wall racks. They made me feel statuesque, a rare and delightful feeling. One asked if we needed assistance; she had an Asian accent and spoke English well. Her hair shined as dark as her eyes and as bright as her smile. She offered us a glass of water and motioned to the spring water dispenser in the corner. In need of refreshment, we accepted the invitation. The second woman never slowed her pace, hanging shirts. We thanked them, browsed the low racks with no intention of buying anything, the fashionable European clothes too young looking for Marie and Kathy Jo and too pricey for me. We exited the slate threshold.

"I did not realize there was an Asian population in Rome," Marie stated. Kathy Jo agreed. Kathy Jo and Marie might not have expected to see many ethnic cultures living in Rome. As in any big city, Rome has boroughs that are Asian, Hispanic, African, and others. We happened into the Asian section with many people roaming the streets of many different cultural backgrounds: some tourists, some residents. Being used to this type of experience in many other cities, I roved the streets wide-eyed and curious but feeling the need to guide and protect the ladies with me, to stay within their comfort zones. Marie and Kathy Jo were taken aback and feeling uncomfortable. Only three hours ago and five blocks away was an agreeable walking tour. A small distance creates a dramatic difference in cityscape and mindscape. I led them back to the hotel.

Tony was at the reception desk with two others. We greeted him in the warm style in which we had become accustomed; he was our interpreter, our friend. Agitated and concerned Tony quickly bid us farewell as he sped to his motor scooter. His son was still stranded in Los Angeles. The doubts and threats to security ran scenes of horror through his mind. His son was to call home from the airport. He must be home for his son's phone call or arrival, which preceded the next, Tony explained. We empathized with his anxiety; we were living it too. With quick phrases of hope and best wishes, we watched Tony depart through the hotel gate and into the swift avenue.

With plenty of time before dinner, I chose to dress up, show Rome my best side. An ankle length black dress with white flowers printed along the bottom will do. At eight o'clock the group ambled to the gate of the Arralian walls to Tempio di Minerva Ristorante. In the historic evening glow of gate millennia-old, we ate a sumpuous four-course dinner. Flatbread with rosemary and red wine would warm our appetites. The kosher salt and rosemary supplied the sharp flavor to contrast the fruity wine. Bruchetta was next, toasted crusty bread with garlic and sun dried tomato pesto spread. I would have indentured myself to the cook if he gave me this bruchetta recipe. Everyone fawned over it. If licking plates were acceptable etiquette, all would have been spotless.

Rosemary and Frank were speaking of his experiences being a police officer in a small town. Amusing stories of police calls over raccoons ripped laughter through the cooling night air. Dad swiped the last bruchetta before anyone noticed, most still laughing. Fettuccini in a marinara sauce and salad with white wine was served to cooing party. I clapped at the presentation, a sprig of fresh basil in the center of each heaping plate. Conversation ebbed. The food was too good to distract with chatter. Yet we were not prepared for the spectacle that was dessert: chocolate mousse and cappuccino for me while others chose from a selection of fruit tarts and gelato. The chocolate mousse was a rich mixture of dark and milk chocolates not quite combined. The texture was more pudding-like than conventional mousse, but the melding of flavors offset the texture perfectly. I ate it as slowly as possible, savoring every dripping spoonful to remember it as long as I live. It was that good. If I were not already indentured for the bruchetta recipe, I would be for the double chocolate mousse.

For three hours we ate and ate with delight on the patio. Conversation flowed easily with no mention of world events. We were too enchanted by our surroundings, pulled out of global concerns and into the presiding welcome of eternal Rome. The awning and candlelight provided just enough intimacy while the open street provided entertainment of people watching. Mad traffic swurved. Busy pedestrians strutted.

Dick was telling stories of his family getting ready to attend a friend's wedding with Lou adding details. I could imagine their family, pristine and punctual, gathering for the special occasion. Dick and Lou were one of the few couples that were not retired, although nearing that age. Dick was a plumber. Lou was a plumber's wife. They were of one mind, finishing each other's sentences. Their hallmark of perception was familial: their sons, their business, their garden. Their life focused within their gated house even while traveling, especially while traveling today. Usually their stories were captivating, and, necessarily, always about themselves, their opinions or their family. After two glasses of wine I had this evening, they exuded boundless charm as verbose storytellers.

Rome hovered in a timeless dream, above the modern race and below the ancient remnants of boundaries. Nothing could disrupt this evening; we tried diligently to make it so, as the Pope had already blessed the day.

A street vendor, jaunty and young carrying a half-barrel of flowers, gave me a long-stemmed red rose.

"Che, Bella!" he said to me. With a smile I accepted, reaching for my wallet.

"No," he replied with flattened hand as a stop sign.

A sweet gesture of fragrant kindness, and business move, he made; every lady at our table was then given a red rose by her husband. I could not be the only lady at the table with a rose. Dad offered to pay the vendor for two roses, which the vendor denied the offer with a firm downward wave of hand only taking money for the rose for Mom.

"The rose was a gift for Bella," he explained grinning at me. I have received many gifts today, I thought as I returned blushing smile.

Happily the vendor left, and happily we made a bouquet in our empty wine bottle. The vendor approached our second table. Doris and Kathy Jo shooed him away quickly, not interested in his wares or his charms. As the vendor crossed the street stretching toward more prosperous avenues, Marie surveyed our table from hers. She told Doris and Kathy Jo that we all had roses. They shrugged. Marie grunted.

Marie deserved a long-stemmed red rose. Delicate yellow lights illuminated the precarious remnant of domed gate of the Arriulian walls, illuminating our street corner full of life.

It was very late yet the city ran at full force. We reclined in our chairs, most to finish the meal with a healthy glass of spring or seltzer water. I enjoyed one more glass of white wine. Its earthy bouquet was agreeable to the senses and the palate. Two young men rode by on bicycles as if in a competitive race. There were no expectations, only surprises. What can one expect when the unimaginable has already occurred?

Peg claimed her red rose, eager to keep it as long as possible. Following suit, Rosemary, Theresa, Lou, Mom and I retrieved all roses.

Romanced by Rome itself, we sauntered back to the hotel ready for a good night's rest. The ladies arm clutched their roses as if school girls in a pageant. I gave my rose to Mom. The roses would not be lonely and Mom could enjoy twice the fragrance. Peg proclaimed that she would dry her rose so she could take it home as a symbol of the day. I suggested that increased security would confiscate it immediately. Undaunted, she would try it. They could not confiscate it if it were not there to confiscate. If security does not confiscate the rose then all the better for her. On this, as always, she would not waver on a fine idea.

For the next day's schedule promised to be a rigorous one.

ember 13, 2

SEPTEMBER 13, 2001

Sometimes there are no fitting words; gestures speak instead.

ROME

THE SUN GREETED us this morning as brightly as the rooftop gods. The salamander pink tiles of the floor glistened, freshly mopped. As always, coffee and croissant were escorted to marble table and short slit-back chairs. The morning was so lovely that many sat outside the glass café, under umbrella tables. No outside seating was vacant, so Marie and I sat in the enclosed café, the usual corner table. Zeus bid the morning splendor.

VATICAN CITY

It was only eight thirty and the bus was frantically driving towards Vatican City again. Once parked outside the Vatican Museum we realized the reason for the early rush: the entrance line wound down the block of medieval ramparts and curved around a new one. By the minute the line grew as others were dropped off in great numbers.

43

Delphi, our guide, jumped from the bus, not yet stopped, to secure our place in line. The museum walls slid to sidewalk, circumvallating many irregular city blocks. The rest of us followed as hurriedly as age and temperament thought possible.

The line was long. We had time. The jokes and prodding began. Doris and Kathy Jo inquired into Delphi's personal life: forty, attending graduate school, of Greek origin, moved to Rome several years ago, single. Kathy Jo shrieked for me. From the end of the line I was pushed and grabbed to the front where Kathy Jo and Doris proudly announced their newly acquired knowledge. He asked me if I could cook. I said no, but I can bake. That was no good, too fattening, he said. Doris and Kathy Jo insisted if one knows how to bake, one could learn to cook easily. The ladies continued to tell him of my accomplishments in life. I slipped to my former place in the crowd. A street vendor in colorful vest was selling books of postcards for a dollar. I bought one.

Surprisingly the line moved quickly; once admitted into the great complex it is easy to disperse. The fortress walls gave admittance into a modern lobby of glass ticket booths, gift shops, and a concourse to the main buildings.

In the piazza joining the four major buildings of the Vatican Museum, a humble courtyard stood. In the midst of lawn and narrow brick paths, a spherical sculpture burned. The hot morning sun reverberating from the bronze globe caused eyes to dilate, adjust. This was the modern globe: cracked, exposed, and dark in areas and highly polished in others. Another tour guide spun the globe to impress his group. Alas, it impressed many besides. Spots of white light blazed, then were engulfed only to jolt a second later. Its cavernous richness created a whole that was not physically there. It entranced. Quickly mentioning this abstract sculpture as new, our guide directed us towards the far building where posters of the ceiling of the Sistine Chapel hung on easels against the wall.

Delphi explained the history, symbolism, and painting techniques involved in the construction of the Sistine Chapel. Then, the tour of other buildings commenced. Through rooms of ancient Roman artifacts we meandered until we came upon an interior garden. At first it seemed a circular garden with trees and fern in the center. On closer inspection it was hexagonal, each wall housing troughs that were once Roman bathes, or grand sculptures of gods, lying in sumptuous pleasure or strutting to luxuries unforeseen. In a niche within a pediment column, a sculpture of Dionysus heralded news, message in extended hand. What could this important message be? I would not guess as our group was plowing ahead, no time to wonder. The next ancient marvel would come and go in an instant.

Lean windows allowed soft breezes to enter the vast corridors. Soothed by breezes, I stepped to one window and bent over the sill to see contemplative gardens: lanky evergreens draping as willows to protect the gardens from singular viewers, true green lawns swirling by palm trees and fountains audible flow just out of view. I took a deep breath, closing my eyes to the late mornings rays. Marie tugged at shirttail. We would lose our group if I did not hurry along with her. But first, Marie must take a quick glance at what I saw, curious. Just as the gardens greeted her, she darted in the window, not to lose sight of the task at hand. We must rejoin our group.

Too fast, too fast, we traipsed, having to finish the tour by noon to comply with Delphi's schedule. The travel agency had paid him to escort us until noon. Next, the Egyptian collection bared examination.

Delphi rushed us through at steady clip, pausing only when another group blocked entry into gallery or to explain a single artwork in a sea of masterpieces. The pace annoyed; the tour mapped by a cartographer with Attention Deficit Disorder. I felt time fleeting with sterile first impressions of countless treasures. The passageway drove by vision until I forced it to halt in front of a small sphinx to size of a crouching golden retriever, and just as loveable. Our group treaded past. I doted.

Even though it is gouache, I touched the marble paw of a miniature sphinx guarding the hallway to St. Helen's room. He didn't seem to mind and it was no longer than a brief moment: two fingers grazing the bottom of his immortal paw. This was the moment: two histories interacting, one of the ancient past and one contemporary. What could be gained from a quick, cold touch? A connection-- an understanding that you are not alone, nor ever have been. A feeling that expression of thought and culture has been not only acceptable but also revered throughout time. I am imbued with a momentary sense of immortality. However, there would be no more transient clandestine touching, however perceived as harmless, for the rest of the journey. It is in spontaneous experiences where one finds oneself through instant reaction.

At regimented pace, we marched, unable to pause at the many wonders of art and history unless on Delphi's roster. Now in the building reserved for religious artifacts, paintings and statues from many generations' display their mighty representations. I was most impressed with Raphael's tapestries. One hallway housed twenty massive tapestries. There was no time to inspect any of them. Parading through the room, we zoomed. Hurried by a relentless guide, I was forced to stay with the pace of the group, or lose them for good. One wall was showing the tapestries with biblical scenes, the opposite wall housing tapestries depicting scenes from the lives of the Popes. The weaving was intricate and beguiling. They were calling to me, just for a minute to introduce themselves. Acquaintances could not be made, not one. Our group was already in the next room. Rounded forms and lush backgrounds captured Raphael's intentions and my imagination: a Renaissance pope strolling the gardens, a counsel of cardinals with spectating wild-life. Rafael grandly introduced the walkway to Michelangelo's Sistine Chapel.

In six different languages announcements rang through the hall, saying that cameras, videos, and talking was prohibited in the chapel. Signs on the walls resembled street signs requesting the same as the announcements. The line of people in the hallway was dense, taking half an hour to funnel into the passageway of the chapel. The announcements rang every five minutes. All these warnings are understandable; they are exerting to protect the chapel while creating a special silent moment of awe. Delphi announced we had ten minutes; he would be at the exit—waiting on the threshold.

Carefully stepping into the chapel, one odd angular step down, I was overcome by the lively colors: blues leapt from the ceiling, background overtaking foreground before focus. The expanse was mystifying: heaven, hell and purgatory sprawl behind the altar; the creation of the world languishes on the ceiling--what astonishing beauty. Small murmurs blanketed the floor. It is difficult to keep silent when experiencing something so massive in proportion and history.

The altar calls first. Drooping toward oblivion, Michelangelo's body hangs, gray and dull juxtaposed with ethereal blue. He is weary. His fate resides in the whim of the man clutching his back, no choice of his. Enemies are active in hell: pulling spirits from purgatory, torturing, burning. Not even his friends in heaven attend to Michelangelo's depleted corpse. Alternating focus from figures to background, the stunning blue returned to braise eye against the commingling clouds, an atmospheric juxtaposition. There he is again. A cloud himself, Michelangelo is. A dreamy means of transport beyond this worldly existence. He is the only figure in and of the clouds. Drooping becomes suspended emotion. Oblivion is just a means of communication with nature. Michelangelo is not in heaven or hell, but a constant, sentient, natural state of being, floating. Brilliant colors of life and death in heaven and hell cannot compare with the unbleachable nature of Michelangelo, a charcoal cloud.

They stood directly under the famous panel, Mom, Marie. Dad marched ahead, alone, to view Adam backwards from the golden gates dividing the room in two unequal halves. God reached for Adam with a cautious finger. Marie was deeply moved. She grabbed Mom who had tears in the corners of her eyes. They embraced. In this holy and beauteous place, she wanted to reach out to those who touch her life, to her best friend; Marie explained her emotions to Mom. In silence Mom nodded and squeezed Marie's hand. All this while I stood, head back, open-mouthed, in awe. There is a purpose here, in this room, throughout. A spiritual journey of hundreds of years culminates above our heads.

I stand directly under God bestowing life unto Adam. The vibrant colors fill the air, my lungs, my blood. By osmosis, heavenly life seeps into my being. God gazes not at Adam, but at all of us gathered, shoulder-to-shoulder, expecting a blessing of artistic illumination, guiding muse. A middle-aged, obese American lady photographs it with a disposable camera, taking aim without looking. Immediately I glared at her with vicious rigor.

How dare she not only be imprudent but disrupt the moment, my moment. The American woman is looking through snap shot vision: a superficial experience captured for instant recall of disposable memories for proof of being physically present at a given moment, not dwelling within the experience.

When two Italian young men confronted her about it, she said, "What picture? I didn't take a picture." I was boiling at such ignorance.

"That is an American for you," the Italian men shrugged as one said to the other.

I was so angry I could not speak, only shake my head emphatically no. When traveling we are diplomats, personal ministers of culture and discourse. Any impression made on others has the pleasure and the danger of being transposed into a generalization of a country or culture. How could this woman not know that? Or worse, how could she not care? Taking that picture was not American, it was ignorance. She could have been from any country. Ignorant people are everywhere, crossing any culture or country.

Waiting for the rest of our group to finish their Sistine Chapel experience, I pulled off to the side by the partition, golden gates. On that half wall of marble gilded with ornate edging and angels carved into the base, someone had left a shining candy wrapper. Frustrated, I had come for inspiration and was leaving with insolence and ill will. Consequently, what have I learned? I mused. Nothing is irreparable. What one has destroyed, another may mend. Not in the same moment or, perhaps, with the same people, but to live wisely one must learn from every experience and apply that knowledge. That candy wrapper, offensive beast. That candy wrapper could be tamed, could save another's shocked experience of it. That shining candy wrapper is my opportunity to exercise new wisdom, the wisdom of Michelangelo and God. I tucked it into my purse.

Cutting through the masses, Dad found me, as he had just finished his independent explorations. We did not speak, only huddled together waiting for Mom and Marie. Norm sat on his cane chair while Dorothy stood by his side gazing astonished at the brilliant Renaissance vision overhead. Even the bustled curtains within arms length were frescoes, separating ordinary people from the genesis of muscular swathed characters posing above for eternity. Blurred, unfocused vision folded a ka-

leidoscope of flying colors in energetic accord: magenta swags on coral
bodies, turquoise robes clothe landscape, saints and sinners, burnt
sienna bodies contort to hide in crevice and corner, stark marble entablature gates all. Delphi wove his hands over head to signal that our
group should gather and depart. It had been ten minutes. Ten minutes
was not nearly enough.

The outdoor corridor leading from the chapel to St. Peter's Basilica
framed an interesting space of complimenting buttresses and arches
with beckoning domes in the distance. For a brief rest our group collected there. Then, we ventured on to the basilica for more adventures
in holy reverence. Mom was in her glory: deeply heartened by the sa-
credness of the artwork and massive proportions of it. Heaven could
hardly have been as grand to her. To see the fervor on her face made the
entire trip worthwhile.

Inside St. Peter's the scale remained immense: alcoves and side
altars strode from wings while the ubiquitous dome took flight.
Michelangelo's Pieta was housed behind a wall of glass--spectacular. We
pressed close to the glass; unable to conceptualize that we were in the
same space as the famous Pieta. The profound spiritual measure of this
sacred edifice left Mom and Marie in religious bliss, and me speechless.
To the right, to the left, straight ahead, every visible distance was a
marvel and miracle. Days could be spent appreciating all works of art
of each chapel, crest and niche in St. Peter's Basilica. We were children
in a dream, finally experiencing in flesh the fables and characters from
favorite storybooks. The altar of St. Peter commanded with the presence of a sleeping giant: the dark canopy and white marble gave weight
to the circle of luminescent vigil lights, eternally aglow to light the
spiral way to the tomb of St. Peter below. Mom, clutching her heart
with fist, was spiritually moved, not knowing to cry, pray or gasp. She
did all three. Dad, in monk-like silent reverie, walked behind us alone,

hands held by each other behind his back. No one would disrupt his meditation.

Do people leave flowers on altars in St. Peter's Basilica? The stately grandeur of the basilica almost precludes the thought. Masses of tour groups may trample a bouquet of prayers.

Along the main aisle, the statue of St. Peter had a long line of pilgrims waiting to visit it. Each person would hold a dear one's wish and ask it of Saint Peter while touching its right foot. The foot had been rubbed so much so it did not resemble a foot any longer, just a smooth round lump of marble. The statue of Saint Peter needs prosthesis. Observing Peter's loss of limb, I realize the paradox: every touch that attempts to connect erodes. No one artifact, regardless of its accessibility to the public, should be exposed to hands of deterioration. Could a rose be placed at St. Peter's feet instead? Could a fingertip graze be replaced with a bow, a penetrating stare? Connections made from here on will be mental and manifest in words and action, not physical proximity.

Is an offering of a flower different from spiritual transcendence through touch? Some relics are accessible, known conduits of spirituality, while others are restricted works of art and history. One is not invited to be moved by or to interact with any or all of them, but touch those deemed touchable by credible institutions and popular experiences. A sphinx paw is an unacceptable conduit while the worn foot of the statue of Saint Peter is acceptable. Why?

But one last stance: it is human to want to touch and to hold a connection to something or someone. It is a reflex thwarted by discipline. Greater self-discipline must be practiced. Intentions were honest.

I leave an ethereal rose with all that inspires, from now on.

Our steps retraced the main aisle to the front doors. Once again our group assembled to walk through the square, a finished tour. The

Pope's canopy under which he addresses the general audience was still erect, and now empty. I stood beside it, not having the nerve to stand under it as the Pope does. It was the reverse view of yesterday: colonnade arms encircled huge steps and cobblestone space where throngs of people once were, Saint Peter's obelisk at the heart, at the center, aligned with myself right now. The experience is a beautiful embrace.

We meandered down the side steps and into the square to be among the cobblestones once more, Saint Peter's obelisk to the right side. With other people's cameras I took pictures of our group. Vendors not allowed within the square linger at curbside. The moment one passes from square to street, the sacred passes into the marketplace of the sacred secular. Dad and I purchased rosaries from a street vendor. Theresa surveyed another vendor's table of figurines of popular saints. Delphi led us into an official Vatican gift shop. Dad, Frank, Don and Jozef Maszerkevicz wondered if he received a kickback, or some percentage of sales, at this "official" gift shop.

"Buy everything quickly." Delphi insisted. The bus was waiting. Those not interested in shopping boarded the bus immediately, Mom and Peg among them.

No matter, the shop had an excellent book department from which I purchased few books on history and art while Marie examined necklaces with gold charms of the Pope. I left the official gift shop happily, bag of books clutched in arm. Marie left disappointed, no necklace suited her taste, which she could not discern quickly.

TIVOLI, ITALY

On the bus after the Vatican tour, the group agreed that we did not want another unstructured afternoon to fritter. Most would have brooded in hotel rooms. I sat with Delphi and planned a tour based on his suggestion of what complimented what we have already seen. He suggested an excursion from Rome into the southern mountains for an afternoon tour. Since this was not scheduled, I bargained for a price and everyone gave twenty-five American dollars for the tour of Tivoli. We escaped the bustle and hum of Rome to discover the charms of rural Italy.

Tivoli is half an hour south of Rome, where Roman emperors then Popes would vacation in the summertime. Cacti and palm trees dotted the roadside. As we traveled the mountain air was cool in contrast to the tropical habitat.

Driving past olive farms and open land, we hugged the curving, slender road leading to a mountaintop restaurant where we would stop for a small lunch. From the restaurant the view stretched: mountains on the right plunging into an expanse of openness splotched by farms and small villages, in the distance the Rome skyline.

The attentive reedy waiter, Martini, served red wine and salad to start. Don emphasized that we wanted a small lunch quickly. With a nod, Martini knew how to abridge the meal so it was fantastic and speedy. This was his profession, his craft. The salt and pepper gray of his hair revealed this experience as much as his perfect timing and attention to every detail. As Michelangelo painted with God and Bernini built toward heaven's embrace, Martini presented the perfect meal, his life-long art of impeccable service of fine cuisine.

Naturally, I chose to sit by the picture window. Dick and Lou sat with me. Dick spoke of his exotic hat collection and how he procured each one, as Lou supplied the characteristics of each hat. Mom, Dad and Marie sat at a parallel banquet table with Frank and Rosemary, and Theresa and Jozef Mazurkiewicz. The ladies spoke of changing the way that they cook to adjust to more healthy living. The men, for the most part, stayed silent, drinking the wine and eating the first course before us. Frank, a police sergeant too dedicated to retire, sat beside

Dad. They became friends. Frank's wife, Rosemary, was a moderate personality: calmly absorbing all events in even manner, commenting in pleasant firmness occasionally.

Martini entered the room with trays of ravioli and cannelloni. Circling the room, he served each person what they specified. The cannelloni was an unusual delicacy: similar in concept to manicotti yet lighter, more dynamic: a crepe the size of a dinner plate ensconced a whipped cheese filling with garlic and basil. A drizzle of sun dried tomato sauce topped the cannelloni with a kiss. Martini was pleased when we requested more. We were pleased when we ate more. A quick lunch was no longer essential. Enjoyment was paramount. The wine and excellent meal soaked in as the village slept beneath us, and sun blazed impressions on mountain and valley. Kathy Jo and Doris finished their second glass of wine with laughter. A joke was made out of my earshot, which sent our second table in a roar of levity. Doris laughed so hard her eyes were teary. Dick mentioned a fez he purchased in Poland last year; Lou told of Dick giving Matthew money to buy a fez for him in Ukraine. The meal was affecting Mom as well: she wrapped her table's attention by describing her recipe for low fat eggplant Parmesan and telling the story of its invention. The mood was as light as the food.

Did anyone cancel the special lasagna at yesterday's café? I wondered. The question softly circulated around the table before it was addressed. Don answered that he said he would call the café this morning if we were eating lunch there, giving the chef time to prepare the special meal. Since Don never called to confirm, he assumed that no preparation would have been done, no fresh lasagna waiting. In his mind all was reconciled. In my mind, a polite phone call explaining changed plans would have been in order with sincere gesture of gratitude. Don was our leader and as he labeled it finished, so it was. No one spoke more of it. I still thought a call was the least we could have done. Hopefully, no special lasagna was made without gracious recipients.

Apple tart with lattice top next was presented for dessert. The fine cinnamon beige fruit glistened under lattice as if stained glass windows, so beautiful I stared at it before casting the fork the first time. Martini slyly placed cornucopias of fresh fruit at each table. Green grapes were eaten with apple tart, a succulent combination. Pears, oranges, and plums also poured from the cornucopias. As we finished the wine with the fruit, Martini surveyed the range of our content expressions. His suave attitude lit. I instructed him to give me the bill, as I was elected the group's accountant and money exchange firm.

Collecting money from each person, I paid the bill including tip. Together Martini and I balanced the bill; the extra money collected was given as a tip, all of it. Martini was so happy with the tip he charmingly kissed my hand, calling me a generous young lady. On the spot, our group was willing to leave me for married. Please take her, they teased and pleaded. He laughed and told them he was too old...but wait a moment.

Now it was getting embarrassing. He returned with a teenage waiter, handsome and spry in an awkward adolescent way. Upstaging the jest, he introduced the young man with pomp and demanded that the young waiter kiss my hand as well. I had had enough. I am not a teenager in need of a prom date. I told them it was an unnecessary token, gesture of hospitality already accepted. Italian words were exchanged between superior and teenager, producing a suspect glint in the young man's eyes. Anyway, he sweetly took my hand and kissed it dutifully as if I were his distant cousin. As quickly as possible I thanked him for the introduction, wished the teenage waiter well and sped to the exit where the pure mountain air reconfigured my unraveled continence.

Dick and Lou were waiting to board the bus. "Thanks for taking care of the money for us, young lady," Dick said.

"We are impressed by your money skills and traveling smarts so young. Our boys were savvy at a young age too," Lou added.

I smiled and drank the intoxicating view: villas and farms clinging to waves of earth while mountains parade in triumph.

Refreshed, the tour of Villa D'Este began with a stroll through plaza and avenue to the villa. Since it was riposo pomeridiano, we were the only tour group there. Aside from a dozen stray travelers, we had the villa to ourselves. Entering through the courtyard, one could view all wings and floors from the open center. The villa itself was splendid: first floor of rooms piled on top of each other with various themes in frescoes and furniture ranging from religious to myth to hunting and outdoor life.

The first room, the dining room, impressed with landscapes and seascapes ornamenting the walls, all skies leading to the curved ceiling where a ban of puti introduced a heavenly fresco of activity: angels and birds fly among clouds and saints. An enormous marble fireplace of sculpted figures took up most of the far wall. This decoration was not of Roman care, highly polished with attention of a staff of conservators. These works of art had the dust and weather of centuries coating their morals. There were no guards present, requesting one to keep a specified distance. Photography was allowed. We felt as visitors, true guests, allowed to wander at leisure. Delphi drew our attention to the floor in the upper-most corner. The wooden floorboards were replaced with glass, exposing archeological ruins of a Roman bath. Apparently this site has been a summer retreat for millennia of Roman citizens. Amphoras were toppled under glass. The cracked and severed remains of mosaic floor and basins beamed in the floodlights, calling the imagination to picture their original splendor and utility. As in this room, we slowly filed through many others, ending in a small chapel that lead to stairs. The second floor was not open to the public. We descended the stairs to enter anterooms to the gardens. A moss-covered fountain trickled a meditative tune, inviting one to sit at the marble bench below it, slightly less moss-covered. Yet the gardens were the most mystifying of the estate, hailing attention.

Careening down hillside, the gardens formed an unending labyrinth of greenery, medieval cobblestone paths and fountains. Two and three story fountains told the myth of the founding of Rome or explained the personal lives of the Greek and Roman gods. Next to this alcove of fountains, stretched a quarter mile row of a Hundred Fountains that would launch the rest of the gardens. Erect, a hundred gargoyles, griffins and beasts cast parabolic curves of water into a trough of stone and ivy. The sidewall of the trough has one hundred fish heads and sea serpents spitting into another trough that expanded into retaining wall and seat. Paths in front of the Hundred Fountains were mosaic works of art: colorful circles in cobalt blue squares, a patchwork of alternating, vibrating hues. A tree, millennia old, rooted along the mosaic path by the top spray of the central Fountain of Dragons. This tree had the girth of five oaks, at least. Its trunk resembled an open hand, dense fingers tipped in green. I climbed into the palm of the tree hand and happily sat for a short reflective time. The tree was amicable, accepting and soothing me. The Hundred Fountains pranced and cajoled as if performing on stage. Delphi called the group to assemble once again.

Standing at the first balcony attached to the villa anterooms looking down at the acres of gardens, Delphi gave us five Italian minutes to explore the gardens on our own. Most of the group could not handle the grade of the medieval stairs and chose to stay on that veranda, with several fountains to see along the corridor of a Hundred Fountains. Mom and Dad fondly retreated to the moss marble bench to sit and enjoy the view. But I could not be stopped. I ran down the steps, eager to absorb as much as possible in a few short minutes. Marie chased after me.

She was no match for me. By the time I was at the base of the fountain of dragons, she was still carefully scurrying from the top. The breeze was just enough to guide the water away from the circumference of the serpents in the base toward the front walkway, right where I stand. The wriggling serpents incite mischief and exploration. The mist is inviting on this hot autumn afternoon. I took Marie's picture along the side of the dragon fountain and scamper on to see what amazement presented itself around the corner. Looking at the underside of the balconies and the vast white stonewall of the villa, Kathy Jo and Doris stood waving. I waved back, enthusiastically.

"Run! Run!" Kathy Jo and Doris implored, "See everything you can possibly see, there is not much time!" But first I photographed these ladies hugging each other while leaning over balcony railing, giddy. My spirit leapt at their gloomy countenance evaporated. Then they disappeared from view.

Down a long passageway of cypress trees and bushes, a quick turn leads to a steep slope of cobblestone. Natural momentum has me running. Cobblestone gave way to slate at the base of what appeared to be a building façade complete with columns and turret, the Organ Fountain. The only music I hear is that of tumbling, rustling water being continually propelled two stories up, splashing down two stories, bubbling. I am staring the penetrating look of meditation. The water waves and conducts, the moving water a picture of stillness. In the pluming mist, I see a single rainbow contained in the base of the fountain. The organ is calling fractured light to parade in colorful symphony of nature. For, this is where the Organ Fountain derived its name. Marie is questioning, where am I. Sitting at the base of the organ facing away toward the reflecting pools I reply; I am waiting. Gurggling water at my back, placid waters in front, my heart cannot comprehend the satisfaction it feels this moment, only this moment. Marie finally arrived delighted to find me, but more importantly delighted to see the magnificence of the domed fountain with eagle statue, in taxiing stance, crowning it. Now she wants her own moment to ponder at the fountain, in private thought I would not invade. During that moment, I continue down to another labyrinth, which ends in fantastic gardens of flowerbeds and forest. Vision enough, I turn to retrace the path that led me there. After that moment, we amble together back up the steep graded lane.

"I'm looking for you. Come back!" Delphi yelled as he trotted past us, attempting to consolidate the group once more. Marie's knee provided the perfect excuse to dawdle. While she slowly plotted up the steep stairs, I ran to the top of the organ fountain to see the view. Mist from cascading water filtered a scenic overlook of mountains with pools in the foreground. Quickly making my way to the main stairs, I almost passed a small arched opening.

Suddenly turning, I discovered a fountain not functioning and well hidden in ivy-laden walls. There was a small stone bench, moss covered, in the far corner of the alcove. This cozy hiding space would have been ideal for a moment's solitude. No one would have seen me unless one entered the alcove, approached the silent fountain and turned to face the entrance but veered to the left. Arched moss in ancient mortars supply, I thought. A poem was aching to be born, with muse the midwife. Holy precipice enshrines disabled fountain; the poem flowed imaginary waters. Scrambling through my purse, I could not find my journal— no journal. Where is it? What was the first line? Arched moss, remember arched moss, I instructed myself. Fretful I tried to recall where I last saw it…in the hotel on my bed. All lines lost with no instruments to hold them fast. Arched precipice, that was not right. The lyric beauty for the moment had past. Muse floated overhead, just out of reach. By now Marie caught up to me and admired the silent alcove from its entrance. My moment was gone; that sudden moment of quiet inspiration flew—a missed opportunity. Never again would I be caught without my journal. Around the labyrinth of manicured shrubbery to the plotting Fountain of Dragons, ascending cautiously, we tread. The aisle of Hundred Fountains beckoned our return in orchestrated repose. Perhaps the Tivoli muse would fancy my dreams the poem to bestow, another chance.

Marie and I returned to the veranda where Delphi waited. Others decided to shop in town; we were not holding up the group, only holding up the guide in wrangling the group. His reclining stature and puckish smile implied we were not detaining him; we seemed to be an entertaining spectacle for his personal audience.

"Your energy amazes me. I did not think you had that kind of stealth and vigor in you," Delphi was bold enough to expostulate. Flattered yet dismayed by the sedentary preconceived notion, I reflected the puckish smile, speechless. An Italian five minutes equals half an hour, a half-hour of playful glee. I asked Delphi how much time he gave the others to shop.

"Ten Polish minutes, since you are a Polish group; a little less than five Italian minutes I would say," he replied with a grin.

I am Polish.

Ten minutes in real time, but many in the group would take longer, not allowing a trivial thing as time to interrupt their agenda. There were views to explore, a market square to scour, and a pedestrian walk through wooded mountaintop to meander. No one would proceed to the bus without being satisfied with one's impressions and experiences, perusing the whole. That is Polish time.

Delphi, Marie and I exited Villa D'Este at leisurely pace, stopping in the gift shop first. As we dawdled and browsed kiosks lining the path to the plaza, Kathy Jo and Doris were examining amphora and sculptures in the pottery kiosk at right bend in the path. Shopping was their element. We waved as we passed. Scarves are next! Doris joked, although I was sure they would visit every kiosk in the market before pointing in direction of our meeting place, our bus.

Mom and Dad were in the heart of the market square when Marie and I found them. Mom discovered a kiosk of ceramics and purchased a wall sculpture of flying cherub holding a cornucopia of fruits. Briefly we walked through the wooded park, enjoying the view of fountains rushing from mountainside into the arid landscape below. Large groups of tourists began to crowd the piazza. Riposo pomeridiano was over and the afternoon tours commenced. The private estates of our independent wanderings yielded to a bustling town of maximum occupancy. Our private Tivoli was now relinquished to the masses. We aimed our sights at the bus parked across the street where Delphi was hailing us to board.

He was nervous, almost frantic, as frantic as his relaxed disposition would permit; we were running overtime and the bus was due for another group in Rome. Even with Delphi's flailing and gestures, we were one of the first to take our places on the bus. He was forced to run through the crowded streets to implore others to board in haste. If our time were clocked, it was about twenty-five minutes in ordinary time. Delphi was right; ten Polish minutes is a little less than five Italian minutes.

Cacti and palm trees, ruddy ground and olive grove pass by the window as the bus slips back to Rome. Mountains released scrolling hills of terra cotta and burnt sienna. Lost in the landscape of honey and wine, the senses could not get enough. Floating, pleasure soaked, in motionless air, life seeps: into the craving earth, into the exotic, stretching flora and fauna, into the timeless spirit of bounty. The open, honest beauty of Italian countryside will not be easily forgotten, ever.

The yawning, brittle countryside gradually gave way to the traffic and clustered living of the city. The Tiber bowed in greeting through hill and expressway. The Aurelian walls crept into view as a sunbathing cat. Our hotel approached much quicker than it should. Delphi flittered goodbye and good rest for another day of touring together tomorrow morning. Shaking hands, I thanked the driver for his day of service and patience. Half of the collection of bills and coins I garnered from willing participants on the bus ride back I gave to the driver who seemed pleased. The other half will be saved to tip Delphi tomorrow after the morning's tours. We had two hours before dinner and would create our own siesta to rejuvenate for our last evening in Rome.

To end the visit, our group ate a farewell dinner at Rom Antica, in which we first ate. The travel agency instructed the manager to serve the best meal on the menu to the stranded American tour group as a symbol of friendship: seafood pasta, prawns, and calamari. The waiter was offended when I refused to eat the pasta course of seafood pasta and risotto with scallops. At this point I had to tell the waiter that I was vegetarian and that any meatless pasta would be fine for me to eat. The travel agency was informed of a vegetarian being among our group; yet the agency had neglected to incorporate that information into its planning. A few minutes later he returned with a plate of fettuchini in mushroom sauce. I was very happy and voiced my appreciation. However, others began to complain about the calamari being served cold and that the portions were excessive.

Deeply frustrated and insulted, the manager cleared the pasta course and served tiny portions of the main course to each person. The music stopped. The soloist who serenaded me the first evening vanished into the inner rooms not to be seen again. Tension built. People muttered in whispers. Servers congregated in the kitchen. Parties at other tables would not look beyond their immediate circle. What could happen next; no one knew or would be surprised at any outburst.

The salad course was served next: a variety of lettuce, black olives, beets, carrots and sweet corn. The varying tastes of sweet and salty were pleasing. Everyone enjoyed the salad and dessert courses. We expressed it so, attempting to assuage the insult of the other courses. The manager's icy attitude slightly defrosted. Hazelnut gelato. The exquisite dessert was faultless. Hazelnut gelato soothed all nerves in creamy tranquility. We began to joke. We began to laugh. Everyone complimented the meal. The manager appreciated the gesture and the sincere enjoyment of food. Thankfully, the music started once again: traditional Italian folk songs played over crackling speakers. A little dessert wine came, just a touch, and then coffee to seal the evening in a bouquet of splendor.

Finally when we were leaving, the manager asked what he could do to satisfy fussy Americans. Expounding, he told that this was not the first incident with Americans not eating all of his carefully balanced dishes on the menu. Marie explained that we were not trying to be offensive but not used to exotic seven course meals. Succinctly she illustrated that if he came to her Polish American house for dinner she would serve him the best cabbage, sausage, and perogi. Serving salad and dessert, three courses would be at most presented. He cringed. She explained that she could not be offended if he would not eat the meal because she did not know his tastes. If his tastes were known, she could plan a fine meal, but without knowing the other, one can only extend from oneself and hope for the best. The best is not accomplished in every instance. Our welcoming banquet was marvelous, perfect. And, it was all right that this one was as intended.

I told him that we truly appreciated all of his efforts and that it was a great experience even though it did not turn out as perfectly as he planned. What he presented was thoughtfully prepared and gorgeously presented. For the rest, I am deeply sorry. He kissed Marie on the cheek and shook my hand. All three of us felt better. Tonight the sentiment meant much more than the food. No one should be difficult to please when offerings are sincere.

The night was warm. Mom, Dad, Marie and I strolled and lolled through the streets as the others steam rolled to the hotel. Rushing traffic could not compel us to move faster. We were intoxicated on wine and spirits, Italian affable spirits. The city was incandescent without neon and billboards, but with the electric glow of streetlamps and internal lights of buildings' private activities spilling into streets. Eventually, we returned to the hotel and parted for the night. Dad would not sleep much; wine and a good walk could not calm his worries for a safe flight. As Marie resumed her nightly rituals, I scrambled through my purse for the stray candy wrapper. Without hesitation I threw it into the wastebasket under the desk. Now I was able to sleep.

Puti flying amidst clouds of sound, an organ churning would wake me from a cautious sleep. Dionysus and the grotto of Roman bathtubs from the Vatican Museum commingle with Martini kissing my hand and the eerie stillness of the mossy alcove. Dreams destroy the order of experiences the mind creates in wakeful consciousness. With one eye open I comment these lines to page to banish them from dreams.

Everyday Saturnalia

Villa of medieval cardinal envisions
God through timeless hourglass
Refracted and rejoined
Many one, one many.

Gods rest within
Cracked remains once a bath.
Oiled Jupiter reclines; mirthful Bacchus splashes
Where bronze serpents wreathe.

Trickling brook of cast fountains
    Flow downhill:
Seraphim chasing griffins and goblets
    Through plotting stream.

Arched moss on ancient mortars
Supply holy precipice
    Enshrining disabled wellspring.

God is in the brush, is in the vine
Weaving through fountainhead,
Mystical and divine waters
Rush immortal spring.

Reflecting pools my eyes,
My ivy covered arms a basin
Of tranquility retreating
Into shadowed wall

For eternity to frame
My bones in stone,
Blood circulating clear truth
Of waters' rebirth;

Tourists come for leisure, stride
Reprised Muses proclaim
Fluid message from marble lips,
"We are with you."

"Have a pleasant continuing journey."
– LOT PILOT, LANDING IN WARSAW

ROME, ITALY

I WOKE EARLY with a start. It was our last day in Italy and I did not wish to miss a wink of it, especially not for something as trivial as sleep. Marie was lying in bed waiting for me to stir, rising, as usual, before I did. We dressed and went to the lobby to climb the only staircase that led to the rooftop café. Tony was attending the reception desk. He smiled at us, good morning. Ease and pleasure returned to Tony's gait as we exchanged morning greetings for the last time. His family was safe, where they belong, he offered. Marie and I did not know how his son managed to get to Rome, or was he safe in Los Angeles or on a boat or plane currently, and we were not bold enough to ask. We did not wish to disturb a placid temper. He told us of the marvel of having his family together after a catastrophic week. They knew how to cherish each other now more than ever. The bride's parents bought a villa outside of Rome, near Tivoli, and will renovate it, making Italy her and her parents' new home.

The head maid walked past us, her gray curls complimented her black linen suit. She waved and said hello without stopping. We inquired if she was Tony's wife, as we had concocted stories of them as owners, managers and partners. They were cordial enough with each other that it seemed possible. Tony said no, no emphatically. His wife was beyond hotel work, he said.

"My wife," he clasped his hands on heart when speaking of her, "is beauty and love beyond earthly bounds—so lovely the angels weep." His eyes reflected inward the tenderness of thirty years of adoration. He was genuine love. His wife was lucky to have him as a husband. Yet this sentiment, this demeanor goes beyond them as a couple. This is Italy, I thought, its people so affecting the angels weep.

Tony bid us go eat. We said goodbye in case he was not at the desk when we would check out later this morning. He insisted we visit again; he would see us next time under better circumstances. Tony would not be at his post when we checked out an hour later. I was relieved we said goodbye when we did. It would have been sad to leave with no goodbye, without knowing if his son was safe. We ascended to a marble heaven with croissants and popovers waiting. The coffee this morning was the best of my life. The strong aroma and rich texture awakened the senses to myriad pleasures. Sipping. Sipping slowly. Sipping softly the bittersweet liquid was as medicinal as natural spas of pure water, a panacea. I would not leave Rome without a bag of coffee. Venus, head tilted, peered approvingly.

After the usual breakfast with the gods (I could not say goodbye to the gods of the rooftop café, only farewell), the scheduled tour started: the walking tour of fountains then the tour of ancient Rome. For months I had been excited about Trevi Fountain. Being an old movie hound, the lure of "Three Coins in the Fountain" drew me to it with all its maudlin charm. Friends had sent coins with me with wishes already attached. The three coins were ready.

The expanse of Trevi Fountain is remarkable: gods stand aloft watching the floods of water stream from remote corners while winged horses give chase to mermen for half a city block. The immense oval pool collected the teaming horses and water with a curved lip of retaining wall. My knees caressed that lip as I fished the coins out of their special holder for safekeeping. With no ceremony I threw them into the water. Delphi walked over to me and said I had done it all wrong; for wishes to be granted you must stand facing the street, not the fountain, and throw the coins over the right shoulder. Now what do I do? Will my friends' wishes come true? I have to do it again.

Delphi was keeping close eye on my coins. One thrown means a guaranteed return to Rome; two means a love affair in Rome; three means marriage in Rome. Stepping back for space, I would not let him see my handful of coins (after all this is my last day and my wish and my last chance to get it right). Turning to face the street, I fisted three coins then released them over proper shoulder as required, thinking good thoughts. So whose wishes will come true? This is a bungle. Six coins in a fountain: three right, three haphazard. Do I get the marriage in Rome or is that transferable to my friends since the original coins were for them? Or do I get two marriages in Rome? That is more interpersonal activity in life than I care to handle (one, eventually, is fine, two is no good). I will at least return to Rome of my own account. I am young and will make sure of it. Perplexed, yet hopeful for one of all these wishes to come true, I rejoined the group to walk through the thin alley to the next wonder, the Pantheon.

The wiry alley twisted to reveal expensive boutiques and cafes, inexpensive street vendors and an open-air market. Pyramids and domes of jewel tone fruit glistened, from cart to cart an extravaganza of fresh produce, so many potential desserts. Pushing forward with head turned back, the avenue flushed into a whirling plaza of ancient commotion. An Egyptian obelisk marked the plaza in front of the Pantheon, one noble fixture of history paying homage to the other in turn and force.

Corinthian columns support the coffered dome of the Pantheon to heights unimaginable. The elegant facade of column and pediment did not betray the purity of the interior architecture. This ancient house of gods and goddesses turned Catholic church impressed with essentials: a vacuous center filled with natural light from the oculus in the dome dispersed fragmented light to side altars. The main altar, in shadow now, is a lesser cousin of that of St. Peter's Cathedral: twisting columns of marble baring canopy over altar.

In one side altar the tomb of Rafael resides. Bronze doves in flight with beaks sharing an olive branch protect his resting-place. Above, an eight-foot tall marble statue of the Madonna compassionately holding upright the infant Jesus presides over his tomb. He requested to be buried in the Pantheon, buried in the creative grandeur of this house of gods. I stepped closer to the doves fluttering about my knees. Upon inspection, they were not sharing a branch; their beaks are touching, as if food, or something more intimate, is being consumed by both. One bird is upside down, spiraling to keep in time with the other's pace. Yet all wings are visually upright and extended: feathers aflame, flickering rapidly, perpetual haste of love's ignition. The doves' bodies align poetically, although one is inverted. And there he is, not a meter below doves' feet, the symbolic remains sealed in marble and bronze. Rafael loved his fiancé and his mistress model. Which does the dove represent? Rafael, the spiraling inverted dove, lunged to meet his muse unabashedly. Any moment the doves will fly through the dome. Their spirit permeates the atmosphere. Muses are everywhere. I linger a moment, still, while Delphi guides the group to the center.

The sunbeam through oculus was too tempting to resist. Our group congregated under the center of the dome, where in the exact center of the Pantheon and dome is a fleur-de-lis of gold inlaid into the floor. Each person took a turn standing on the golden floret looking up and wished for inspiration. Some told wishes aloud, others did not. Mom whispered for world peace. Dad wished for a safe journey for all and a safe return home. I stood, head bowed, thanking the forces that be for what I have, for what I am experiencing, for the peace I feel within, and for what I know will be eventually. Then, looking up into hallowed light, an inner voice told me to embrace what comes. The light burned instantly as my once closed eyes dilated. Golden light, not white light, streams bronze. The moment now past to the next wishful individual, I left the sunbeam eager to see what wonders are yet waiting to behold.

Another walk down slender lanes led to the Plaza of Fountains and the Church of Saint Agnes, every brick of the church ornate and impressive. One fountain housed four men of marble, the cardinal directions. Fearing God, the sculpted man to the north shielded his face from the Church of Saint Agnes. On the tips of his index finger of the hand posed to block sacred heavens, a pigeon was perched. I was captivated. Pigeons lit on any surface in Rome, any fountain, any newsstand. Yet here was a clever bird surveying God in a natural position. The pigeon made the man seam as if he was not in fear of God but enraptured by the presence of the pigeon—the miracle of ordinary creatures. I approached the fountain and quickly photographed the pigeon before it took flight for other remarkable views.

Artists gathered in the plaza to sell their work and paint in front of watching tourists and marble protectors of Rome. Approaching one lady's easel, she addressed me in Italian. I asked her if she spoke English, which she did a little. She asked where I was from, and when I explained, she expressed regret and sympathy for New Yorkers.

"Don't you miss home?" she inquired.

There was no possible way to get home, I explained. So, we try to contact home, but this is very difficult as well. I was glad to be safe and in Rome where everyone has been very hospitable. Nodding her head slightly, her long black hair fell from shoulder to shoulder blade. If Rome were crumbling she would race to be here, protecting her city in any way she could. I fell silent, looking down. She noted my gloom.

A variety of pastel drawings and charcoal sketches were exhibited on an easel while larger works were stacked in a wooden rack. She graciously allowed me to pour through her work, settling on a pen and ink sketch of the Pantheon. With a handshake we parted, once again words of sympathy given. I was reassured by her kindness during this time of uncertainty.

Hugging the picture I returned to the fountain of Neptune where the group was to reassemble. Marie also purchased artwork but from a different artist in the square. When we showed the pieces to the group, Mom and Dad smiled and agreed on the excellent choices. Delphi did not care for street art, he stated. I stared at him speechlessly, abhorred.

Back on the bus, Delphi announced that there would be a world-wide moment of silence at noon to honor the victims of the terrorist attacks. The tour would continue as planned, but wherever we were at noon, we would stop to honor them. In Ancient Rome the bus tour turned into another walking tour. Mom, worn out from the tour of fountains, chose to stay on the bus with a few others.

The Arch of Constantine welcomed us to the ancient city. The Coliseum stood proudly in the background right. Ruins of the Roman forum hid in the background and foreground left: foundations and column bottoms exposed with only remembrances of the structures they once held. We did not have enough time before our flight to tour the Coliseum. For half an hour together the group walked the paths outside the arch and Coliseum, without getting neither too close nor too far. The arch was under renovation, gated off from the public. A black cat was on the prowl for a fat pigeon.

At exactly twelve noon, we stopped.

We were walking back to the bus along side the forum ruins. Most of us chose to sit on the wall next to an arched entrance to the ruins. Grieved by the moment and our tenuous grip on family and country, Dad could not sit still but paced under the archway searching the archaic stone for answers. Did the stones respond favorably? Could he interpret their answers?

Now everything was still and silent. Traffic halted. Tours paused. Pedestrians slowed and some stopped. We bowed our heads.

Not for long, just the length of a traffic signal--a minute or maybe less, Rome was in reflective silence. Yet Rome, the giant city of chaotic passionate movement, paused.

It was a solemn and awesome moment of reverence shared with strangers at a memorial of a place of martyrdom and gruesome entertainment. This moment we make a memorial for just as gruesome an act as feeding people to lions. The Ancient Romans would turn in their graves, savage as they were to anyone other than themselves. May the American government learn a lesson from the Roman Empire: does it want to be remembered for brutal retaliation against an incomprehensible other, or does it want to be an example of tolerance, endurance, and understanding of world cultures and religions? In this moment no questions will be answered, only emotions will have a chance to be expressed. Our group remained quiet well past the Roman moment of silence.

After a short bus tour of City Center, driving past the Spanish Steps, the Palace of Culture, government buildings, and more ruins. We were scheduled to have an afternoon walking tour of these sights, but the increase protocol at the airport shortened the last day's events. These sights sped by in the blur of a city block at highway speeds. The Palace of Culture struck most: Pegasus guarding each side of the ornate columns and busts lining the pure white building. Delphi expounded that the Palace of Culture was built by order of Mussolini as a gift to the Italian people. Italians do not like it. "The wedding cake" they call it, too ornate and showy for real Italian taste, Delphi illustrated. Poland has a Palace of Culture; Italy has a Palace of Culture. What is America's Palace of Culture? The domineering Twin Towers jutting into the New York skyline with the presence of a hero in triumphant glory after completion of a quest for a global democracy and community welcoming all in one vision. No, the towers reached beyond culture. It is now a pile of debris drenched in the tears of a nation in shock. Throughout the Union, America has many palaces of culture: The Empire State Building, The Sears Tower, Disneyland, The French Quarter of New Orleans, Mesa Verdi, Falling Water. Many different symbols comprise an intricate nation of vagabond idealists and steadfast natives. On a billboard near the street a sign was pasted over advertisements of plays and concerts. The sign read in Italian "Condemn terrorism. Stand with America." Along the bus route, I began to notice that these signs were everywhere. They consoled vaguely, as an unsigned greeting card.

Once again we were late and rushed, keeping Delphi from other obligations.

In front of ruins of the Roman senate, Delphi moved to disembark, turning to say a word before jumping to sidewalk. I was designated by our group to give him tip money collected. So with thanks and an Italian kiss, a single brushing cheek to cheek (sometimes brushing of each cheek in turn, in this instance only one), he was tipped, thanked and slightly taken aback. I was astonished that I was brash enough to venture an Italian kiss with a near stranger. Flushed, he said goodbye, threw some bills at the bus driver, and ran down the block to catch the city bus. I waved as he ran past my window and he returned the wave and yelled, "Ciao!"

On the way to the airport, I begged the bus driver to stop somewhere, anywhere for a WC. Along the roadside, ten minutes outside of town there was McDonalds. The driver did not mind; he took an unscheduled smoke break.

Da Vinci Airport had increased security since it reopened on Thursday for European travel only. We made it through customs and security without any problems. From receptionists to security guards, people are being exceptionally nice to us as traveling Americans.

Mom, inspired by her pilgrimage and the Pope's words, decided to reciprocate the good wishes. There was an hour before our flight to Warsaw. To calm their nerves, Mom and Dad chose to sit at the gate facing the windows during that time. They watched planes landing and planes taxiing on several runways. Mom said the rosary, and then began to bless each plane she witnessed in flight. At first it was in words only, a short whispered prayer of blessing. Then she became more avid: blessing each plane with a sign of the cross gesture toward the window, a quick Hail Mary as the jet either landed or departed, and then either a "thanks be to God" for a safe landing or a short prayer of safe trip to airborne plane departing. In the interim, she continued the rosary. Dad did not partake in the blessing, but sat in meditative silence two seats away from Mom.

Marie and I went shopping. Marie was on a hunt for unique souvenirs for her grandsons whom she missed more than anyone else. I was on a hunt for coffee. My hunt was satisfied first, as we stepped into an airport café for water and a newspaper; a display of packaged coffees stood in the doorway. Marie's quest took longer, but was successful: identical Pinocchio dolls, carved wood, on stands with highly moveable joints and limbs. Feeling pleased with ourselves, we browsed the duty free shop. Eyeing a sale area, I convinced Marie to peer further. Two angora sweaters lay on a twenty percent discount shelf. They were men's size large, but we did not care. We tried them on. One was speckled black and navy; the other was periwinkle, a grayish blue. Marie fit the sweater in proportion and looked stylish. The sweaters swam on me; yet, as a jacket or lightweight coat it would be suitable. I prefer loose clothing. Without hesitation I bought the black and navy sweater, which prompted Marie to buy the other one. This was a smart decision, as the weather in Poland was cold and rainy and I wore the sweater everyday thereafter.

We settled ourselves next to Mom at the gate with just a few minutes before boarding. She was elated with her blessings, as if she had personally guided each plane to safety. Her eyes flashed in holy symbiosis. Noticing the sweater, she complimented it and my acquisition of it. Dad thought it handsome. It fit him well. I promised to give it to him as soon as we were back home. For now, I needed it.

Our plane boarded and taxied with no commotion. A blonde Polish businesswoman sat next to me, while Marie sat on my other side. The woman repeatedly crossed herself with no apparent soothing effects, her edgy disposition never changing. She sniffled and coughed for almost an hour. I offered her tissues and hard candy. With a sweet smile of appreciation, she waved a broad no gesture, declining; however, offered us cough drops, which we accepted. Marie began to speak to her in Polish, to calm her spirits. Thankful for the common language and the gesture, she happily conversed with Marie. She thought that Marie was my mother, an idea that Marie would not confirm nor deny. At landing, an ovation guided us to gate. The pilot took it as a compliment and a blessing. With one more cross, the woman shook our hands and greeted us to her Poland of deep and wide tradition.

Antoni and Edward picked us up at the airport. Once gathered on the bus, the first expression Antoni made was one of condolence and sympathy of Polish heart with America. He explained what reactions were in Poland at the time of the attacks: dismay and disbelief, a flood of phone calls to relatives in America, and instant solidarity of spirit with the American people. His words resounded through bus and boulevard until we reached the hotel.

Once in Warsaw, our microgroup of nineteen felt more at home. We settled in the Forum Hotel and ate dinner in the hotel banquet hall, intending to meet the rest of the group. A buffet of salads, fruits and breads stood adjacent to a hot table of meats and vegetables. On the far side was a table of desserts, coffee and tea.

Since our flight was delayed, others coming from Ukraine or various areas of Poland chose to eat early. We met those who were still dining, but not the entire group. That would wait until tomorrow. There were no shortage of topics of conversation; yet very little was said. Everyone had a story of where they were when they heard the news about the tragedy, and stories of their travels and genealogical research. Hurried, abridged stories were told as most were not eating for pleasure but eating for nourishment. Those who were very weary where already in their rooms, resting.

As he roamed and greeted each table of our group members, the first thing on Matthew's lips was "did you have a good time," remaining in vacation frame of mind. I did not overhear what others said at various tables. I was the first to answer the question at my table. I said, "yes." Mom, Dad, and Marie also affirmed the question. Pleased, Matthew proceeded to other tables.

I hailed him to return. Sitting down, Matthew nudged me as if I was flirting with him by coyly waving at him.

"Yes, if you were only forty years younger," I suggested. He would settle for me being twenty years older, he retorted.

"Sorry, I don't want to rush it," my final reply.

Seriously, we compared stories of travel, news, and emotional responses to each. His travels to L'Wów, Ukraine were unstructured and unruly. They saw some interesting sites: churches, castles, town center, however they had much time of country wandering and hotel room dwelling. No guide was hired to focus their travels. His group of six relied on him as a tour guide and interpreter. This would lead to some organized site seeing, some disarray, and always humor.

Nestling into his upholstered chair while firmly planting elbows on table, Matthew launched into what would be the story of his group's Ukrainian adventure: Dinner in the hotel restaurant provided the evening's entertainment. Drinks rotated in hasty gesture as soup and bread began its course. A platter of jerky was presented: a strange delight, shriveled and cured to salty perfection. Matthew held a strip in midair for inspection before pressing teeth and jowl into the labor of ingestion. The waitress passed his chair. Inquisitively, Matthew addressed her, showing the remaining stub of jerky as evidence. "What is this?"

"Do you like it?" the pleasing waitress retorted in Ukrainian.

"Yes, but…" Matthew reiterated this questioning sentiment.

"It is coin," she finally replied, encouraging the tourists to eat well.

Matthew's Ukrainian was conversational, but his Polish was fluent. Coin. In Polish kón means horse. This can't be horsemeat. Is this horsemeat? Visions of Black Beauty and Budweiser stallions colored his face a doubtful hue. He inquired, hoping for a negative response. The waitress would not fail; of course it was horsemeat.

"You don't like it?" she asked, becoming nervous at the thought of rejection.

With resolution, Matthew ate heartily the stub of jerky while reaching for another piece with other hand. Wonderful. Thank you. Then he informed the group, in English, that they were enjoying horsemeat. Gasps and chuckles reverberated. The platter was cleared when empty, with relief from the hostess and no requests for seconds from the tourists.

Matthew could not keep his composure while telling this story. The vigor of his elbows ground into tablecloth and the excitement of recapturing the moment increased the volume of his speech. For the rest of the trip he would repeat the story. "Kón" was the joke at every meal whether it applied or did not.

Matthew's group unknowingly booked rooms in a hotel outside of L'Wow, about ten kilometers south of the city. This was not an easy walking distance for self-guided tours. They required a shuttle bus to transport them into town; however they did not book the shuttle bus beforehand, so they were forced to shuttle at the hotel's earliest convenience. The first day of their trip was spent in the hotel or walking around the hotel grounds. Partially this was due to the attacks.

Arriving at the airport at nine o'clock for a ten o'clock flight, Matthew's group had only an hour and a half flight to L'Wow. As Matthew and his troupe were settling into the hotel and scurrying to arrange plans for four days, they saw the news of the attacks on television. The shuttle would not run that day. No matter, they thought it best to stay in the hotel for news bulletins.

Of the remaining three days, only one day and the morning of their last day were spent touring the city and its sights. Open countryside surrounding the hotel became their gardens, their entertainment, and their confines. Overall Matthew was pleased with the slothful pace and easy touring, but he feared that his troupe felt disappointed. Frankly, he directed the conversation toward pressing issues now that our group was reunited.

As our group coordinator, he wanted to know if anyone mentioned abandoning the trip to go home. As far as we knew, in the hours of open conversation, no one had mentioned it. There was no way to go home, he pointed out. Why lose the money and the experience of the trip to ruminate in Warsaw while merely waiting for the chance to be on a plane heading west? We must continue the tour. He did not have to convince us, for Dad deduced this logic yesterday. Matthew was happy that everyone agreed to continue the tour. Not one person broke away from our group to attempt to go home.

In the privacy of our Metropol Hotel room, Marie confided in me her thoughts. She had already lived through war and conflict. She knows what it is like to ration for the war effort. If we were in Europe, now in Poland, by the grace of God then she was going to make the most of it. If war breaks out there will be no more luxurious international travel. And if war does rage, its duration is indefinite. She is old. At this I balked and incited her vigor and youthful spirit. She quieted my attempts with a cold stare requiring all of her perspective to be heard. Silently I listened with complete attention. She is old and may not live to see the end of another world war. Then she is going to relish every experience in Poland: eat as she wishes, drink as she withstands, live each moment fully, and shop with abandon accumulating heirlooms for her daughter and other family members. Tomorrow is uncertain. Now is all we know that we have.

I shook my head in agreement. I understood her perspective although it was not my own. We will embrace what comes. With courage we will handle what we must. She accepted this response and ordered me to strict confidence. As friends, I would not jeopardize her trust.

Marie and I relinquished conversation to survey our room and settle ourselves for the evening.

I was happy to become reacquainted with Polish comforts: a huge feather pillow, puduszka, ensconcing head and shoulders, and thick perzina inviting warmth. The perzina is an outer casting in linen or flannel that neatly gathers two or three, thinner wool or fleece blankets inside, acting as one mechanism of slumber. Lying in bed was as if I were an inner layer of cake, concealed by dense sweetness of perzina ganache. With dim bathroom light guiding pen, I must stop and sleep. My head was already stuffed with the cold of the lady seated next to me on the plane. Energy is needed for tomorrow's journey. There is much more to come.

"Look at that mushroom picker!"
— Matthew, tour coordinator

ROUTE 7, HEADING NORTH

Morning doves were cooing outside my window, misty light of dawn gently waking. Is this my Polish lullaby to continue slumber or the sweetest alarm one could wish for? I lay awake, eyes closed, listening to the doves on the opposite side of the glass as if there were no barrier. I flew on their contented songs, jetting threw curling melodious clouds. Cooing meditation.

Marie woke sometime later and we began the usual morning scurry before meeting our group for breakfast.

Polish breakfasts are wonderful: croissants filled with butter cream, sweet rolls and savory breads, hard-boiled eggs, and fruit both fresh and preserved in light sauces. Black current juice, rich and dark, is as potent as wine for the start of a good day. The most important part, of course, is the coffee. Strong and freshly perked, I could drink a dozen cups. After a hearty breakfast each day, we packed up and boarded the bus headed for new sights to behold.

Entering the dining room late this morning, seven thirty, the room was filled. As others left to pack their luggage, we sat and stacked dishes to the side to make ample space for our breakfast. A waiter came to collect the dishes, and Dad addressed him in Polish at which the waiter looked cross. No one thought anything of the exchange, accept Dad. During the meal, once again, Dad addressed the waiter to ask a question in Polish. The boy did not understand, wincing as if in defiant pain of youth. From that point on Dad would not speak Polish, thinking that his language was weak and unintelligible.

Dad knows the Polish of early twentieth-century immigrants, the Polish his grandfather brought on the ship through Pennsylvania. His grandfather spoke in Polish to his children, and in turn Dad's parents spoke in Polish to him; they even sent him to a Polish speaking elementary school. Yet being severed from Poland the language took on a life of its own: accumulating slang and dialect differing from that developing in continental Poland. The basics of Polish, though, should be the same. Yes, this young waiter could not or would not understand Dad. But Dad took this too much to heart and would not speak in Polish throughout the remainder of the trip, not unless implored to speak. He would rather be viewed as a confused tourist than have his Polish, his American Polish, his first language, mocked.

Before departing, we gathered in the lobby to check out of our rooms and organize luggage. While we waited, we sat on sofas designed in two rectangular forms adjacent to each other. A large group of about twenty-five occupied the neighboring set of sofas.

"We have no place to go. We will be out on the streets." I overheard one couple talking heatedly.

The Asian American couple faced us and began to explain that their group of twenty was from California. They were touring Poland for two weeks and were scheduled to fly to Los Angeles on Wednesday,

September 12th. With all American airports still closed for international flights, they were stranded but still with accommodations through today. However with the hotel booked and no outbound intercontinental flights, they were at a loss as what to do next. The travel agency would not offer any further assistance with many other Americans in the same situation throughout Europe, their hands tied at the unprecedented events. There was no possibility to fly to Toronto or London, Paris or even Amsterdam, every flight booked. There was no way to fly anywhere along the Atlantic coast, where at least the notion of home being across the pond would stir hope. Anxiously, they waited for their group leader to report his findings after making several calls at the reception desk. Our group was assembled and readied for departure. With empathetic words, we wished them safe travel and good fortune in getting home as quickly as possible. They collected in a nervous huddle, banded together.

On the way out of Warsaw heading north, the bus passed by the American embassy to show us the response of Poles to the terrorist attacks. Guards in militia gear stood at attention outside closed embassy. Metal gates lined the sidewalk in front of the building to keep people at bay. Yet these gates were decorated with flowers and banners and flags. Memorial candles and flowers paved the sidewalk. This makeshift retaining wall turned into a living memorial constantly being augmented by the next person's story, feeling, connection. Letters attached by string to the metal bars breathed in the wind. Deeply touched we tried to stop the bus to get out and observe the monument closely, letting each petal and flame of emotion trickle into consciousness, but no traffic was allowed to stop in front of the embassy for security reasons.

A brief pause was all the chance we had; yet it was enough to spark mind and spirit into pensive thoughts of wounded home and soothing condolence. Edward held his position although the traffic light was green. For another moment we could witness this manifestation of peace and mourning. The light flashed green. This instance Edward was forced to drive by traffic pushing behind. This experience led to storytelling: a representative of each mini group sat in the guide's seat with microphone and shared each group's experiences on independent jaunt and reactions to hearing news of the attacks. First, Matthew told of his unpredictable ventures in L'Wow that he relayed to Mom, Dad and I last night after dinner. His story was identical in public and in private. Matthew then asked Alma and Steven to speak. They looked at each other in their bench, and without words Alma proceeded to the guide's seat to tell their story. Her petite frame was invisibly cradled in the guide's large chair. Instantly she stood to face our group rather than the chair's view of the front window. She began in neutral tones, with a keen eye of assessment, not nostalgia.

Alma and Steven met their guide, Iwana, in Warsaw, thinking they would begin ancestral searches in Warsaw Archives. However, when they arrived at the archives a researcher told them that the information they sought concerning Alma's grandparents was in Mlawa. Without hesitation they drove about an hour or so to discover that the archives in Mlawa were transferred to Nidzica for renovation of the archives building. A castle paraded in the center of Nidzica. Iwana suggested the castle restaurant for lunch. When they discovered that the castle is now a renovated hotel, they booked a three-night stay. From there they could drive within a couple hours to all the hometowns of Alma's parents and grandparents.

Nidzica Archives was a goldmine of information: grandparent's marriage license and birth certificates of their five children (including Alma's father). Researching for the afternoon, Iwana translated these documents from Russian to Polish for Alma, fluent in Polish, to copy. After the archives closed at 3 p.m., Iwana led them through

Old Town Nidzica where they browsed through shops. Steven stepped into a woodworker's shop and began to speak with the clerk in Polish. The clerk informed them of the attacks, offering empathy. Fear struck. Thoughts rushed to their daughter who lives in Brooklyn and works in Manhattan. Where was she this morning? Immediately they returned to the Teutonic Knight's Castle; news of the attacks was everywhere, every television, every radio. Where is she now?

Iwana rushed them to an Internet café where they would send messages to all three of their children. With no other recourse, they lightly dined at the castle then returned to the café to check for messages. Their son replied that all family members were safe. Relieved, Alma and Steven thanked Iwana for her swift action and thoughtfulness. The next day they would receive messages from their daughter explaining some facts, alluding to chaos, wishing to move back home in Ohio, thankful for their safety in Poland.

Over the next three days, they traveled to several villages in search of archives and cemeteries. First, Iwana took them back to Nidzica Archives to completely translate information housed there. They discovered her father's birthday was two years earlier than he claimed. Immigrating to America promised new life, for some new identity. Why not make one a few years younger as well? With excitement of new knowledge, they roamed through villages. Alma wished to see her grandfather's grave, or any relative for that matter. None were to be found.

At church of her father's village, the parish priest abridged his activity to assist them. Alma inquired of records of baptism or marriage from a century ago or further past of her father and grandfather, but the priest explained that his village, in fact all of Poland, had been through so many wars and occupations in the past century that if records survived one, they did not survive the other. He was fortunate to have records from the past fifty years, he stated ruefully. However, he invited them to search the old section of the cemetery.

In Poland, relatives care for cemeteries, not companies, parishes or government. As they passed the new section, neat rows of flowers, potted plants and candles formed beautiful tributes to the living dead. The old section was a field with rocks protruding. Overgrown weeds, grasses and bushes masked headstones of the old section, the forgotten dead. Iwana was the first to tear through bramble and weed, and brush stone with hand to read names. Steven and Alma followed suit until all were exhausted. They began to leave the old section.

Iwana tore a piece of bark from an ancient tree and presented it to Alma. "You're father was surely here at some time; he may have stood against this tree, sat under this tree. Take this. It is a remembrance."

The wonder of this symbol was not lost on Alma, yet she usually scoffed at the maudlin as sickeningly sweet. Steven, sentimental at heart but functionally an objective businessman, appreciated the gesture quietly. Alma accepted the bark with a simple "thank you." As she relayed this story, Alma grinned and pantomimed in animation, despite herself.

They returned to the medieval castle for lunch and luggage. Wiling away the afternoon on a leisurely drive to Warsaw, they peered onto woodlands and farmlands with natural appreciation. Iwana bade them farewell in Warsaw as they expressed their gratitude and complimented her expertise. That evening, they were glad to rejoin our group. We clapped for her story as she sallied through corridor to her bench where Steven was waiting with a broad grin. Matthew asked a representative of our Roman group to speak. Each gazed at each other. Marie wanted me to speak. I shook my head no. Finally Don stood and clenched the microphone. Pausing for first words to frame themselves, he breathed in deeply and began.

Don told of our flight into militia guarded Da Vinci airport, of the traffic jam, misinformation, and our arrival at the hotel to see the attacks on the television. His story roamed into details of Italian television and English rebroadcasts in the late hours of the night, and of staying in hotel rooms and trying to call relatives instead of touring. Monotonously he reported all events with equal weight. Briefly he mentioned the Pope speaking of the attacks to the General Audience, our touring the Vatican Museum and St. Peter's Basilica, our wanderings through Tivoli, and our whirlwind touring of fountains and sights of Rome yesterday morning before flight to Warsaw. Our whole group applauded Don's efforts to condense stories while remaining interesting. Matthew requested Brendon and David tell about their journey next. Neither would allow the other sole commentary.

Since theirs was the first seat behind Edward, Matthew stretched the microphone cord to their bench and they proceeded in exacting detail. Brendon and David traveled to northern ancestral towns in search of church records of baptism, marriage and final rites also in search of cemeteries, headstones relaying basest facts about one's life. Brendon began slowly, describing their guides: a husband and wife team, amiable in every way. David grabbed the microphone.

In Sokolniki they began. The lucid village of central Poland hid no secrets, only pointed a tree-lined path to its church and cemetery. David was in search of his mother's family. His mother, as a child, survived the Dakau, Germany concentration camp and then was transferred to the Polish resettlement camp, Altenstadt. When free, her mother with four children immigrated to America. Who could David find living or past? The cemetery held a row of family members: mother's cousins, uncles, aunts. With great excitement David photographed all tombstones for his genealogical records. At the local post office, David found several relatives in the phone book, correlating with addresses and relatives with whom his mother corresponded. Immediately setting out, David could not stop his drive to know more.

At the first address, a vacant tattered cottage greeted him disparagingly. Aggressively he marched to the second address on the list, discovering people at home. Awe struck, his cousin and great-aunt introduced themselves, which commenced an afternoon of visiting, storytelling and eating. A younger cousin turned on the television and news of the attacks blared. For only a few minutes they sat silently around television and table, watching. Then David turned off the television. Nothing would intrude on his moment of discovery, nothing.

David left his cousin's home with a promise to return with his mother next year. Then, his cousin would share records of family history already charted for centuries, but only share when he would see David again, face to face.

"It is insurance that we will meet again," his cousin endearingly manipulated. There was no need to barter; David would return willingly in a moment.

Comfortable hotel room awaited as thin moonlight lit the path. Even now world news would be neglected in preference to idyllic remembrances and reunion planning. The following morning David, Brendon and their interpreters ate breakfast at a restaurant in village. Their waiter was thrilled as they entered. Overnight news of prodigal American relatives spread wildly throughout village. Their waiter was related to David, a third cousin. With extraordinary attention his cousin served them, speaking of mutual relations all the while. David felt exhilarated, a local celebrity for having interest in estranged family. His cousin spoke of an uncle and cousins who relocated to France after the war. David resolved to visit France as well, scratchy microphone proclaimed.

The microphone was at home in David's hand, relinquishing nothing but enthusiastic wanderings. He continued. David has living relatives in Poznan that own and manage the music shop in the square, centuries old, selling instruments and sheet music. These relatives were delighted to meet him and they exchanged information to correspond and share knowledge of family history. He visited tended graves of relatives long departed, photographing each headstone as a chronicle, documentation. Brendon requested the microphone.

Then Brendon and David ventured for two days to Kashubia, a province in central northern Poland. Brendon was in his glory, the province of his father's ancestors he studied for years and changed his name to reflect his dedication to the province. At a restaurant, Brendon fancied a pretty brunette waitress named Ewa. The forty-year-old bachelor complimented her and her homeland. To him everything was better, more beautiful, more plentiful, more meaningful in Kashubia. He would have loved to have a Kashubian bride to be a constant reminder of this paradise.

At an old town square, they wandered through an open market. Selecting many souvenirs including a tapestry of the Kashubian alphabet, he engaged the vendor in conversation. Brendon did not know much proper Polish but had studied the Kashubian dialect and could quote Kashubian proverbs and folktales in native tongue.

"Na codzen to Kaszeba je Kaszeba a na swiąto Kaszubowski." To the vendor he quoted. Translated: "For everyday a Kaszeba is a Kaszeba but on holidays he's a Kaszubowski."

The vendor was much impressed by an American's knowledge of his language that he offered Brendon forty słoty discounted from his purchases. Brendon glowed in pride as he recalled the story through tinny microphone. His stories persisted. Stories of church records and

cemetery visits stretched for long periods of time, which strained my
normally rigorous attention.

In Wiele, another town in Kashubia, their guides toured them
through a park. Trees and path gave way to an obelisk commemorating
the poet Hieronim Derdowski. A bronze plaque of Derdowski's profile
centered the obelisk with the inscription: Nie ma Kaszub bez Polonii a
bez Kaszub Polsce. Thrilled with this discovery, Brendon insisted David
photograph him next to the monument. Indeed, in Brendon's heart
he believed the epitaph: There can be no Kasubia without Poland, or
Poland without Kasubia.

Brendon asked David if he wished to speak anymore. David nodded no. David was finished. Brendon fumbled, deciding whether or
not to continue with more stories of genealogy and Kushubia.

Finally, Matthew retrieved the microphone from Brendon and
entreated the last two adventurous members of our group to speak:
Charlotte and Jean. With a concentrated look of business, no frills,
Charlotte proceeded to the guide's seat and adjusted microphone in
hand. Her spirit commanded more attention than her slender phy-
sique.

Charlotte and Jean became natives of Warsaw for four days, staying at a bed and breakfast that was once a dignitary's home. They
were checking into their bed and breakfast when the attacks were announced over television. Both called relatives at home to be sure of
emotional well-being, neither of them had family in New York City
or Washington D.C. The innkeepers were generous and consoling, offering them to stay as long as necessary, attending to their every wish.
That day they spent in their rooms, calling home and planning the rest
of their days. Each morning they awoke to the filtered light of white
lace curtains and homemade breakfasts. Each day they ventured to museums or galleries or to the market. Both fluent in Polish, they meshed

into society as refined older ladies entertaining themselves on afternoon jaunts. The highlight of their trip was certainly the bed and breakfast, its steadfast attention and homemade delicacies. There was no elaboration on any of this information. Skeletal facts did not acquire flesh of a story. Succinctly Charlotte spoke, then replaced the microphone as we began to applaud and advanced to her bench where Jean sat in dignity and brevity, complimenting Charlotte's efforts.

Affected by trickle and stream of stories, Antoni wrangled the wandering microphone into its rightful place and began to convey his story. Antoni's older brother, Adam, was a doorman of a prestigious hotel in Manhattan. As a child, Adam plastered a map of New York City in his bedroom wall, memorizing addresses and placements of architectural and cultural phenomena. For ten years, since immigrating, Adam lived for the sights and experiences of New York City, the only city, the American City.

When the Twin Towers were attacked, Antoni was frantic to contact his brother. With several unsuccessful attempts made, he finally broke through the congested telephone wires on Wednesday. Adam worked the early morning shift on Tuesday. From this hotel, Adam witnessed the attacks: first unsure then horrified, but always safe. Antoni's voice trembled with unspoken thoughts of potential loss of his brother and the chaotic danger that surrounded Adam.

Antoni empathized with our group. His family was part American, part Polish as ours were. Obligatory kindness towards all of his tour groups transformed into sincere regard for us and empathy for our present situation. And as one of us, we accepted him into our ranks with appreciation.

This exchange of experiences occupied the first hours of the ride north. Matthew began to speak of his impressions of all the experiences and of political ramifications of the attacks. Our group fell silent. Matthew allowed us this space and switched the microphone off, resting it on its hook. He sat in the first bench and began to read the Warsaw newspaper to himself. This behavior keyed others into independent activity being acceptable. Marie leaned forward to speak with Jean and Charlotte. Mom and Dad conversed softly, then Mom pulled book from purse. I was thankful for a quiet moment.

Unmolested forest peaks out from behind farms and cradle lakes before hills. Some forests hug the road where you can see people picking mushrooms: an ancient art passed down from generations identifying edible mushrooms and harvesting them for sale along the roadside or in the nearest town. Small cars park in the shallow woods; the ones with back seats packed with open boxes of fresh mushrooms are headed to market.

Quaint farmhouses in Prussian style, terra cotta corrugated roofs and adobe-like earth tone walls dot the landscape with the natural excitement of being close to the land. These farmers love their inherited land to the point of fighting and dying for it. Regaining farms after war with Russia or Germany, reunited farmers would kiss their land and eat soil, a symbol of appreciation, a holy connection. To love a way of life so dearly, to be symbiotic with Nature, is noble and just.

The bus passed by a leggy woman, dressed in miniskirt, heals and leather jacket, a contrast to the forest behind her. Just a mile before was a colony of mushroom harvesters plying their trade and selling their natural gems in crates at roadside. Matthew, with his raw humor, yells for everyone to get a look at that "mushroom picker". Mom grimaced. Dad glanced to the point of reference and then looked at his feet. Marie whooped. I sat neither offended nor entertained, peering again into the forest for a glimpse of filtered light tickling forest floor, which responded in chocolate brown with liquid yellow, white and red dots, fallen leaves accompanied mushrooms. Prostitutes along the countryside are an oddity to naïve American tourists. They are restrained to cities in the States. Not in Poland.

Antoni, embarrassed, grabbed the microphone and stumbling for words began to explain: these women come from Russia and other former communist countries that have worse economies than Poland; cities are policed very well and would deport them if found; therefore, they find customers on the country highways, truck drivers mostly, who should be ashamed of themselves; we try to deport them but they come back and sometimes travel through to Germany and other western countries; it is unfortunate that some women think that is their only alternative in life; it is a grave problem that our government is addressing to remedy.

I appreciated Antoni's honest speech, however that would not bar Matthew and Jozef Mazurkiewicz from adolescent jest. Throughout the trip Matthew and Jozef Mazurkiewicz howled at the sight of these women alongside the road, insighting others to joke or scoff, sometimes rating them, as if judges in a Miss Universe pageant, for fun. Yet Matthew's term is misplaced, the truck drivers are the "mushroom pickers" as they are the ones choosing, the active pickers. Prostitutes are mushrooms, wild gray offerings from dark territories with little control of sustenance or selection. Suffice to say that all sorts of mushrooms are picked on the side of the highways.

The long bus ride was curtailed; we stopped to tour the largest medieval castle in all of Europe, Malbork. During the war about half of it was destroyed, and later a fire consumed some of the renovation. Still, little by little, Malbork is being restored today.

The large imposing structure has many strong features: gothic peaks atop massive walls, long buildings stretching for city blocks, protective towers and gates surrounding all. There was too much to take in on the whole. I looked for the small fixtures that a knight would see every day.

In the main courtyard there was a vaulted door with curved top. The diamond shaped vaults had a striking fleur-de-lis pattern carved into each one, except on the top row where stained glass replaced carved wood. The glass was subtle, not noticeable until the right angle of sunlight shone through it-- beautiful. In a small room with a scale model of the castle, there also was an exhibit of the destruction and renovation of the castle. Some pieces that were salvaged stand in glass cases: a column head of stone carved to resemble a man's head with wide-open mouth and elongated limbs. Was he hungry? While walking, the guide pointed out an intact column head of a gargoyle holding himself in distress. The guide explained that these sculptures were used to point the way to different rooms since most people did not know how to read in the Middle Ages, very clever. The intact gargoyle was pointing the way to the Gdanisko Tower, the bathroom and area of last refuge if under siege. Necessary, it is to be able to relieve oneself while under heavy attack.

At this point there was an adorable young couple tagging along to hear the tour in English. The young man was from Australia and the young lady was a native. I do not remember their names, but we only briefly exchanged greetings while Matthew and others spoke with them at length. They were perfectly matched in height and in character, and it was suitable that they were touring the castle on Saturday, wedding day. For they were on their honeymoon, searching for the romantic history of Poland to kiss before venturing forth on their new life abroad and within.

As the tour progressed we saw three different wedding parties in the castle for pictures. One bride in red, one in white, one in eggshell were led by professional photographers to scenic areas for portraits. They were beautiful.

Down the vaulted gallery to another museum room, we saw even more salvaged treasures: a book with gilt edges, various ceramics and decorative pieces. Yet the most striking was the tapestry done in gold and red hues, very much like the Rafael tapestries we surveyed in the Vatican Museum. It was an outdoor scene with animals in the foreground and landscape in the background, and a marvelous tree on the left of the main figure. I do not recall what the tapestry represented or who created it (I had but a moment to view it, not studying the identification card), but it commanded the room and the attention of the observer.

In another similar room, more religious salvaged artifacts were displayed. By lingering at the end of the group I was able to steal a few extra moments while to group moved on. I dawdled at the end of the group often. At that time I was able to get up close to a small frame of stained glass. It was a picture of Christ, or possibly Joseph, holding a staff. The edge work around the frame was the most interesting because of the intricate detail work done with a very simple repeating pattern of swirls and circles. The pattern continued on different pieces and colors of glass, transforming its effect. What a wonderful effect: simple yet ornate. Photography was allowed. Our group filtered through passageway into another gallery. I was alone with my passions in this gallery. Quickly and slyly I took a picture to study later.

The last cavernous museum held a showcase of amber pieces, some historical in significance, some rare in quality and proportion. One wall near the entrance displayed every variety of amber. This rich chromatic scale began near the ceiling with honey colored strands and progressed to darker hues of rose, burnt sienna, green, and black. Other cases across the chamber exhibited amber pieces with a whole insect, or large chunks of wood. At the other end of the gallery, historical crafted works sit behind glass. A medieval chess set, an ornate chest of drawers, and royal presentation jewelry highlighted this magnificent collection.

After the tour concluded, most people were hungry. It was agreed upon to have about a half-hour to eat at one of the restaurants, walk the ground, and then meet at the entrance to get back on the bus. Dad was tired and did not want to eat a big meal this late in the day because it would ruin dinner. Mom, Dad, and I separated from our group and bought ice cream at a kiosk. Antoni was eating bigos at a picnic table outside the kiosk. We walked along the cobblestone path between the Vistula River and the castle. Antoni finished his bigos as we did our ice cream. He walked the same path as we, few steps behind us. Enamored by a local fisherman, Dad wanted to speak with him but did not feel confident enough in his Polish to do so. He settled for me taking his picture beside a boat, twenty feet away from the fisherman. When Antoni saw me composing the picture, he turned his steps and retraced the path to the castle entrance. He did not wish to be in pictures, I supposed.

The rest of the half-hour Dad spent taking pictures of the long side of Malbork Castle, and its many curves and turrets, with Mom and me in the foreground.

"Tell me what to do. Direct me." I ordered Dad to compose each possible picture.

He was happy as creative director and photographer. In one shot I was dwelling in the shadow of the turret while Mom stood before it casting a long afternoon shadow parallel to my hiding place. In another composition, we alternated Mom, tree, me, trees lining wall before moat. In this way we laughed and progressed along shields of stone, chasm and river, the warm mid-afternoon sun beseeching jackets to be disrobed. We turned to retrace our steps.

Near the food kiosk, there was another we seemed to miss as we first began to walk the path. I approached it as Mom and Dad veered in opposite direction, intrigued by other vendors and displays at Malbork's drawbridge. A linen covered table exhibited a variety of woodwork: carved and painted figures of knights and saints lined the outer edge of the table with larger nesting dolls, chess boards formed the bulk of the exhibit, along the front were miniature jewelry and trinket boxes in various sizes, shapes and colors. Each piece varied from the next, each a gem of its own design. It appeared that each was the last, the only example.

The gold swirls and squares against the dark wood gleamed regally. I wished to purchase this small jewelry box thinking it was unusual, that if I did not purchase it there would not be another one found like it. With a smile I greeted the vendor who had been watching me for the moment I scanned his wares. I inquired about the small jewelry box in front of me, afraid to touch it. He leaned across the table and showed me the price on its underside. I shook my head in agreement and affirmed my choice, as it was very inexpensive. He wrapped it gingerly in newspaper, then in a small plastic bag. I thanked him as he accepted the exact amount. Exuberantly I turned to finish the path to drawbridge.

On the way to meet our group, I noticed a walking path through what was the moat. Under the drawbridge there was a couple sauntering, arms embracing the other's waist. The man was loosely guiding his bicycle with his free hand. I imagined he rode his bike to discretely meet his sweetheart, possibly flower in hand. It was perfect. With the zoom lens I framed the shot with a portion of moat path, bridge, and castle with the couple directly under an arch of the bridge. It was a beautiful day, wedding day; the sun was brilliant, the breeze slight and refreshing, moment perfect and unobtrusive. A couple that knows how to seek intimate spaces deserves to be pictured in them, even if it is from a far off stranger.

As I continued to walk I craned my head to see the kiosk of wood-work. Not comprehending my vision I stepped closer until I reached it once more. The vendor had replaced my jewelry box with a replica, a twin. My box was not one-of-a-kind, singular, or unique. Upon closer inspection, he had boxes under the table he used to restock the table so only one of each of his items was on display. Deflated I stepped away, but with each retreating step I realized that it was still a beautiful box.

When I returned to drawbridge, Mom was buying a pen and ink drawing of the castle from a street artist. Approvingly, I compliment-ed her choice and helped Marie pick one out as well. Since we were American or since we were nice (who knows), the artist asked for fifty zloty, fifteen American dollars, very fair price. When we were leaving a German lady asked him for a price on a sketch the same size and qual-ity of what we just bought. He quoted her sixty zloty. He gave us a deal, nice sympathetic artist.

Since we were to be living off of the bus for the next ten days, Matthew initiated a number system to keep everyone accounted. My assigned number was sixteen. Around the bus we shouted our numbers in order, ensuring that one through thirty-four were present.

Sixteen I said, in usual tone of voice.

Edward bowed to Antoni and whispered, "Who is sixteen?"

Antoni replied, "Sixteen is alone."

"She has a nice voice." Edward stated in English before converting to Polish to continue their conversation.

Marie and I occupied the fourth bench from the front on Edward's side, the driver's side of the bus. Wanting variety of views, Marie stated that we would not always sit there. Everyone else was settling into their seats as if benches were assigned for the entire journey. Peg already referred to the second bench behind Edward as her seat. Mom and Dad cozied into the fourth bench on Antoni's side, behind the guide's seat near doors. Some people do not like change. Marie was not one of those people.

I told Marie of my experience at the kiosk of woodwork. That is the communist style of selling, she pointed out. I should have thought of this but have never seen stores of that system before. My naivety invoked her to chuckle.

Looking back from the departing bus, I studied the red brick towers along the meandering river one more time. What an enchanting place Malbork is, especially that day. If one looks long and hard enough, unblinkingly, the sight, the moment is burned into memory. Anyway, that is my theory.

GDAŃSK

In the late afternoon, we drove into the misty streets of Gdansk ready to be off the bus and in the hotel. When checking into the hotel the receptionist mentioned that the elevator was broken. I took the opportunity to get exercise and run luggage up the stairs, at least my luggage and my parents' luggage. Feeling better for it, Marie and I settled ourselves and then went back to the bus for a driving tour of the tri-city area: Gdańsk, Gdynia, and Sopot, all connected by a main artery of train line and tree-lined boulevard.

The cities are sheltered on one side by the Baltic Sea and on the other by hilly forests. One may orient oneself by looking for treed hills and head north or for a panoramic view of water and head south. The local guide was very cheerful, as we entered each city or came upon a building of significance he would exclaim, "ladies and gentlemen welcome to..." While Dad was displeased with this formal greeting,

pretension without substance he submitted. I was charmed by its diplomatic undertones. The enthusiasm and pride he had for his home
was apparent in every excited sentence.

Unable to retain specific historical and architectural details through
storm and crowd, I grasped the gist: the tri-city area is an international port with a corresponding international flavor of culture, not
always a part of Poland. Gdańsk was always an important port of trade;
therefore, kings would visit Gdańsk from Warsaw parading through
the arched gates to Old Town (which was probably most of the town
at various points in history). Many treasures of Gdańsk, the Fountain
of Neptune for example, were hidden from Hitler's destructive hand,
as in other cities in Poland. Famous for amber, salt mining, and Lech
Wałęsa, the cities are industrial and political hotbeds.

Walking through Old Town at dusk, even the granaries looked picturesque. The group ate dinner at a fancy local restaurant along the
river. The baked potatoes were exceptionally good. I could eat nothing
but Polish golden potatoes all my life and be a happy person. Baked
fish in a lemon glaze accompanied the golden potatoes. Greedy for a
second helping, Dad gleefully accepted my fish. We had a system: he
would eat his meat or fish while I ate the rest, then we would switch
plates and finish each other's remainders.

Conversation between Marie, Dorothy and myself focused on
travel and the Sistine Chapel experience. They had interesting stories
to share. Marie found a spiritual experience in the Sistine Chapel;
where Dorothy thought it rich in artwork yet so claustrophobic that
the chapel could not be deeply enjoyed. The vegetable coleslaw was as
heavenly as any cathedral stained glass windows: shards of pure color,
rich carrot orange, gleaming celery green, exotic opal parsnip, bathed
together in a deeply understated oil and vinegar sauce. Each bite of reverberated splendor danced on tongue and cheek, a bittersweet festival.

Thankfully, Dad left me an extra portion of coleslaw in exchange for my fish.

The Sistine Chapel conversation blended into a discussion on arts in America and at home in Western New York. Richard talked about Chautauqua Institution at the end of the table; I listened and added a comment or two. Chautauqua Institution is a center for the arts only open in summer. It draws the best of the music, writing, lecturing, and visual arts world to it for a host of functions. Its curricula and events are select, exclusive. Richard experiences Chautauqua from the perspective of a comfortable patron of the arts, while I have experienced it as a poor student listening to concerts from afar, walking past the gated road, unable to purchase a ticket. Very different perspectives, I tried hard to compliment his statements instead of contradict them. I suggested that Richard visit Chautauqua in winter when its essence lays bare without crowds or fanfare. He responded with raised eyebrows and an assertion about the delicate dessert just served. For dessert, preserved peaches in light syrup were served, delicious. The peaches, warmed and sprinkled with cinnamon, were simple and satiating finale to the meal.

Old Town at night along the river, lights playing in gentle waves of commotion in river and on cobblestone, the beauty resonated. Each moment's beauty overpowers the rest, as it is alive with reverie and discovery. I could not keep pace with the flood of beautiful moments experienced and to come. The romance of the moment swept me away on undulating pools of lamplight. My shadow consorted with the angular shadows of turret and lamppost, which were happy to introduce themselves.

Music and laughter was pouring out of the banquet room at the Hotel Posejdon, after all it was wedding day. A few of us huddled in the doorway to see the party. A circle of bouquets designed the floor as the party ate dinner, and then were moved to a table for dancing.

Some started dancing in the hallway as the wedding party danced in a circle just as the flowers were. Swirling, clapping, radiant bodies leapt. Smiles and cheers formed a halo of energy. Exuberant dancers came to the door and grabbed Jean, Irene, Marie, and Doris to join the festivities. Charlotte watched from doorway with me. Jean, a sprightly lady with curly blonde hair who, although almost eighty, in body and spirit seemed a dignified sixty, kept time with her young partner. Irene was a round and jovial soul with a pleasing, subtle demeanor. Her body had trouble paced by the rhythm of the song, but her spirit was parading about her face and through every gesture. Charlotte took a turn around the dance floor with a happy groom's man. She could not help herself, watching became the temptation. His offer came just in time. It was delightful, the party glowing. With a few Polish words of thanks, they returned when the song ended. The wedding party entreated us to come for another song, but with energy spent, we wished them a lifetime of good fortune and headed for our rooms. Marie continued to hum the tune and dance with phantom partner ascending the stairs to our room. Wedded bliss, part memories, part wishes for this hospitable couple, rallied Marie's thoughts to sound sleep. I was happy to dream of tomorrow.

"Look at my salad plate. It has walnuts and peaches in it."

— Marie in her sleep

GDAŃSK

Today I succumbed to the pressure and went to church, St. Peter and Paul, with members of the group who cared to go. I am a spiritual person, not a religious one. Spiritual guidance may be found, not only in the sheltered saints of buttressed cathedrals, yet in anything, in any moment, of any experience that is willing to linger. The rote ceremony of Catholic mass feeds my spirit inconsistently, as a pigeon given scraps by tourists.

Sitting with Dad alone, while Mom and Marie sat in the front row to hear more clearly, I studied the features of the small honest contemporary church since I could not understand much of anything in the Polish homily. Above the altar loomed bronze statues of the twelve apostles with Jesus in the middle. The apostles, as if apparitions, sprayed out from Jesus elongated, six on each side. None of the statues had eyes, only eye sockets, so the altar light coming from below lit the eye sockets furiously. Spooky Jesus and the apostles looked like Halloween decorations that would frighten children. They frighten me.

Dad strained to listen to the faint homily, brows furrowed in concentration and internal translation. During the sign of peace I asked Dad the topic of the homily. He responded that the priest spoke of politics and the religious life of the candidates running for office, although he could not describe details as the priest was speaking too fast for Dad's speed of translation. Dad was happy to attend mass but uncomfortable participating. We, he and I, decided to forego communion and spent those moments studying the blonde wood of the pews and aisles, the bronze of statues and vigil stands. I squeezed his right hand with my left; he smiled a short appreciative simper.

After mass, Mom and I lit two candles: one for John and Ann, my brother and sister-in-law, and their efforts to move into a new house and have another child, and one for victims of the terrorist attacks and world peace to prevail. I believe in lighting candles. Mom knelt to say silent prayer for one moment. I bowed my head in reverence and prayers of peace and stood alone, off to the side of the radiant vigil flames, now the only lights within the darkened church.

Walking two blocks through misty rain and puddles, we returned to the hotel for breakfast before the day of touring began. The ubiquitous bus was waiting, our primary means of transport always at the ready with an agenda and a roster. Edward at the helm, prompt and courteous, would know the day's plan and the routes to drive. Although we never needed to be aware of our trek, the narrow Gothic streets and the country highways that more resembled back roads than interstates, we played an advanced game of follow-the-leader: purchasing road maps at a gas station and highlighting the circumference we traveled in mind and vision. Always efficient, Edward in quiet dignity maneuvered the tour bus with the agility of a Roman sports car.

The misty rain of the early morning gave way to downpours in the afternoon. Nonetheless, we began sight seeing in the mist of the Baltic Sea on the pier in Sopot. This pier, stretching into the sea at least a quarter mile, invited people from all walks of life: fishermen on pier and in boat worked their gear, young people sallied for entertainment on beach and pier, guides with tour boats floating empty in the off season, and we the tourists flit around absorbing the sights. The clouds and mist seamed together any distinction between sky, water, and land. This played with my imagination more so than if it was a clear busy morning. The chill of moist air seeped into clothing, a shiver. At the end of the pier a bright red lamppost made itself known, the only color besides gray. Dick took my picture with it. Looking back to shore, Japanese buildings hugged the ground while a baroque lighthouse squarely towered. A Prussian style castle now hotel and casino occupied the right side of the vista before the hills and trees of the peninsula demanded attention.

A touring boat launched from the far side of the pier for its daily cruise to Hel and back. There were no passengers on the boat today. Hel, a village at the tip of the peninsula a mile distant, relies on tourist boats as the primary industry besides amber mining. Many in our group delighted in the name of the unassuming village, taking the opportunity for jest. Why don't you go to Hel? Let's tour Hel; it must be warmer there than here. There was no time in the schedule to visit Hel, although from the pier it looked charming: a small cluster of buildings at seaside with forest ensconcing it. The forest became denser as the peninsula attached to mainland. The easiest way to get to Hel was by water. Fists of fog wringed the bracing village. I would gladly travel to Hel… and back.

Mom did not walk the pier, too long for her. The dampness aggravated her arthritis. She discovered a street vendor behind a small white building on the pier. The vendor had all sorts of amber jewelry displayed on folding table draped in linen. Mom bought two rosaries while speaking with Jean and Charlotte. They also purchased rosaries from the grinning vendor who resembled a worn retired fisherman. He enjoyed their company, at length talking with them in Polish in happy tones and grandiose gesture. I approached them from the lamppost meandering back to land, my creaking footfalls indications of the thin crust separating one from frigid ocean.

Ladies from our group swarmed around vendor and table before I reached Mom's place. She called me excitedly from afar to hurry my pace; she discovered something wonderful. I bolted directly to her. In her palm she unfolded a silver bracelet with perfect oval amber stones, multicolored representing the entire tonal spectrum: pearl onion, honey, maple, wine, and black olive.

"That is the most unique bracelet I've ever seen. Really beautiful." Peg interjected. Amorous greed invaded her complexion in an instant.

"It's… It's Grace's," Mom stammered, "I mean… Grace is going to buy it now." She handed it to me with the import of talisman. Then Mom walked away.

I asked the vendor how much it was, not concerned with the price. It was mine already. I paid the requested price with a smile and handshake. Peg stared all the while, then abruptly departed for other shops on the beach. Antoni began to call, beaconing I rejoin the group. I waved him off with a similar gesture to hold just one more minute. Grabbing a few baubles for friends at home, I once again paid the vendor now drunk with delight of prosperous businessmen. With a hearty wave a bid him farewell as I ran to our retreating group: the pier over, now the beach to explore.

There were other shops and kiosks on the boardwalk at the base of the pier; we peaked through them all. The first whitewashed boutique along the boardwalk was a shining amber jewel itself: a window display of lamps with amber and stained glass shades threw light on the gray morning while inside amber jewelry of all sorts glistened from backlit glass cases. All the women of our group crowded into the tiny boutique and assailed the two sales clerks for assistance. Diligently I surveyed the cases of rings and already chose the two I wanted before a sales clerk had opportunity to serve me: one oval ring with scrollwork for myself; one perfect circle in an edgy art deco setting for my sister. The clerk was relieved I knew what I wanted. Dorothy received her assistance next, asking to try on many items at once. Mom and I left the packed boutique for the openness of the cold beach.

Marie insisted on stepping into the Baltic, since she has dipped her toes in every body of water she has ever visited. We took this opportunity to go on the beach while others finished shopping. Surrounded by jellyfish, Marie took off a sneaker and sank one foot into the chilly water. I would like to have jumped in completely this morning instead of going to church, but some things just do not happen as hoped. I resolved to soak my hands and take pictures of Marie and the beach. Ducks swam close to shore as if protecting their sea from curious foreigners. Waves tickled my fingertips with icy affection. A gray and black striped cat pranced on the sand until she realized we were there; then she ran back into a crevice under the pier. My hands were imbedded in the moving sand, slightly warmer than the peaked waves. Grains of sand tucked themselves under fingernails, a small shelter. Marie had had enough; she dried her foot with Mom's handkerchief. Antoni called for us to return to the boardwalk, as our group was moving towards the castle.

We found Dad waiting for us while speaking with Richard. The time wasted shopping annoyed both. The path to the castle was lined with street vendors. Marie, Mom and I would continue to try Dad's patience by looking at each stall. Mom and Marie moved ahead of me. Outside the amber boutique at the start of the boardwalk, I stopped in front of a young man selling charms for necklaces, rings and peculiar drawings.

Half way down the walkway, Kathy Jo and Doris perched to look at jewelry again. Most of our group passed them on the way to the castle. They greeted the elderly woman vendor and began to touch rings and broaches with gliding fingers.

I greeted the young man with a robust hello, to which I received an elegant and wordless smile. I assumed he did not speak English. There was a lovely amber heart with silver leaves strewn through the center. Other charms were pretty but none as this. The young man watched me carefully as I progressed from one end of his table to the other. I complimented his wares. Another smile. The right side of the table housed pastel drawings of churches and castles with what appeared to be sand glued to certain areas of the drawings: along the steeple of a cathedral, at the base of a castle following the chasm. My attention drew to a picture of the beach with sailboat in the distance and trees in forefront. The sand was glued to the beach and more course stone outlined trees and shoreline. It was odd and beautiful in a strange folk art way. It was labeled ten złaty.

In broken conversation, the elderly lady asked Kathy Jo about our group and the trip. Kathy Jo replied that we were from New York and were already traveling when the attacks occurred. Now we could not go home. I could not hear this gentle conversation, remote from peripheral vision. The lady began to weep.

"America is our sister. We weep with you, we weep with you. It is terrible. Terrible," the lady stated in high tones of emotion.

The elderly lady walked to the side of the table where Kathy Jo met her. Both in tears, they embraced for a long moment, hugged in solace not in need of words in any language. Doris stood motionless, overwhelmed by her own emotions.

With another greeting and smile I asked the young vendor for the charm and the drawing. Noiselessly he retrieved and prepared them in bags for sale. I handed him a bill as he presented the items. A quiet moment passed as he gathered my change from his cash box. I shoved it into my pants pocket quickly in wadded handful. Before turning to rush toward the castle I thanked him for his help and his fine charm and drawing. Expecting no response, an excited grin launched across my face to convey my feeling across language barriers.

"That is not sand, it is crushed amber not good enough for jewelry. Too small." The vendor explained in proper English. My grin morphed into dropped chin. He understood me all along.

"Thank you. Have a safe trip," he said with fluttering gaze and sheepish grin.

"Thank you very much," I said with waving hand; my smile returned with new hope. My spirits leapt in solidarity. At last shouldered glance, he was still looking in my direction grinning. We affect others in many ways, not just those ways openly apparent. I strode to rejoin our group.

Kathy Jo and the elderly lady ended their embrace, wiping their own tears. They whispered conversation of family and global worries.

"America will recover. We all will recover." The lady murmured in private solace. Kathy Jo and Doris shook their heads solemnly in agreement, held each other's hand and began a slow, plodding walk towards the castle where our group waited for stragglers. The lady walked behind her kiosk and sat in her small folding chair facing the direction of the young man. Last with most ground to cover, I rushed past her stall, her heated face now stoic.

Inside the castle we rested for a few moments as Edward retrieved the bus for the next tour. The luxurious interiors of lobby and sitting rooms were a welcome sight in contrast to the misty gray of the gothic exterior. Mom's arthritis raged in the humidity; she needed the rest. I took this time to adjust my change from pocket to wallet. The young man had given me more change than I should have been given, by five złaty. An inner beam of illumination struck with gratitude, appreciation and kinship. I wished I could go back and say thank you. Edward pulled the bus to the moat and drawbridge entrance. It was time to go.

Dad and I waited for Mom to refresh herself in the ladies lounge. How slowly, painfully she moved. We were the last to board the bus. Antoni would not give Edward the signal to drive on until Mom was seated comfortably. On the bus Kathy Jo relayed her stirring interaction with the lady at her kiosk. The moment would linger with her and Doris. Timing correlated in my mind of interactions, elderly lady and young man. I smirked at my picture of amber dust and sea.

The downpour began; as did our walking tour of Old Town. The local guide persevered and we followed. Would kings have walked this way in the rain? Colorful and symbolic facades introduced the use of the structure: gilded statues of Justice and War surveyed the plaza from City Hall, figures of medieval people (tradesmen as well as distinguished families) cover the entire facade of one building, lions facing the same direction point to the Royal Way in anticipation from a museum front. The Fountain of Neptune rallied courage off center in the town square. Sea serpents reared their heads from tumultuous waves as Neptune fought them with golden spear. This fountain represents the spirit of Gdańsk. Ever since its unveiling during the Renaissance it has been a cherished piece of art. Through several wars the fountain was disassembled and hidden from invaders; this treasure would not be pillaged.

Most recently, Neptune went underground for years during the Second World War. Hitler would have destroyed Neptune, if he could. The people of Gdańsk triumphantly proclaim the Fountain of Neptune as industrious, as beautiful, and as resilient as their eternal community. Looking up at Neptune from a rain-streaked hood, his determined face coaxed and cajoled. In an instant, we were friends.

The rain was relentless. The local guide led us through alleys, by-ways, and avenues to an upscale amber shop to wait out the rain by shopping. This was the Tiffany's of Gdańsk. Opalescent display cases starkly offset the artistic jewelry. Mom and I just browsed, admiring the various settings and colors of amber, while Marie bought an elegant multicolored necklace for her daughter (similar to my bracelet but with much bigger stones and settings).

Peg stood over a case with a friendly sales clerk. As I walked past, Peg selected a long necklace of varying reds and browns. Amiably, I complimented its shape and colors, matching her hair and eyes.

"It's not as nice as your bracelet, but it will do." Peg commented blankly.

I slithered away noiselessly, recoiling from unintended adversarial position to watch rivulets slice picture windows in torrent and conviction. Others bought some lovely pieces as well, but after half an hour I was ready to move on regardless of rain.

Someone ran over to the cathedral and ran back reporting that mass was finished and we could walk over to start our tour. When we entered St. Mary's, mass was only half way done because of a special procession and service to honor the victims of the terrorist attacks. Once we understood what was happening, some wished to stay and partake in the service. Mom, Dad, and Marie stood behind the last pew, concentrating on the procession of rhythmic prayers said by a line of priests carrying candles. The last monsignor in procession deftly swung incense onto the silent congregation, pure blessings waft toward the turrets of newly released spirits we recall. Solemn faces hung. The local guide rules, after fifteen minutes he ushered our group into a small gallery for a lecture on religious art within.

Our group gathered in a side room for a brief introduction to the uniqueness of St. Mary's Cathedral. The door to this room resembled an enormous arrowhead, slate colored, studded panels crowned in a sharp tip. Inside a Dutch painting of heaven, hell, and purgatory hung on the left, and a wooden pieta sit straight ahead behind protective glass. These works of art have had tumultuous lives: being hidden for safety during the war in Warsaw, then not being returned after the war as promised, finally after diplomatic negotiation one was returned and one copy was sent instead of the original. This wooden Pieta of elongated, yet remarkably exact detail, was said to inspire Michelangelo to create his Pieta. This artwork also struggled to survive the destruction of war, hiding in various catacombs. The long mass concluded, and so commenced the tour of the main cathedral.

Mom could not walk any longer so she sat in the center to absorb all she could. Dad remained with her, watching the tour from afar as not to become stranded. He clasped Mom's hand for an intimate moment. I walked to the group, joining the guide in progress. St. Mary's, the largest church in Europe made of brick, housed an unusual clock by the left-hand entrance. The clock was built into the wall and had one large hand to point to the hour; all twenty-four in brass Roman numerals highlighted the circumference. Inside the clock circle, stars shone from the heavens while puty flew as if playing tag. The guide from Gdańsk led us around the cathedral, then to the main altar, where he thought Mom and Dad were locals and spoke to them in Polish. Dad understood the guide and responded in English, Mom needed rest.

The rain did not stop when the tour did, so we ventured again into the weather to find a place to eat lunch. Along the front steps of each building, two gargoyles pout rainwater onto the sidewalk sewers. The entire lane looked like the Hundred Fountains in Tivoli. Streaming water bowing from snarled lip and jagged stone teeth, these gargoyles seemed happy to be functioning. By this time, Mom's knee was quite sore so Mom and Dad chose to head for the bus to eat snacks for lunch. I offered to walk them to the bus three blocks away, and then return to our group for lunch. Dad insisted that I stay with the group; he knew the way across the cobblestone bridge to Edward waiting on the bus. I relented and watched them hobble in slow measured footsteps along the embankment to the bridge. Before our group turned the corner out of eyesight, I rushed to meet them. The rest of the group bounced between two different restaurants that did not have the accommodations for a large group with no notice.

We wandered along the canal in Old Town, the medieval restaurant strip where we ate last night. A foreboding, dingy factory building loomed over avenue and canal. Hundreds of years of smoky apparitions engulfed the stout factory. This was the grain elevator, constructed in medieval days of commerce and still functioning. The far side of the edifice jutted into the canal, threatening expulsion. This is another symbol of Gdańsk, Antoni explained. Without protection, like moveable artwork, this grain elevator has withstood over five hundred years of war, peace, and change, and still remains useful. With a hard look, its dark, angular beauty united water and sky without being cajoled by the clean, renovated facades of adjacent Old Town structures. With new respect, I bid the grain elevator farewell. It flexed its indestructible pride, watching us parade over bridge into a gray mass of the future. Then the group decided to go to the bus and drive to someplace to eat closer to the hotel.

From the breakfast buffet, Mom had taken two apples and two rolls. As I climbed aboard, Mom and Dad were just finishing their lunch buffet out of Mom's purse. Edward was in his own universe in the driver's seat, ready to be employed at any moment. Many people wanted real, simple Polish food. Someone spotted a diner. Edward stopped and a couple people jumped out to see if the small diner could accommodate us. Not waiting for a response, people got off the bus ready to eat. The diner was cafeteria style, real, simple Polish food. Theresa and Jozef Mazurkiewicz helped me order a bowl of vegetable soup. When my turn came to pay and sit down, I turned to scan the room for a seat. A Polish lady tapped my shoulder and told me to sit at a small corner table with an old lady (I think she said that but she was speaking in Polish so I do not know for certain). Gladly, I walked to the table and asked her if I could sit with her. She shook her head yes.

Over the next fifteen minutes while we ate, I attempted to speak with her in gestures. She reminded me of Nana: permed gray hair, short and neat to match her soft blue-gray eyes. She was eating potato pancakes for lunch. I motioned to the pancakes and said that they looked good. She gestured happily to the pancakes and then made waving steps with her flat hand, then back to her plate: she had eaten them ever since she was a child and growing up. Memories of Nana and growing up with the sounds of Polish in the house flooded my perception. If she would say anything melodiously in Polish I would be two-years-old again being rocked to sleep with lullabies in Nana's cradling protective arms, softly, softly singing…

Ah, ah kotki dwa,
Szare bure oby dwa,
Nic nie beda robili,
Tylko Gracja bawili.

Translated:

> Ah, ah two kittens,
> Gray stripes on both,
> They will do nothing,
> Only Gracie to play with.

A grin crawled across my face at the familiar Polish melody playing through mind and spirit.

She gestured to my bowl and then to her throat, venturing pointed words—a question. I shook my head yes and gestured to my throat saying that I had a cold and the soup felt very good, especially on this stormy day.

The soup did feel like home with every salty smell and chunky slurp. As children we always knew what was for supper the moment we walked in the doorway from school. The warm odors greeted us before Mom or Nana did. Dinner was already being prepared. Our favorite winter meal was chicken soup and homemade bread. I would step into the radiant kitchen to find the chairs draped in noodle dough, drying. The rectangular sheets yawned over wax paper covered chair backs. Dishtowels protected the dough from little dirty hands but allowed the dough to dry before being cut into kluski noodles. At just the right time, the entertainment would begin as I sat on a green aluminum stool to watch: Mom would get out Teddy's bread board and lay it across the kitchen table; he had made it for Nana from parts of an old printing press, the patchwork of wood grains duck-tailed beautifully; Nana would tenderly handle the dough from one chair as if it were a bolt of expensive material, and present it to the floured board, a gift; expertly, Nana would slice the dense dough thin with a butcher knife, shake the noodles gently to separate them, and throw them into awaiting boiling water. Each chair's dough would receive the same treatment in turn. At the precise moment, Mom would drain the noodles and shock them with cold water before pouring them into a ceramic bowl for serving. At the dinner table, boiling chicken vegetable soup met cold kluski noodles to become the perfect temperature for eating and dipping crusty warm bread while melting butter dripped from the center. Nothing could approach that exquisite soup, until this bowl in this warm small diner in Gdańsk. I looked from my bowl half expecting to see Nana, waiting for a compliment on her soup. The gray-haired lady stared at me with cautious gentility and searched for a way to convey her next idea.

She made sweeping gestures to the crowd, to ask about all the people I think. Her language was so fast and adamant that I was not sure what she was trying to convey. I told her that we were a group of American tourists who wanted authentic Polish food. All together I said as I made circular gestures. She shook her head yes and we sat a few moments in silence. I was thrilled with our conversation. She tried to break down barriers and connect. I was embarrassed that I did not know the language. Marie was just about finished with her lunch, so I approached her and double-checked how to say "thank you and have a good day". Then I went back to her, said my best Polish and offered my hand. We shook hands with smiles, and I left feeling overjoyed by the interaction, hoping that she enjoyed her lunch with me too.

On the bus, I relayed my story to everyone who was there: Kathy Jo, Doris, Piotr, and my parents. Enthralled with my animated story, Piotr listened eagerly. The bus was filling up as I finished the story, so I took my seat. For the first time in the tour, Piotr, the attractive young Polish cousin of the Prorok Brothers, spoke to me, asking my age. Telling the truth, I stunned him and many others who thought I was ten years younger. He said I did not look my age, and I thanked him before he took his seat. This would finally end the age guessing game that had been taking place ever since the first day. I really enjoy looking young, and enjoy acting young even more. Yet, being treated as a teenager was never fun. So finally that uncertainty was over, and I was still the youngest in the group (besides Piotr) so what did it all matter?

During the rest of the afternoon's activities, Piotr was very sweet to me. He held the elevator for me and we spoke briefly of the pier and Gdańsk. Although neither of us knew what to say, friendly smiles were exchanged. He was lovely, and young, six years younger than I am. Since he lived in Gdańsk with his family, he did not partake in the rest of the tour.

After a brief rest at the hotel, more like a WC stop, an organ concert at St. Oliwa's Cathedral was the next activity on the agenda. The church was beautiful: the main altar vanished into ethereal clouds swirling white with gilt stars caught in haste. In the eye of the cloudy heavens rests a stained glass window of golden colors mixed with blue. I could not discern the figures in the middle of the oval window, but a white dove flew over their heads. The church housed the largest organ in Poland. As the music started we were asked by the organist to think "higher" thoughts. For about twenty minutes the organ rang through the church, parts of songs juxtaposed to use the entire range of the organ's capacity. I thought I almost heard a lullaby or a bit of Andrew Lloyd Weber. Thank you, Mozart, for writing "Twinkle, Twinkle Little Star." The pieces were alternately sentimental and reverent, and a carnival of holy amusements. It would be fun if the organist broke out in a little Dave Brubeck, maybe a little Theloneus Monk. Wouldn't "Take Five" on the organ be crazy? I will burn in hell for being irreverent. Higher thoughts sometimes plummet.

Everyone enjoyed the concert and flocked to the church gift shop. One small nun was attending this kiosk of religious gifts. In front of her there was a stack of flashcards with prices written on them. As a person would inquire about an item, in whatever language, sister would hold up a corresponding flashcard. Did she take a vow of silence? Or did she assume this system to avoid confusion between visitors? I asked her about a cd of organ music, pointing to the item behind glass. The solemn sister retrieved it, and held it in one hand, the price card in another. I shook my head yes and presented a bill. To make change, she replaced the card on the stack efficiently. With a bow she presented my purchase and with a smile I returned her silent warm before departing for the windy cool awaiting outdoors.

Others had found small fieldstone shops hiding along the courtyard of St. Oliwa. Dad was reviewing free pamphlets inside the door of one of the shops. I went to meet him. Mom and Marie perused as they wished before joining us to walk to the bus. Edward was patiently nestled in the driver's seat.

Roll was taken once all aboard. Sixteen I called.

"Who is sixteen?" Edward inquired of Antoni.

"Sixteen is attentive and calm." Antoni responded with short smile. He sat behind the driver's seat and proceeded to converse with Edward in Polish.

For dinner tonight, the group went to Old Town again, to a restaurant in the basement of one of the medieval buildings. This was an interesting space of heavily arched ceiling forming columns throughout the dining room. The green walls were painted in black acanthus leaves. The setting and the meal were feasts for the palate. As the tables were set to seat five around, Antoni sat with us. During the course of divine cream of asparagus soup we discussed family and the possible ramifications of the attacks.

Lemon and chive chicken was served with glazed carrots and beans and whipped golden potatoes with a crust of paprika. Antoni noticed

that half way through the meal Dad and I exchanged plates. He inquired into this curiosity, to which I alluded to my vegetarianism. He
offered to arrange for all my meals to be vegetarian. I told him not to
trouble himself with the extra work of calling each restaurant ahead
of time. I was full each meal with this system already in progress. Dad
was happy with his portions and arrangements as well. This response
did not appease Antoni. He wished to please; he wished for everything
he could control to be more than accommodating, perfect. Our world
was crumbling into a sea of uncertainty and potential terror. What we
could control should be a manifestation of heart. Without further discussion Antoni set his mind. I did not know exactly what this meant,
but had no time to think of it or question it as Matthew called for
everyone's attention.

Matthew had invited family friends to dinner: the daughter,
Katrina, (and her daughter, Rena) of his friends in the States that are
Katrina's parents. Katrina, the lady with golden hair and soft disposition spoke to our group about her reaction to the terrorist attacks; she
began to cry. Rena stood with her, mother hugging daughter around
the shoulders. They were holy, a sacred portrait of Madonna and child
with classic features of gentility. Their story was touching, although
the length of the room and strength of emotion muffled her speech
where I strained to hear. Katrina spoke with her parents in America
and none could believe what was happening. Rena was at school. Over
the intercom, the principal expressed the details of the tragedy as it was
unfolding. Teachers began question and answer sessions with students
on aspects they did not understand. Most children sat silently, Rena
added. Katrina expressed her deep sympathy, which everyone accepted
at a generous and heart-felt gift. All were one: all capitalist countries
in the free world united. Everyone applauded her for sharing her story

and joining us not just that evening but in her thoughts and philosophy as well.

Venturing to the hotel, Peg and Don finally, successfully telephoned
their daughter. She was going to relay a message to my brother that we
were fine and proceeding with the tour as planned. Now our family
would know that we were fine, but we still did not know if family in
Washington and New York were all right. If anyone was harmed we
were sure that my brother would somehow contact us. A chain of communication was formed: Peg and Don would call their daughter to give
information about our trip, and she would call my brother who would
in turn call others. In this manner all relatives would be kept informed,
soothed. Then, we hope for the best and continue to be excited for the
next part of the trip. We will venture into the Polish countryside for a
day at a farm.

A short nightcap in the bar with David, Brendon, Doris, Kathy Jo,
and Marie recapped impressions of events thus far. David intended to
locate cousins in Poznań, and told the story of his Internet search for
living relatives in Poland. Brendon's fascination with the Kuszubian
province of Poland, which his family originated, drove him to change
his last name to Kaszubik. Although most surnames from that region
are some derivative of Kaszubowski, Brendon opted for the contrived
Kaszubik. While drinking orange juice from a wine glass, he spoke of
his research's progress when we were in Rome and addressed hopes to
uncover more information in Warsaw later this week. Kathy Jo and
Doris, drinking partners since school days, just enjoyed Polish beer and
overstuffed chairs. Listening astutely, I enjoyed the drinks as much as
the conversation, a dry red wine good for the blood. The bottom of the
wine goblet sent Marie and me to our room ready for sleep.

I feel Polish in America and American in Poland.

ROUTE 7, DRIVING AWAY FROM GDAŃSK

ANTICIPATION MOUNTED THE closer we drove to our next destination, a Polish farm turned bed and breakfast. Some anticipation was positive, an excitement to be in nature, in ponderous vegetation of lifestyle harmonious with Nature. Some anticipation was negative, the anxiety and prejudice of not having the myopic expectations, comforts of city dwelling. My disposition rested in the first camp, and stubbornly would not be moved by ill tempers flaring.

This excursion into the countryside was added into the typical itinerary. Matthew was bored with the usual tours after seventeen years. He longed to see the pure spirit of rural Poland, the origins of folk ballads and family life before immigration. Our trip needed this variation, a welcome contrast, most agreed beforehand; and so, democracy prevailed. The majority ruled. However, the minority grew louder and louder. Kathy Jo and Doris were put out, fancying themselves too cosmopolitan to condescend to sleep in a renovated barn. Nonetheless, we were off to the country.

We waved goodbye to the amber streets of Gdańsk and rode past river, lake, forest, and village. For a couple hours the lush landscapes of greens with just a hint of autumn yellow and red scrolled by the window. Farms without fences meshed into the surrounding lands. Cows tethered with chain links grazed or just sat in the midmorning sunlit fields.

To amuse the group, Matthew played word games, supplying the Polish word or phrase and asked the English translation. Billboards were interpreted with common words and objects. This game meant to entertain and educate those of us who knew little Polish. Those fluent in Polish were challenged by more obscure references Matthew would throw in to keep all awake and amused.

Richard, fluent in Polish and bored of the game after half an hour, began telling jokes. "What do you call someone who speaks three languages?" the joke began. Trilinguist.

"What do you call someone who speaks two languages?" it continued. "Bilinguist," several shouted proud of themselves.

Therefore, "what do you call someone who speaks one language?" The punch line: American. I scoffed. Others chuckled.

Matthew put the question to Dad, "why didn't you teach your children Polish?"

Dad never permits being pinned or prodded. He dodged the question, launching into a story of growing up in the Polish section of town. Everyone began to speak of growing up together, the good old days. American Polish reverberated from wall to window in excited giggles of memories almost forgotten.

The truth is complicated. Although language may be one of the first cultural elements to be lost when immigrating to America, Dad's family took pride in retaining the language as well as the culture. Yet culture is highly personal. Nana, and residually Dad, used American

Polish as a secret language, their private language, the language of adult arguments and discussions. The world of adult negotiations was in American Polish, a world in which children were not invited. As children, we knew our place and would not attempt to enter that universe.

That adult universe was changing as well. The neighborhood, the community, morphed into a conglomerate of diversity as the old Polish families either moved or died. American Polish was no longer the language of the neighborhood, as it was in my father's youth. One spoke American Polish only in club, in church, or in family circles. Dad could no longer assume that at the market or the corner drug store his Polish would receive Polish or English response.

American Polish was used as a tool of extreme emotion in regards to us children: the last command before consequences was yelled in American Polish, and we knew what it meant. Conversely, the sweetest moments were in American Polish: cradling arms rocking me to sleep when small or ill, always accompanied with Polish lullaby or hummed ballad; Polish nicknames whispered tenderly, playfully. Those were the special moments, reserved. The everyday language of ordinary existence was American English. As children we understood this, and as adults we prize those American Polish memories while functioning in American English society.

HAJDUCZEK, BED AND BREAKFAST, GÓRZNO

By lunchtime we arrived at the farm in Górzno, our hosts greeting us and directing us into the chicken coop turned dining hall for our first meal on the farm. The red tile floor offset the dark wood walls and white lace curtains. A loft above the bar sheltered musical equipment, enough to satisfy any disc jockey. The long banquet tables were draped in white linen clothes. Prints of still life, bowls of fruit, and portraits adorned the walls leading to exposed beams on the ceiling. The only remnant of a coop was the barn-like shape of the exterior walls. I enjoyed the sloping shape of the dining hall as we waited for lunch to be served. We ate tomato vegetable soup, and when others ate pork dumplings I was considerately offered an egg, sunny side up. After this rustic and pleasurable meal, most were ready to see what Górzno had to offer.

The enormous bus seemed completely out of place cruising down gravel and then dirt paths of Wilga, the nature preserve five miles south of the farming community of Górzno. Tree branches scraped against windows and roof of the bus, a high-pitched symphonic welcome. Stopping at the entrance of a trail, everyone who was interested and able got out of the bus for a walk. Mom was not able to manage the terrain so she, along with a dozen others, stayed on the bus looking out the windows. With book in hand, Mom relaxed. Kathy Jo and Doris extracted rosaries from purses and began to pray in loud whispers intended to be heard by all. Overcome, Doris cried for this calamity befalling her. There was not a high rise or castle in sight.

The hearty travelers began to walk a short decline through woods to see protected bog land, the home of rare white owl and tree inhabiting ducks. Certain mosses and grasses were also being conserved in the wetland habitat. The bog rested in a bed of thick vegetation, trees, brush, and amphibious plant protecting the shoreline. Although I strained to see wildlife, a duck, a lucky frog, none were detected. The local naturalist was brilliant: explaining the Latin names of plants in the hopes that it would cross the language barrier between English and Polish.

She did not have hiking boots on, just plain, black leather, dress boots. This took me by surprise. In America the guide would be in beige suit, ready for safari, with thick-soled heavy boots. In Poland, ordinary dress, nice black pants, green jacket, and dress boots are acceptable, unpretentious. The simpler and unassuming way of our knowledgeable Polish guide seems more sincere. I felt comfortable in my flat, black everyday shoes. Everyone else managed well in ordinary shoes.

Getting back to the bus, we drove a short distance to another trail, this one longer and more rugged. The group of hearty travelers became smaller, the group remaining on the bus larger. A few people chose to stay at the entrance of the trail where there were benches and a sign explaining the trail and what could be seen on it. Dad, Jozef Mazurkiewicz, and Matthew started with the small group down the trail, then turned around after the terrain became too temperamental: curving trail inclining and declining with little notice, muddy passages, sometimes pools of standing water.

Kasia, the niece of the owners of the bed and breakfast farm, and I walked together in the back of the group. Kasia was an elegant shadow of myself: a taller, elongated figure with swift, gentle awareness of her movements and surroundings, small wire-rimmed glasses framing her face. We chattered about the tour, where we had been and where we were going. Half listening to the guide illuminate our vision of the forest and half conversing with Kasia, I observed the scenery: lush rolling hills with forest floor dark and rich, sinuous river cut deep into the land, brush housing field mice or chipmunk close to the path. Kasia caught me off guard by asking my thoughts on the people of Poland and how I would compare my interaction with the people of Italy and the people of Poland on this trip. Her tones elicited a negative response towards Italians and imploring favor for Poles. I stammered out something banal.

"I liked them both for different reasons. The people of Poland were very kind and very sympathetic with Americans. I admired the history of the Polish people and the way they preserve culture and rebuild history."

This fumbling, thoughtless answer was not satisfying for me or for Kasia, but it made due for now and would lead to greater discussion in the late hours of the night.

The naturalist pointed out maple trees with great angles cut into the trunk, tens of these wedges stacked on one another for lengths of three or four feet. In the center seam of these stacked angles, sap would collect, run, and fall in waiting bucket. Sap would then be processed into syrup. This was a century-old practice that was not done in this fashion any longer, too scarring to the trees. Some trees had wooden birdhouses mounted on them. We would learn that those were bat houses.

Along the way Kasia and I swapped stories of travel: her stories of the fjords of Sweden and crop picking in Wales and Ireland, mine of Newfoundland's pristine splendor and car travel across North America. Interested in the structure of college in America, Kasia and I talked about lengths of different program degrees and how students pay for them. Kasia explained that one does not pay for school in Poland, only living expenses during school, which parents help to provide. The group halted to observe a deserted woodpecker colony in a hollowed tree trunk. The bark stripped, the treetop a dream of the past, this trunk was beautiful in its refinement. Even Polish wildlife renovates, rebuilds and uses old spaces in new ways.

Surrounding the woodpecker colony were small, slender trees indigenous to Poland. I cannot remember the name of this species of tree. The silver dollar leaves distinctively shone in the filtered, canopy light of the woods. Marie asked the naturalist if she could take a couple leaves home to show her son who was an American naturalist. The local guide tentatively agreed, showing Marie what branch of what specific tree of which she could take leaves. Before she ripped them from limb, I took her arm and asked if I could just take a picture for her—Carl, her son, would be wise enough to identify the unusual tree from good photographs. Marie insisted on taking a specimen. I was horrified. If every person walking the forest ripped a branch, nothing would be left, I attempted to explain to her. She would not relent.

"I asked before I took anything, and she said it was all right," she defended her position. The naturalist was only being generous to the first American group of tourists to the area, not approving of Marie's actions.

The naturalist mentioned that an orchid on the endangered species list grows in that forest. It is illegal to pick it, of course. Sightings of these orchids are rare by tourists, but one may try to scan the trail as we walk back to the bus. Although the trail continued winding into the heart of the forest, our exploration along the trail was finished. Turning around for the kilometer (three-quarter mile) walk, I correlated and expressed ideas to Kasia: Newfoundland also protects an endangered arctic orchid, which I saw on a hike in a valley. Then we conversed of Poland's wildlife, as I had many questions. She thoroughly described life of the forest. As she spoke, pride shown in her subtle, firm tone, gliding on the forest wind to greet every branch with affection. This was her forest, her playground as a child, her refuge as a student. From her content face and agile feet, one could plainly see that the forest loved her as much as she loved it.

The bus led to the hilltop field house of Wilga, the nature preserve. From there one could see a kidney-shaped lake in a valley adjacent to the forest. The view on the right was deep hilly forest. The view on the left was bumpy farmland of grazing cow and undulating blankets of green and brown crops nestled between woods. With this vista in the background, several people took pictures of the group. Not careful of our tracks, a few of us almost stepped on a frog until I motioned to the spot where he was for others to sidle.

It was prearranged that Kathy Jo and Doris would stay with Marie and me in a suite for four. Upon viewing the room, which to me was spacious with all the necessary amenities, Doris threw a fit, crying. Waling, she demanded a separate room. Her tantrum descended on Kathy Jo who began to pout and whine. Why should they be shoved in a hovel like rats, Kathy Jo persisted. Matthew wanted to slap them. Antoni appeased them, arranging for separate rooms on the top floor of the bed and breakfast down the road. Doris was too much in a fit to carry any of her five pieces of luggage. Dragging luggage from our room, I managed Doris's while Kathy Jo maneuvered herself. Now Marie and I would have a suite ourselves. Each of us had a king size bed. A sitting room and accommodating bathroom made for luxurious conditions. The view of village and tumbling farmland was picturesque. Marie and I did not take offense to their comments. By default, we had won.

There was an hour before dinner for everyone to entertain oneself. Marie and I thought it fun to walk the main street of the small village or the road leading to farms. The doors to Hajduczek were locked and the back gate padlocked. Were we locked in to be secure or to be contained? The locks could be undone, upon request. We decided to play card games in our private lounge instead.

Dinner was a diplomatic event: the Mayor of Górzno as well as a local journalist was in attendance. The first American tourist group to this struggling farming community transforming into a resort village were newsworthy and a business opportunity. Before dinner, I bought Kathy Jo and Doris a glass of wine as a peace offering to relax the spirits, accommodating everyone for this brief rural respite. They appreciated the offer and accepted the wine without hesitation, yet the easy and affable rapport in Rome and Warsaw dissolved with no trace elements to be salvaged. The dining hall converted to an evening's elegance of red linen on candlelit tables.

At table, I asked Mom and Dad of their accommodations at the other converted bed and breakfast. Their cozy third floor farmhouse room lit green and gold with the view of fields ready for harvest with protective Wilga in the distance. Very pleased, Mom beamed a contented smile. She continued, sharing thoughts first in mind.

It was time for all to meet for dinner. Those housed at the auxiliary bed and breakfast began to walk the short path to our farm. Mom and Dad strode with Dick and Lou. A local couple their age passed the group at intersection of main street, aimed toward the steeple one country block up the hill. In Polish, Dick and Lou greeted their local peers and asked where they were going. The lady gravely stared at ground and said that America was attacked; there will be another world war; we must go to church to a special vigil and pray for all souls. All eyes fell solemnly on ground as Dad whispered translation to Mom. Thoughtful gratitude and wishes for peace united these six before pursuing the road that lead to a wistful evening. My mind savored their experience as ruddy purple soup was served in bone white tureen.

After a fancy dinner of borscht (beat soup), homemade breads (rye bread and rape seed bread), gołabki (cabbage rolls filled with rice, tomato, and beef or pork), mushroom strudel (made special for me, the odd vegetarian) and a host of desserts, the Mayor addressed the assembly. A huge man of over six feet, he explained his history of leaving Poland to become a successful businessman in America and returning prosperous to contribute to his homeland. The struggling economy worried him: as it was no longer possible to make a living from farming, alternatives are sought. Since the village is adjacent to Wilga, he would like to promote the village as a resort town for vacationers. Then came the part that caused Dad to shield his eyes and the rest of us to wonder; the Mayor begged our investment and support financially and entrepreneurally.

Did the Mayor know that most of the group was retired blue- and white-collar workers on fixed pensions? There might be a couple people in the group with financial resources abounding, but the majority did not have the assets. I felt for the Mayor. He was doing what he thought best, seizing an opportunity not being able to access the outcome. Luckily he spoke with the right people (Fran, Stella, Matthew, and Antoni). Fran and Stella were Matthew's friends and dignified widows. Their witty humor and good-natured caprice fit the diplomacy required this evening. Antoni suggested avenues in Warsaw to pursue; he also could recommend Górzno to his tour agency for future touring routes. Don, former small town councilman himself, was strangely silent this evening, not offering opinion or suggestion. The journalist interviewed Matthew. Being a loquacious attorney with affluence, Matthew was the correct person to represent American success, and possibly aid in connecting Górzno with economic resources.

After the speech and interview, music revived the mood and the Mayor danced with forlorn Kathy Jo, a striking couple. Redheaded waitresses danced in the kitchen doorway, mouthing the words to the Polish folk songs, half in jest. They caught me giggling at their antics and broke out in laughter themselves. Kasia rolled her eyes at them. Everyone was asked outside for a bonfire.

In Poland kiełbasa is the food of choice for cooking on bonfire flame. After a lavish dinner people were hesitant to eat more, but a short while later some had the fiery sausages of mixed spices. I tried to explain marshmallows and the concept of heating candy to make it crispy on the outside and melting on the inside. Sometimes the roasted marshmallow is then placed on a graham cracker with a piece of chocolate, delicious. The explanation was returned with incredulous, perplexed looks of almost disgust. Candy is not supposed to be heated. Crispy and melting at the same time is strange. It was very good; I tried to reassure. I gave up.

Campfire songs broke out, of course. First lead by Matthew with alternating Polish and American traditional campfire songs, the journalist was impressed. We sang "God Bless America" and "My Country 'Tis of Thee." After the diplomats left, Jozef Mazurkiewicz took reign, stood in the center by the fire and lead the band with gusto. Old songs were then sung: "I've been working on the Railroad," and "You Are My Sunshine" topped his list. I joined in for the most maudlin and romantic "Let Me Call You Sweetheart." Then I was done, and most of the rest of the group was too. Half the group went to the bed and breakfast down the street and the other half lingered at the fire a few more minutes. Brutus the dog was let out of his cage for a run around the yard and a tasty kielbasa. When everyone went to their rooms, Kasia invited me into the bar for a drink and lively conversation.

As we sat down at the square table, Kasia asked me the question foremost in her mind: why are you traveling with old people? I had to laugh before I could answer: my parents were interested in Dad's heritage; this group was loosely structured around discovering family and family history. A friend of my father was initially supposed to come but then she unexpectedly found herself overwhelmed by personal turmoil and chose not to go. Two of my sisters would have fought to fill the seat, but because of their schedules could not consider the trip. I gladly filled the seat, wanting to experience Poland with my parents as they reacted to the real Poland versus the family myths of old Poland. I was honored to be with this group. Yet it was my first trip with "old people."

She retorted, but how do you entertain yourself at night when everyone goes to bed at ten? Simply, I have a nightcap with whoever wants a nightcap that evening, and then go to my room to read or talk with Marie. (I was too embarrassed to say that I scrawl in my journal impressions and events.)

We talked about where I was and where she was when we heard of the terrorist attacks. She has a cousin in Washington, DC for an exchange school program. He was safe but experienced the chaos. I still did not speak with family at home, but rather relays of messages passed from one group member to a network at home, not the same as speaking with home directly. I thought of my brother James having information on my family in Washington and New York City. All must be fine, or else James would have made a concerted effort to reach us directly. Stay hopeful. She expressed sympathy, for which I was grateful. Possible ramifications of the attacks, mention of war, methodical acts of terror, and mobilizing troops, kept the conversation somber. Kasia, knowing the topic was too much too late at night, with a smile and a wave said on to better things. Her whimsical manner was appreciated.

Asking of student life in America, we quickly changed tones to various activities. Student life in America is a juggling act: working some job (most likely in retail or in restaurants) to pay for books, supplies, and living expenses; going to school during the day or night; completing school projects constantly, and entertaining oneself in spare time, not too often. In Poznan, where Kasia goes to school, there are several universities. The government paid for school, only living expenses out of pocket. Her parents were paying her living expenses so she could concentrate on her studies, which is typical she explained. Kasia was shocked that students work in America. When do you study? Whenever you can. We don't sleep much. A small smile rose from that comment.

The real question was posed: don't you have discos in America, don't students drink?

Thus began a swap of stories of American bars and nightlife and the Poznań club scene. I also talked about other entertainment: movies, poetry readings in cafes, concerts, camping excursions, and theatrical productions of all sorts. Yet the stories that eclipsed all others were the ones of drinking. Apparently Russian students have very high tolerances for all sorts of alcohol. Neither of us was a big drinker, but had enough stories to entertain. Shots lined the table as one is slugged between each song, each dance. The drunken stories progressed as well sipped bottled water. Somehow a divergent topic was introduced, Kasia asked, what do you call black people?

There were Africans coming to Poland and Kasia heard an American say that there are proper terms to call people. I explained that slang terms exist that are meant to be derogatory and other terms that are respectful. Outsiders always should use the respectful terms only. For people of color they would be African Americans (if from or in the States) or Africans, the term black is all right if you know the person well and the person is comfortable with the label. People from the East are called Asian Americans, people from Central and South America Latino, and natives are called Native Americans or American Indians, or Mohawk, for example, if you know the person well and the person is comfortable with associating with the specific culture or tribe. Friends usually do not call each other by categories, only by endearment or offense—ruled by emotion not objectivity. In America, one is who one wishes to be. Kasia found this interesting at a distance but troublesome in homeland. Why should we accept foreigners when there are barely enough good jobs for natives, Kasia thought aloud. Poland is one of the more successful former communist countries, yet it struggles with

prosperity. I could not answer this age-old democratic question of turmoil between the established and the new immigrant.

This spiraled into discussion of big city existence, immigration and
gangs. In city living there are boroughs (little Italy, China town) but
that does not mean that you only interact with whom you live. If you
want a good Italian dinner, you go with your friends to little Italy. If
you like dim sum, you go to China town. If you would give an exotic
gift, you shop at a boutique in the French Quarter, or anywhere else.
As long as you are respectful, knowledgeable, and understanding, there
is no problem. I have had positive experiences in many cities across
North America in many different boroughs. The troubles are related to
local gangs of diverse composition who are not willing to understand
the perspective of the other, not willing to respect another out of fear
or ignorance. Kasia gave me a lovely compliment; she called me open-
minded.

She explained that many Turks are settling in Poland, which is
cause for some alarm. Muslims immigrating to a mostly Catholic, if
not ninety-five percent Christian, country was treated with tentative,
questioning regard. This observation led to a conversation on immigration. Many Latinos go to Florida and New Mexico; many Asian
come through California, but people come from all over the world
to the States. I explained how my neighbors were Bosnian and across
the street live Puerto Ricans. Taken aback she asked, don't you feel
like they are invading your home and they should go back to theirs?
No. If you say that, I should come back to live in Poland where my
father's family originally lived. Or, should I go back to France where
my mother's family originates? America is based on the welcoming of
others, or the entire country should be given back to Native Americans
with apologies. This flamboyant statement transformed into a discussion of culture.

You are lucky to be in a country that honors history, and has cultural fabric so strong that it continually rebuilds itself; I addressed her. Kasia smiled at the compliment. I told her she should be proud to be Polish, another smile. In America culture is a choice. Freedom of choice allows for responsibility for oneself, one's personal culture. And, one may choose not to participate in any culture, or choose to create one's own tradition. There are no buildings to remind you of honored kings of homeland, no kiosks offering bigos. Families keep culture by cooking the food and following the traditions, telling the stories of homeland, and sometimes practicing the language. By living in communities of the same derivation or establishing unions or clubs, culture is also kept. Yet all these require the will of participation. Nothing is assumed or expected; therefore no cultural framework is given save what one gives oneself and one's family. Kasia put a difficult question to me, how do you feel touring Poland?

I feel Polish in America and American in Poland. Much of the history and culture I am trying to absorb while observing, curious to discover more and more. Yet at every turn I am American, different dress, different manner of speaking, different everything. In our group, we are birds who thought we were flightless, learning to soar alone, trying to remember how it was to fly in pointed formation. One holds dear the speckled markings that create oneself and the long wing feathers that steer on wind's edge of history—the marriage of both is the wholeness of experience.

By the way others look at me, I know I am different, and that is not bad nor good, just different. Not speaking the language is a real barrier; I must learn Polish. I complimented Kasia on her perfect English. She refused that compliment, saying that she is still learning. Endeavoring to encourage me, she illustrated that Polish is a difficult language to learn because of the many dialects. Polish of the north, as in Gdańsk, is very different from the Polish of the central mountains or southern cities. Extrapolating, Kasia herself could not understand the Polish of mountain dialect. However the northern Polish dialect is understandable to her, as she knows proper Polish taught in school as well as her native dialect of the northwest farmlands. Appreciating the gesture, I mentioned the dialects of American English, which would be difficult to learn as a second language as well. Describing the dialects of the south, of the west coast, and of various inner cities, not to mention the many translations of slang everywhere, I entertained Kasia with awful mimics of dialectical language, intonation.

Kasia then made a point that stunned me. A complete break in flow of conversation, from comedy to icy seriousness cracked, in a moment. The clown in me paused to regroup.

"I wish Poland had more economy and less history," she stated.

I asked her about communism and capitalism, and working life of the people. She explained that her aunt and uncle had a difficult time farming under both systems; at least capitalism allows one to change as one wishes, not as government instructs. She herself did not recall her life under communism. Yet she knew that capitalism was slow in stimulating economy, many people unemployed and frustrated. Small villages, farming communities, were unable to sustain themselves. Now everyone is trying to build a business. Her aunt's best friend opened a bakery (all of the desserts at our meals were from that bakery) while her aunt hopes to run a successful hotel while others cling to farming. Everyone is struggling in one's different opportunities. They choose to struggle in their home rather than move to a big city where there are more jobs.

Some people leave Poland for a couple years to get job experience in France or Austria, then return to get much better jobs. Employers perceive workers who relocate to have better credentials than those who stay home. It is more psychological than skillful. Kasia feared that she would have to move in order to sustain employment in a bio-technology firm. Poznan was big enough for her; she did not want to consider moving to Warsaw, let alone outside the country. Poznan was close enough to home that she could visit once or twice a month, or whenever her aunt needed help in the bed and breakfast. Without the ability to easily travel home for walks in her forest, she did not want to consider city life.

Fascinated, I understood the trouble and relayed my experience of living in a small decaying town in the American Northeast where people are moving away for jobs. New York City is rich; Buffalo, New York is poor. Stubbornly, I reinvent my career to stay home choosing not to move to more prosperous states. In California or North Carolina I could get a job immediately, but I refuse to leave my home.

When abroad our group has been referring to ourselves as New Yorkers. The reaction we have had from this has been overwhelming. However, our home in New York State is a seven-hour drive from the City. Toronto is more commutable. At home, we take great pains to distinguish ourselves, "Upstate New Yorkers," from the typical idea of those in the City. Not so after the attacks, not now. We accept every embrace as New Yorkers. We wipe every tear as New Yorkers. At this point her uncle came into the room and joined us. Kasia translated, as he wanted to ask me a question.

He has relatives in Pennsylvania who are farmers. He wanted to know what Pennsylvania is like since he never had the opportunity to visit. The northern part of the state is very close to where I live, only an hour's drive. It is hilly (like Górzno) but then gets mountainous in the southern part of the state, a beautiful place to live and farm. The land is expansive and fertile. I explained that a large population of Amish and Mennonite farmers reside in Pennsylvania with simple lifestyles, respecting nature. The climate is similar to Poland's, if not slightly warmer. He was happy with this description. He had no intention of visiting, yet wished to have a mental picture of his family's estates and lifestyle. Kasia's translation of my description satisfied his curiosity and soothed his mind of their detachment. Shaking my hand and wishing us both goodnights, he left the room.

Kasia would like to visit America. The freedom and ideas that have been imported with capitalism fill her mind with dreams of cities where everyone wears jeans, eats fast food, and plays more than works while still managing to accumulate wealth. Why wouldn't every country want to emulate America?

Quebec sprang to my mind. I told Kasia about French Canadians who wish for independence from Canada. It is their right to practice their culture and participate in government, yet isolationist to ignore commerce and interaction in North American and global communities. Above all, respect must form interaction between any community and country. This brought on another exchange of family stories.

For holidays, all of Kasia's family meets in the hotel for a great feast and music, a grand celebration. The rooms fill with about forty people when all the relatives arrive. They dance and sing until all hours of the night break day. Being one of seven siblings, when our immediate family gathers for holidays, if everyone is able to come, we reach about twenty. Baking, trimming the tree, exchanging gifts, and feasting highlighted my Christmas stories of home. A few more stories, then the small hours of night crept into the room. We parted cheerily, both excited and grateful for this opportunity to make friends. It was a privilege and honor to have an exchange of ideas and frames of reference with another person.

Reaching the suite, Marie had locked the door. I knocked as quietly as possible, whispering her name. Then I had to knock louder. As drunk and groggy as a lonesome truck driver, Marie opened the door with accompanying gruff vengeance. What the hell, she was forced to murmur, among other statements and postulations. Quiet apologies led her to bed. In the dark I fumbled and tripped over luggage until the stable bathroom light organized my search. Wakeful ideas would not allow my head to sleep. Yet the soft warmth of poduszka and pieriyna ushered sleep to its rightful stronghold, one happy prisoner taken.

SEPTEMBER 18, 2001

"Did you see the cow walking down the street?"
— JOE PROROK

GORZNÓ

MORNING CAME TOO fast, sunlight edging cloudy dreams. Yet it was a lovely, bright day full of potential. Marie and I quickly got ready for the day, as the alarm never went off and we were the last to appear for breakfast.

Marie offered for me to get ready first, which I accepted swiftly. As I was gathering my things, out the window I noticed a farmer walking his cow down the middle of the main street. Enchanted, I watched through the window as others from the group watched from outside where they were walking. I took a picture. A morning walk for farmer and cow is a charming idea.

Nana's face appeared, transposed from memory to half-open shutters in the misty light of dawn. Her blue-gray eyes told the story without need of words. I grinned at her whitewashed faced and listened one more time.

"Be thankful for the milk you have," she said.

143

As the only daughter, and youngest child, Nana's mother doted on her. At the turn of the nineteenth century, they were poor, new immigrants taking nothing for granted. Yet Nana wanted more, as all children do: pretty doll, new dress, or Sunday sweet.

"Be thankful for the milk you have," her mother, Boucha Frania, would say in Polish and lapse into a story from Boucha's childhood: "my mother and father could barely afford to feed us on the farm. Father was upset that he was forced to buy a cow. Milk was expensive for three children. The cow seemed cheaper, but a cow is expensive to maintain, land for grazing instead of planting, a continuous supply of feed, constant attention. Every morning we had fresh warm milk for breakfast and on Sundays we had bread pudding from the saved cream and old bread from the week. Those were our treats and we were happy for them."

So Nana learned to go without and relish simple things and Sunday treats, although she never had the responsibility or the pleasure of owning a cow. Wouldn't caring for a cow be an entertaining chore for children?

At the end of the Roaring Twenties Nana was married to Thaddeus, a dapper young Polish American boy with elegance and vision, and was widowed in the end of the Depression soon after Dad was born. Teddy died of tuberculosis, incurable. Dad was raised by two working widows, Nana and Boucha Frania, and learned to appreciate Sunday treats without the cow. Since they lived on a dead-end street adjoining train tracks, they had a large yard for a city dwelling. They filled the space with chicken coops, practical for eggs and poultry. Not enough space for a cow, though.

In the 1970's our family was securely middle class. Nana lived with us, in the house that she had built when my parents married. She was a second mother, sometimes given more authority by Dad than Mom on certain matters. At the grocery store when I would whine for a last minute treat at the check-out counter, Nana would repeat, "Be thankful for the milk you have."

Although I knew the story by heart, I could not relate to the mundane red and white carton of milk receiving priority over a silver and brown chocolate bar screaming from the aisle to be taken home. Buy the milk tomorrow then, I thought but would not dare to speak. I wanted the novelty of having the cow… or the chocolate. I learned to cherish Sunday treats, stories of Teddy (never Grandpa or Thaddeus, always affectionately Teddy as if my imaginary Teddy Bear), and honored mythical Polish cows.

If I did own a cow, I would walk it down Main Street each blurry morning as well.

I hopped down the stairs and out the door, greeting people who were having a stroll before breakfast. All chose to come in to eat, but Joe Prorok and I walked Main Street following the pavement. Still chuckling at the sight of the pet cow on a morning walk, Joe asked my impressions.

"Seems a good idea to me, keeps the cow fit," I joked as we settled into a leisurely pace.

He told me of the last time he was in Poland as a soldier during the war. The people were left with nothing. Towns, villages were destroyed; most all resources lay in ruin, yet the people were glad to see the American troops cruise in with tank or truck. He remembered their kindness and appreciation. This trip meant much to him, to see how country and spirit were renewed.

We waved to an elderly lady who was watching us from her second story window across the street. She waved back, smiling. We passed the best friend's bakery of which Kasia spoke last night. Villagers were inside having morning coffee and pastry. A young boy came out the door and dropped a paper bag into his bicycle's wire basket, then waited for us to pass before riding home. Knowing breakfast was prepared; we did not stop but peered in to see as much as we could. Reaching the end of the paved way, we turned away from hilly farmland, back towards the bed and breakfast to have our awaiting meal.

This village looked frozen in time, representing the 1940s, Joe pondered, pleased with the notion that life was restored to village and town. Although rural economy is dire, rural lifestyle thrives. I thought of Kasia and her family at this comment, and simpered. He graciously thanked me for the walk together; immediately I returned the thanks, having enjoyed myself as much as he did. With handshakes, we rejoined the group in the hotel.

Plates of hard-boiled eggs, fresh breads, and chocolate pastries lined the tables. Trays of cold cuts and cheeses were also offered. Everyone exchanged morning greetings as each new person entered the room. The best part of each breakfast was the black currant juice. Resembling concord grape juice in color, black currant juice has a distinctive taste: earthy and pungent, unlike the acidic tastes of orange or grape juice. Every morning the first selection for breakfast was always black currant juice and coffee, a fantastic combination.

While half the group and all luggage were being collected on the bus, I had a chance to speak to Kasia after breakfast. She had only an hour of sleep, rising very early to prepare breakfast for us. We exchanged addresses: I gave her my home address and e-mail address; she gave me a brochure for the bed and breakfast because she did not have a computer at school. Any mail I sent her aunt's place, she would receive while home visiting. I look forward to keeping in touch with Kasia. With pleasure and thanks, we shook hands. She asked if I would ever come back to Gorznó. I said I would come back to visit, and next time it would be with friends. She said something to her aunt in Polish and ran to get something. When she returned, she had a small book on local real estate. She presented it to me saying I may contact that e-mail address listed to arrange lodgings for the next trip, whenever that may be. Or, I could write to her at that address and it would be printed out for her aunt to give her. Again, many thanks and gladness for my new friend; I boarded the bus.

Matthew required us to count off numbers. Sixteen, I said.

"Who is sixteen?" Edward questioned Antoni.

"Sixteen is amiable and flexible when plans go wrong; she does not bear grudges." Antoni answered with a relieved smirk.

The Mayor had come this morning to wish us farewell. A small group assembled on the front sidewalk to wave farewell: the Mayor, Kasia with her aunt and uncle, and the redheaded ladies. Everyone on the bus returned the wave from departing windows then settled into the gentle landscape proceeding south.

The soil is dark and rich in minerals. Forest and farm mesh into one fabric of landscape: a kaleidoscope of greens, browns, and yellows. The harsh black and white of grazing cows contrast the scenery. On top of poles or bare trees, huge stork nests loom empty for the upcoming winter. The storks are already in Egypt sunbathing. Yet the nests wait, undisturbed, for their owners to return at signs of spring.

Crosses at every intersection, be it dirt road or major highway, bless people on the journey. Devils, temptation, uncertainty lurk at crossroads. Ancient tribes proclaimed it to be so. Altars to Mary, Jesus or a saint of choice, or wooden crosses bless the roads, the cross section, to keep the devils at bay. These roadside altars, kapliczka, add color to the landscape, but more distinctly they mark the people that live nearby: various altars of size, shape, and decoration speak. The Madonna stands four feet tall on a stone pedestal. A white picket fence squarely surrounds her. Above her head, a halo of white holds rainbow ribbons streaming down to each plank of the fence. Beautiful fresh flowers, sometimes a candle, line the base of the pedestal. The people who live here are prosperous or very religious or both. The next crossroad reveals a wooden cross, plain and sturdy, yet imposing at five or six feet tall. Are these residents more practical or less superstitious? Or could this one be abandoned for promises of city life? The imagination is captive to draw pictures of families or small communities that match their roadside altar.

A saint (but which one protects travelers or small communities?) in a marble case with glass front impressively presides over the crossroads by a small church. Candles along wrought-iron fence pay him homage; has he safeguarded weary travelers along this route? Do those candles represent near mishaps, thankfully kept away? Or are they like indulgences, being stored for future use? Or perhaps this saint is the patron of the community, the altar placed at roadside to combine functions of safeguarding community and traveler.

The altar a backwards glimmer in streaks of field across the window; we stopped at a rest area to stretch. This rest area did not contain a restaurant, but a convenience store. Through the short aisles of junk food and beverages, our group overcrowded. By the front windows I came across the newsstand where many copies of Newsweek filled rows and stacks. On the back shelf there was a Polish news magazine called *Gala*. Hillary_Rodham Clinton in a surgical mask, head lumbering down, forehead creased in worry, was on the cover. She was standing at the site of the Twin Towers. We would not hear it called Ground Zero; that is an American term. Flipping through the pages seized horror in my throat. At a close up shot of the towers just before crumbling, I noticed the specks in midair, trapped people jumping with no recourse. I could not speak.

Antoni approached me, and without word or hesitation, began to translate headlines and subtitles for me. "Poland Stands With America." "Unite For Freedom." "Condemn Terrorist Attacks." "The World United Against Terror." The translations were reassuring, which left me unprepared to handle his question.

"Could the attacks have been from an American group, another McVeigh?"

"Absolutely not," I could not control the tremulous emotion in my voice. American terrorists do not have the organization to destroy the country. As many have gripes with systems and bureaucracies within the capitalist economy and republican politics, most groups agree with the fundamental right of freedom provided within a democracy. They demand their position be heard, albeit in destructive ways. Above all, American terrorists do not kill themselves, but rather relish the twisted glory of witnessing their rancor and dystrophy. Glory lies only in today, not the hereafter. The attacks were crimes beyond American comprehension.

Antoni reverberated my answer with calming tones; he had no intention of upsetting me. "We are with you," he said, as if I was the only representative of the free world and he was the ruling government of Poland.

"And we will fight for you, beside you, if need be," he added.

We rule ourselves in personal behavior, and I studied his words for their beauty and affect as panacea. Soothing words absorbed, I turned the *Gala* magazine in hand and entered the cashier's line to purchase it.

Many people bought snacks for the ride ahead. The two young men behind the counter were pacing themselves, quick but not rushed to cash. Marie purchased a road map and bottled water. For the next half hour we would plot the routes we have already taken with a blue pen, circling the towns explored. Edward, playfully pretending he could not understand our English, would not say the route he would take to Warsaw. The route would depend on the time and pace of the day's events. We would have to attend to the road signs and mark the map as we passed, an inverted use of a map yet still useful. At least we would have known where we had been if we could not know where we were going.

TORUŃ

Soon the rural landscape gave way to friendly street scenes of a moderate-sized city, Toruń. Among small buildings and side by side brownstones, one swift turn lead to surprise: a Teutonic Knight's castle, the front an intact or restored tower with corrugated roof to peak, and the back a crumbling mass of red brick, interior walls and stairs exposed. Along the river we drove until we reached the Kosmos Hotel, very near town center and across the street from the river Wisla.

Immediately, before checking into our rooms, I was given a copy of an e-mail from home: James, my brother, had sent several hotels from our itinerary the same message that everyone at home was safe, family in New York and Washington included. John was fatefully late for work and saw crowds fleeing while he was in his car. The second tower fell in the distance, gray smoke engulfing. John turned and reported to his company's New Jersey office only to watch reports on television and account for his coworkers missing. In Washington, the Trade Building was evacuated, turning Ellen into the street with thousands of others similarly dispersed into chaos. The usual half an hour commute to her home in Northern Virginia took over three hours, but she was unharmed. Our family is safely intact. With relief I continued to read that James would stay in contact with Don's daughter and Marie's daughter for news bulletins of our trip. Now everyone at home was most concerned for our safety abroad. Mom's expression changed immediately when I gave her the message to read. Heavy thoughts lifted; she could now fully enjoy herself. Dad was relieved as well but still kept a stubborn edge of worry, more now about getting home safely rather than the security of family in the States.

The Kosmos Hotel was an older one from the days of communism. There was no elevator to effortlessly convey luggage. Again thankful for exercise, I ran my luggage up three flights, and then ran down to the lobby to convey my parents' luggage. The porters and Edward took care of the rest.

After a half-hour we met in the lobby to board the bus for a tour of Old Town. It took about fifteen minutes to take our seats on the bus. Before and after each bus ride, everyone would call out their number to make sure the entire group was present. My number was sixteen. By the time we finished counting, the bus was moving around a curve and down the street adjacent to the river. The bus stopped. A quarter of a mile no more than half a mile, the bus jerked to a stop and opened the doors for departure—the shortest tour ever. I had to laugh. Departing the bus and crossing the street, we met the local tour guide at the medieval gateway.

Passing through the gate, we sharply turned left to study a medieval watchtower in the corner of the retaining wall to Old Town, the Leaning Tower of Toruń. At an eighty-degree angle the building leans, stable in its instability. In the past it was used for various purposes, now it is a museum. We were invited to try and stand upright along the exterior wall of the facade. Several tried, but the wall pushes; each person fell, stumbling one foot forward unable to be tall and stable. A gorgeous tree nestled into the corner of perpendicular walls keeps the leaning tower company. Moss and carved handiwork covered its trunk until its second story where branches laden with green arrowhead leaves and white blossoms turned back to earth.

Next we encountered a gothic-style building that was a granary but now stands empty. The peaks were covered in crawling ivy. Our guide led the way to Nicolaus Copernicus' home: the arched, wooden door introduced an ornate pattern of stylized flowers in various tones of red and orange. Copernicus was born and raised in Toruń before he moved and changed the epicenter of the universe, let alone human perception. His home was now a museum, closed today. One block north was Town Center, an open square of cobblestone welcoming street vendors and outdoor cafes. Unfortunately, it was cloudy and raining in spurts. On the left of the square, gothic castle now a post office and a Baroque style, cream colored and unassuming, Jesuit Church of the Holy Ghost. On the right, the Town Hall occupied a city block: a quadrangle of buildings connected with spires and clock tower. We passed through the Town Hall gates into the central plaza, observing the city and government offices from the mysterious innards. Misty rain still drizzled as we stood pondering the spire tips and bay windows. The clock tower was under renovation, scaffold and tarp covering the great clock face, rooftop observatory, and catwalk. No one was apparently working on it today.

The tour moving back into the square, we walked diagonally through the square to the Church of the Blessed Virgin Mary. Memorials interlocking into one wall lined the path to the main entrance. The local guide had a thick accent and spoke quickly, a combination that left her unintelligible to the dawdlers at the end of our group. I watched as men stood on a platform ten feet above the ground to rejuvenate the scrollwork and statues along the top. The gray afternoon transformed into a sublime experience of heaven upon entering church. Pure white, ethereal white blazed from vaulted ceiling to undecorated floor. The vaulted ceilings had outlined seams in navy blue and silver, which only enhanced the effect of the stark white interior. This once Catholic monastery became Lutheran in the sixteenth century, then Protestant in the seventeenth century, only to be reclaimed by the Catholic Church thereafter. Somewhere along that historical plane the church was painted white.

We briefly sat down on narrow dark benches to hear more about this church's interesting history and artifacts. Yet all I could hear was scratching. Where was that scratching? I had sat alone behind my parents, which did not help me attend to the guide's lecture. The scratching persists. Behind me, it must be behind me. Jerking more suddenly than I had intended, I swerved to locate the noise. Scratching. I knocked down my purse, which made a horrible resonating noise, but I finally saw the scratching. On a column in a bubble of plastic clothes one bulb illuminates the figure of a man with phantom hand in air holding a small brush, scraping to coax the original splendor of artwork back to life. On plank across scaffold he stands completely enclosed, alone with his work.

It struck in a moment: that is the spirit of Poland. In this small city with the economy in recession, in a church not large enough to be called cathedral, it is important to revive the treasures of history, of culture. Who is the man painstakingly brushing and repainting that piece of religious art? Why does he do it? He is the same as the man working on the clock tower and the same as the woman who laid bricks with her own hands to rebuild the Royal Palace. He is the child at school putting a coin into the collection box to buy material for strikingly new old structures. He is the tenacious spirit of Poland, resilient to turmoil and strife; ready to give whatever it takes to revive, regardless of personal circumstance. The importance of country and culture is as deep as the Baltic and as long as the Wisla to these beautiful people of Poland.

The group was walking around the perimeter at other holy relics. One last time I stared to see through the bubble, only able to perceive the shadow bending for a different tool and repositioning attention. That man must be very proud of his restoration work. I know I would be.

We reached the last shrine by the entry, which was a bronze monument to the founder of the scouts in Poland. Beside the shrine, among the flowers and candles, was a small desk and chair. A ledger was on the desk that contained prayers and signatures of believers and guests. Don signed the book on behalf of our group. Mom wanted to write a prayer but had no pen. I lent her mine and she sat, pensive for a long moment before writing two prayers: one prayer for family happiness and health, and another for world peace without the brutality of war and prejudice. Gently prodding, I rushed Mom and Dad back to our group. We had missed the content of the tour explaining the outside memorials of the church again.

Back through the square to a pierniki shop, we ran to get out of the downpour. A waft of spicy gingerbread filled the air and our heads as we entered the shop. Toruń is the birthplace of pierniki. This fact, to some people (I am included in this grouping), is as important as Nicholas Copernicus. So these were the golden pyramids of the bakery in Warsaw. Never would I have associated this aromatic gingerbread with the cookies we American Poles call pierniki. At home pierniki refers to anise-flavored or butter-flavored cutout cookies, iced and highly decorated. Mom and Dad were disconcerted at the disparity of pierniki forms. Our recipe was secure through generations. How could it be so different from authentic Polish tradition? To us, pierniki are alabaster figures with sculpted icing and candy trim. Here pierniki are spicy cookies similar to gingerbread that may be cutout, and left plain or iced, or may be drops as well. Nonetheless they are delicious.

Nana knew ever since she sampled pierniki as a child that she did not care for it. Ginger, nutmeg, and other strong spices did not agree with her; they were too much like her. One Christmas, when Nana and Teddy were newlyweds, Nana read a recipe in the holiday section of the newspaper for fancy cutouts. Testing it first, she enjoyed the mild flavor and potential for ornamentation. Quickly she dubbed it pierniki, her pierniki. This was America; no one would challenge her right to use the name as she wished. She would create her family's old new custom. Therefore, Dad and our subsequent generations lovingly refer to our traditional Christmas cookies as pierniki. For us, they are.

The dark wood and brass of the counters shone regardless of the downpour outside. On the shelves pierniki cottages and cutouts stood next to bags of pierniki drops. Marie and Mom chose not to purchase any variety. Marie, unphased by lapse in continuity of pierniki, chose not to buy any simply because she did not have a craving for ginger-bread today. As we shared pierniki on the stoop of the shop, the sun decided to greet us with its presence. And, Marie indulged curiosity, not craving, by sampling just one pierniki drop.

The window lavishly displayed the ingredients on red velvet swags: a wooden bowl of whole nutmegs, a glass tray of crystallized ginger and sugars, cinnamon in mortar coarsely ground with marble pestle resting within, star anise sprayed throughout display as spicy drops of heaven christening the recipe. Along the far right side, a basket stood proudly clasping bags of pierniki, the wondrous result of spices and other mysterious ingredients and processes. The rain could not drink through clothes and skin in the presence of these spices, this apoth-ecary of experiences. Scents of ginger and anise sprang from threshold as each person opened the door of admittance. Our group collected itself in front of the warm, spicy display.

The tour was over; the local guide was leaving. Yet it was still hours away from dinner. The group chose to split for a half-hour and then rejoin to take the bus to the hotel. A group of eight of us found a WC and then a Sphinx restaurant for lunch. Frank, on behalf of all of us, requested Dad to translate the menu, which he did with pleasure. For Dad was the only member of this small group to understand Polish. Dad was forced from his non-communicative stance to be our interpreter, and he did so with diplomacy. Ordering for the group, everyone had the same bowl of vegetable soup with two small hard rolls and butter, coffee or tea. Frank offered thanks with a pat on the back to Dad for being our guide, to which Dad responded with a hearty grin, proud of himself. I was proud of him, too. The time went quickly, and most of my little group went back to the hotel.

Surprisingly, Mom was in great spirits and felt enough strength to stay in Old Town to shop with Marie and me. Dad wished for a nap so returned with others to the hotel, giving us his approval to wander. We waved goodbye and started exploring.

In and out of the little stalls that occupied the first floor of Town Hall, we glanced. Hand-painted wooden eggs and nesting dolls stood at attention on display shelves. On the same revolving jewelry rack, rosaries hung beside pendants of angels in flight over town square. Underneath the leather necklaces with pendants, dharma beads swung intimately. I studied them with poor view. Reaching for the one closest to the edge, I grasped one of terra cotta beads. Carved in black outline, Buddha in lotus position was sitting prayerfully on each bead. Slanted rays spring from Buddha's head, a sign of powerful meditation. I thought of the General Audience with the Pope and his council from various religions, including Buddhism. Enlightened, I bought the dharma beads for my brother, the professor of cultural studies. Until they reached his hands, they would help to guide mine. Mom and Marie were already in the next alcove, the next stall. I hustled to meet them.

Richard was keeping pace with us for a while, until interests led us apart. Marie stepped into a swanky art gallery; the window paintings priced in the thousands. Mom and I went into an adjacent fabric shop to buy curtain material, but did not know that only samples were on display. Mom asked if either of the sales girls knew English; they nodded dissentingly. So we left thinking that the shop did not have enough of the lace we wanted to buy. Marie explained that it was another communist style shop where samples indicated variety of fabrics; quantity should have been in storage. Marie asked if Mom would like to speak to the sales clerk again, with Marie as translator. Mom said no. We ambled west.

Continuing down the avenue, we entered the boutique across from Copernicus' home. Alma and Steven were buying rare stamps. There was a folding chess set in the window. It was hand-carved, pieces and board. The sides were ribbed and the top had swirls etched into the outside edge. I bought it for my brother James while Mom and Marie bought painted wooden eggs. Marie flirted with the store manager, tall and gray in brown suit and pocket watch. The manager, with a wink, gave Marie a complimentary hand painted wooden egg.

"For her good spirit." He explained in English.

Marie leaned over the glass counter and planted a blooming kiss on his cheek. Everyone chuckled. And for my patience as he waited on everyone else first, he gave me two postcards of Torun, with wink aimed at Mom and me. Alma and Steven, serious stamp collectors, converted atmosphere to inquisitive politeness, inquiring of vintage stamps in his case. They began a discussion in Polish. Marie, Mom and I left quietly.

We wandered further to discover a small used bookstore. Convincing them to stop, I ran directly to the art section to see if there were any books on stained glass or Polish art and architecture. With little interest in books, Mom and Marie leaned against a table watching me. Typical books filled the shelves: classic architecture, Renaissance painters, Impressionist catalogues. If only I could find books on Polish art and artists. Mom and Marie sat on the table, engaged in conversation. The sales girl stared at them in disbelief. Tables are not for sitting in any country. I curtailed my search, so we could do other things of interest for all.

Copernicus was the center of our universe today, as this is now the third time we are passing his house. We stopped and looked in the windows. A cherry desk and chair, very modest, rest along the far wall. I could not see anything else, nose almost pressed against the glass, breath fogged window into history. Copernicus lived here; as a boy he might of pressed his nose on opposite side of this glass, wishing to explore the world instead of confined to home. The ruddy brick could tell stories of a curious child who would change the structure of the universe. Ideas flowed through entablature and windowpanes. Now Mom was beginning to feel winded; we began to walk to the hotel.

Slowly we stepped on the sidewalk as other pedestrians rushed past in a flurry. There was no reason for us to rush; Mom no longer had the capability and I wanted to extend every moment. Marie did not care one way or the other. A park ran along the Wisla River to the bridge. Picnic tables invited everyone to linger and play, but the rain had left the park uninhabited. Under the bridge and across the street we reached the hotel with plenty of time to relax before dinner.

Mom suggested that I show Dad the chess set; I went to their room to tell him of the afternoon in Old Town. Opening the windows for fresh air, Mom and I noticed two rainbows. One enormous parabolic curve flowing from the Wisla by the bridge past Old Town and into the newer section of Toruń; another much smaller directly above the first, but only extending from one cloud above the bridge to Old Town— near Copernicus's home. This was the perfect sign. The friendship and discoveries of the day were in some way in harmony with nature. I stood at the window staring at those rainbows until they vanished, first the smaller one then the larger waned. By the time every hint of light was surrendered from the tip of the larger rainbow, it was time for dinner.

In the hotel dining hall we learned of Edward's condition. He had strained himself fixing something in the undercarriage of the bus. He was taken to the hospital with chest pains. Antoni was not aware of his condition. The tour company was sending another bus driver so that our schedule would not be disrupted.

We sat at a square table in the far corner next to the buffet, not for convenience; it was the last empty table. It was a sign of luck. The table was abutting a stained glass wall of the Vistula River and hills in the background. The panes were of varying textures, the tolerances impeccable. The wobbling river sprouted tree and sky before settling into mountain, beautiful.

Dinner I cannot remember. The buffet selection was as many others had been: a variety of fish and meats, salads and coleslaws, soup and rolls. The scalloped, sea foam leaves of stained glass tree took my attention from food. I touched the glass to feel its bumps and ridges, the mountainous choreography within each millimeter of glass, for it was not an antique in watchful museum and could be momentarily brushed and surveyed without a commotion. Its tolerances were even.

Its lines were pure. Yet it was no match for the moment along the Vistula River ensconced by two rainbows in meditative protection. One aspect of dinner I do recall: there was no dessert. Few ate many pernickis and fruit, leaving the rest of us with no dessert.

By the end of dinner, Antoni's cell phone rang. He was given news to expect Edward to be better for tomorrow. It was strained muscles due to overexertion, not a real heart attack. Dad was relieved by this news, as he strongly empathizes with any heart attack victim as he suffered one himself few years ago. A release from the hospital would come this evening. With a good rest, Edward should be able to accompany us for the remainder of the trip. There would be two drivers for the rest of our tour. Most importantly, Edward was going to be all right.

When Marie and I retired to our room, I searched through my purse for the pillow chocolate I saved from Hotel Metropol. At the bottom I found it and ate it without haste. There would be dessert tonight after all.

The answer to every question is yes and no.

TORUŃ

DAYS AND DATES are running together like water droplets. Only four more days of adventure—no time to be gloomy about it, each moment must be savored.

At breakfast, we sat in the usual small group (Mom, Dad, Marie, and I) and recapped the experiences we had so far. Each took a turn relaying one's favorite site or event, while eating miniature croissant rolls filled with a sweetened cream cheese, divine. Dad's was the pier in Gdańsk; Mom's was the day in the country and at the preserve; Marie's was staying at the farm of lace curtains and down blankets. I had many favorites. And I expect to acquire many more favorites. For now, the entire day in Gorznó was a great favorite, with meeting Kasia the best of that day.

When Edward appeared for breakfast, everyone cheered. Harry and Joe Prorok got up to shake his hand and wish him well. Many others followed their actions and sentiment. He was an integral part of our group, like Antoni and Matthew our guides; we did not want to

161

consider the rest of the tour without him. Now an older man with gray hair joined our group as second, auxiliary bus driver. He spoke only to Edward and Antoni, unless specifically addressed by others in Polish.

Marie again decided to switch our seats, now occupying the second bench behind Edward, Peg and Don's bench. Severely disgruntled when vision of Marie in her seat appeared, Peg said nothing and proceeded to sit in the fourth bench, our seat. I warned Marie that we should conform to the unstated rules of the bus, sitting in designated seats.

"We are all adults." She responded bushing off my warning.

Marie, and residually me, were the only people perpetually changing benches. Grumbles began the moment Marie chose the new seat.

POZNAŃ—HOTEL 500

The sun shone approvingly for the first morning all week. Passing once more the ruins of the Teutonic Knights' castle, the bus made its way out of town, through country once more, until it reached Biskupin. The hilly forest gave way to flatlands and lakes. Suddenly from placid countryside, we reached the archeological site of Biskupin swarming with busloads of school children.

Biskupin was a Slavic settlement dating from 700 BC. While plowing, a farmer tilled remains of the settlement in the early twentieth century. Notifying archeologists, the land was taken over for excavation and study. This settlement is the oldest in Poland and proves that the Slavic people were the first known to live here. During the war Hitler began to study it, but when his researchers could not link it to Germanic origins he reburied it. After the war, archeologist resumed study and reconstructed the settlement as an outdoor museum. Kiosks exhibiting various skills and crafts lined the walkway to the settlement. Thousands of children were there for an Egyptian festival.

Chariots sped through lanes, horses galloping enough to cause children to dash to the side for fear of being trampled. College students in period costume of gold la meigh and linen strutted though masses of delighted children, handing out informational booklets on Egyptian history and lifestyle. Screams and applause from other demonstrations in remote areas filled the park.

From a teacher's perspective, this was an amazing field trip to witness. Classes of children ranged in age from six or seven year-olds to fifteen or sixteen year-olds. The smaller children were guided by their teacher, and one sometimes two, accompanying adults. Thirty children to two or three adults, and the children were listening and obeying. Older students were allowed to roam in small groups of friends with no adult supervisor. And these groups were behaving, although a little rambunctious yet not at all malicious or disrespectful. This day could not happen this way in America.

Our group marched single file through the crowds. Many would say hello to the school groups as we passed. Some children would call back, "halo, hal-o!" Jozef Mazurkiewicz, Frank and Matthew would yell in warning, "Step!" if there were a step or decline in path. Some children would mimic, "step!" at the odd sounding American English. Through the corridor between the long houses we marched, thatched straw roof scraping head of the taller, to a room exhibiting wall-sized photographs of various stages of excavation, which led to the discovery and extrapolation of aspects of Slavic lifestyle. Then we climbed the escarpment to view a large, period boat docking on the lake on one side, and long houses on the other. The group decided not to have free time to meander due to the overcrowding. Retracing our path, we marched back to the entrance.

I felt like I was in a fishbowl. Staring children were critical and giddy. I stared back. Some pointed and whispered to friends. Others boldly said a word in English. "Glasses," I caught. My wire rims were nothing spectacular; I'll put on my sunglasses that look like the fender of a 1950 mustang—chrome vines and flowers on the sides. That will be something different to see.

"Sad." No, no, no. Not smiling doesn't necessarily mean that one is sad.

Smile a little. Saying hello to groups here and there, I passed the time until the group stopped at a pavilion by the entrance. Edward was eating his lunch, just sitting down. We told him not to hurry. Whoever wanted to go to the bus did, and the others ordered food from one of the concessions and sat to eat. Edward did gulp his bigosh to get back to the bus.

After buying an ice cream cone, I sat alone at a picnic table adjacent to a table of two girls about twelve years old. I said hello and they returned the greeting. I asked how they were. No response. I asked if they knew English. A head shake no. I smiled. They were talking and giggling, until Jozef Mazurkiewicz sat at the table in front of them and began to speak with them in Polish. Jozef gestured to me. I asked if they wanted to talk with me. He shook his head no. Soon others from our group sat filling the tables around us. The girls left and the table filled with six boys, about ten years old, who played cards and shared wedges of apple one boy had in a brown paper bag. Two boys had on tee shirts of American bands. Observing from a distance, it was fun to see them play.

Behind the pavilion ran narrow-gage train tracks for a commuter train. I was unsure whether this train ran solely around the park or through the countryside to neighboring towns as well. In any case, the train was jammed with groups of children as it passed. A few children waved energetically; we returned the wave, which brought smiles and laughter. One eight-year-old boy actually started to jump from excitement; he was adorable with sandy blonde hair and big brown eyes. I reflected his grin for which he waved again. I waved again. We reciprocated until train tracks drew him out of sight, laughing.

Our backs to the train tracks, we exited the park and made way through the muddy parking area. Marie paused to look in a souvenir kiosk, eyeing the wooden and plastic axes and bows. I told her that neither of them would make it past airport security; besides, why encourage aggression right now. She passed them by, agreeing with my point.

The bus parked next to ours seemed as empty as all the others, until it was pointed out that an unusual driver was manning the wheel—a ten-year-old boy, not very happy. I smiled at him and said hello. He did not return the greeting. He was being punished, or just in a bad mood.

"You give out driver's licenses at a very young age in Poland," was the joke that got a smile or two.

Gradually Edward maneuvered out of the parking lot, narrow lanes between tour buses. A stalled bus made the exit lane even worse. Skillfully he drove us out of the populous outdoor museum back into the peaceful countryside to our next destination, Gniezno.

The skyline of this small town had one domineering focal point: the Cathedral of Gniezno also called St. Adalbert's Cathedral. The baroque towers cast no shadow in the noontime sun. On first entry, some people shopped in the cathedral gift shop. We met our local guide, Marta, who was charming and sincere from the first moment of introduction. Her tall, thin stature complimented her soft-spoken character. Her genuine appreciation for her church and her home shone at every monument she highlighted. First, the room of scholars was closed. We viewed the doors and threshold, ornate in black wood and rich carving. This room housed a medieval tome, so large that two people alone could not carry it. The pages gilt-edged, the binding hand-sown leather held together this medieval bible. Marta's description of it rallied my imagination. Gold lettering and columns of illustrations showcase the importance of the pages' content, marvelous.

Next we stood at the beginning of the main aisle, watching the procession of vaulted ceiling and columns to the altar of golden canopy guarding the silver plated tomb of St. Adalbert. Quickly refocusing our attention to the opposite wall where our backs were hiding, we observed a red marble statue of the archbishop, standing one foot out in readiness. I did not catch whether it was a monument or a tomb. Nonetheless it was striking in its ruddy earnestness.

In circular format we progressed around the cathedral in a clock-wise motion. Each side altar contained a tomb of a saint or nobleman, or a monument to a historical religious figure. Pure sunlight glazed the stained glass windows in magnificent clarity of color and shape: a pattern of crosses and circles outline the side windows, alternating in blues, yellows, and reds. The edge work appears simple enough; yet when each window panel is examined individually one can notice that in the central focal point is the joint, the seem, where circle meets slanted tips of x. This creates interesting shapes in between the established pattern: triangles with curving bottoms or sides, interior semicircles suspended from their matching half until the next window.

Many of these windows portrayed nature scenes with flowing rivulets and waterfalls. They were stunning. Looking across the cathedral, a set of three windows portrayed one scene: a glorious tree, each leaf and branch defined, swaying by silvery river with fields and hills in the distance. The heavens were always blue. Movement was apparent. These windows were not static but with each wave of sunlight twisted and played as if alive, as if imparting childlike wisdom of this state of being. I could have sat and studied them for many hours, writing of their forms, noting techniques and inspirations, photographing them through varying light of day. However, the tour continued and I took as many pictures as possible within our limited time. I stared for an extended moment. Possibly there exist books on Polish and/or medieval stained glass windows and restoration, more to research.

Almost completely around the perimeter we had toured, when there was a side altar under restoration. Sheets of plastic were diagonally protecting the far left-hand corner of the altar where a shadow of a person worked diligently under floodlight. Restoration requires creativity and artful decisiveness. Myriad possibilities for successful representation of the originals manifest itself in every stroke, each buff and molding. Antoni crept up close and peaked around the shield, bolder than I. Without hesitation I inquisitively approached him, what could he have seen? The answer came, not much but he is curious. Curious. Curious, the best word to describe this spirit, this thirsting for experience of the new old, the creative history, the sewing of bonds. There is something to learn in every corner. I smiled a big, radiant smile, Antoni returning the smile. For we were all curious, every one on the tour, for a personal reason, curious.

Through the opposite entrance from where we began, we exited to tour the exterior. One of the church bells was made into a monument, as it was damaged in the war and later replaced. Marta unlocked the wooden door to St. Adalbert's shrine with a skeleton key. Inside were the medieval bronze doors depicting the life of St. Adalbert. From bottom left, up and over, and down right, Marta read the scenes to us with feeling, explaining all the symbols. My favorite panel was the central one illustrating the townspeople of Gneiznie trying to buy the body of their beloved patron saint. Some group (Prussian, Russian, German, I do not know) stole the body and asked a pound of gold for every pound of flesh in return. As the panel story goes, the poor townspeople gathered as many gold coins as possible, still not enough. An old lady, giving her only coin, placed her coin on the scale, mystically tipping it to equal the sum needed. St. Adalbert would be recovered and the church would have its foundation. Between the arched doorframe and the rectangular doors, there is a curved space above the door revealing the interior far wall. Colors of the windows projected onto the gray wall: slanted bars and dots of color, an abstract festival hosted by the realistic originals. In this moment of close space witnessing doors of history peaking into fields of marble sunshine, I felt tranquil.

As our group stepped away from the doors into the courtyard, a Gypsy family accosted us with open hands. They persisted after they were told in Polish and English that we had nothing for them. Marta was bothered by the presence of the Gypsies, disturbing the tour. We should ignore them; we were told. They steal and mislead, those Gypsy beggars. Yet I could not discipline myself to not sympathize with them. In one swift current of political action—another terrorist attack, a war of retaliation closing borders and travel indefinitely—I could be her. At the end of pocket money and a line of credit, good for two weeks if thrifty, I could be reduced to street begging to support two aged parents and myself. Could I be her? Give me a moment to tell my story of woe. Call me Gracja and give me a coin. Dad worried about this more than my joking acknowledges. The Gypsy family still follows closely, weaving in and out of the group to create chaos. Marta led us directly into the cathedral to safety. Even Gypsies respect boundaries of some sort.

After the tour, many went into the church gift shop. Rushing, Marie and I bought small medals for friends. To rejoin the group, we walked to the courtyard once more, Gypsies long gone. Mom, Dad, and many from the group were sitting at the base of the statue of Boleslaw Chrobry. A few people went to find a telephone directory or a post office to get information on a relative living in town. There was no need to rush after all.

So, we returned to the gift shop to look more thoroughly and to buy Mom a hand-carved cherry wood crucifix. Marta was just leaving as we were. We thanked her and complimented her presentation and sincerity. Modestly, she remarked that she had just begun to guide tours and hoped that she was improving. I told her to stay the same, as she is perfectly charming. With another round of thanks we parted.

A class of children was in the courtyard when we returned. Norm was giving Twizzlers to them, running out of supply before everyone had a treat. The teachers wanted the children to practice English, yet most were exercising those in the group who knew Polish. I managed to talk with a few saying little beyond "hello, how are you?" But the people speaking Polish carried lengthy conversations with children and teachers. Some teachers began to ask about American life, which launched a barrage of questions from the children. With patriotic fervor Norm and Jozef Maszurkevic answered the inquiries. When the licorice strips were eaten, the teachers assembled the class and began to walk to the hillside park attached to the courtyard.

Still waiting for the few wanderers, I entertained myself by taking pictures. Dad was thrilled to be sitting at the foot of Bolesław Chrobry. Dad's favorite uncle was named after this Polish hero. Would Bolesław Chrobry have been honored by our Uncle Brownie as his progeny? Dad, with pride in his heart and smile on lips, remembers the day when Uncle Brownie was arrested for the fortieth time on his fortieth birthday. Uncle Brownie was very proud of that fact and told it to everyone often. It took hard work for such an accomplishment. Brownie was the town drunk who was only slightly disorderly when deeply intoxicated. Luckily, his brother-in-law was the chief of police and allowed him to sleep it off in a cozy cell until morning. Dad always said that his family were sinners, while Mom's family were saints. Dad loved being related to idiosyncratic characters within moral limits.

I took pictures of Mom and Dad happily resting there with Brownie gallantly surveying the distance, Uncle Brownie not far from mind and heart. Then more of our lounging group came into focus. Soon willing subjects banded together for photographs. We frittered and whiled satisfied. The group once again restored walked two blocks south to meet the bus.

Before we entered the bus, Matthew pointed out graffiti on the half-wall separating park from street. I do not remember the exact translation but it was a sociopolitical, isolationist statement: if communism and capitalism died, Poland would finally be a better place. The statement jarring, I did not know how to react. However, everyone is entitled to expression of thought. The person with the spray paint felt strongly enough, frustrated enough to write it. Is that person contributing to change Poland? What is the complete political philosophy suggested as an alternative form of government? Is the medium of graffiti empowering? These questions rattled the brain as we cruised southwest to Poznań.

Immediately we began the next tour, reaching our destination in late afternoon. A small church surrounded by wire fence stood unused. Excavation was taking place to locate, identify, and rebury nobility from that site into the cathedral crypt. Across the square the Cathedral of Saints Peter and Paul jutted, with Baroque towers very similar to St. Adalbert's in Gniezno. Through the square we processed on this cold afternoon. A blackbird with white tail and stripe on wings lit on the cobblestone beside the right-hand tower. Its robust body resembled a small pheasant, yet its distinctive beak, short and curved, was orange-yellow. Later it was explained to be a magpie. It perched watching us with no particular care, standing in an air of admiration of a moment.

Inside the dark cathedral, light was too weak to display the trea-sures hidden within. Stained glass windows were reclusive. The tour leads down a flight of stairs to catacombs where ruins of an ancient church were being preserved. A baptismal fountain, now a dip and tremor of stone, was the first in Poland. Here we stand above it, plat-form all around. The stones remaining have been covered in a gauze and clay blanket for preservation; the atmosphere controlled by gages on the central stone mound. The seat of Catholicism, of Christianity, is intact with care for longevity. We stared for a long moment in silence, heads bowed from an even vantage point.

The platform channeled into another room, the anteroom to the crypt. Here relics from the small church were exhibited to explain the history of the nobility housed. The crypt was barred. Peering in be-tween wrought iron, one could see the modest altar with rows of ornate caskets on either side. The tour ended and we retraced our steps, once more observing the ruins. In the stair well there was an interesting crawl space where a room ended and another stairwell began. Next to this slanted space of jagged ceiling was a display case built into the wall. The top of a Corinthian column was a neighbor with a larger statue of a white owl. Is this the same white owl now endangered, but then a sight as ordinary as a magpie? Was this statue once protector of buttrice or turret? The sandstone owl drew attention as well as exuded regal supervision, a talisman of safety and wisdom. Mom said a prayer in dark illumination before we left the cathedral.

Across the street from the square was a gilt statue of Pope John Paul II. His arms extend, palms open and up, to bless the assembly. I knew Dad was game. We ran to the statue for a quick picture: I stepped around the backside careful not to disrupt the lit votive candles in the front, and posed with papal mimic. What did I have to lose? I am al-ready doomed by thinking ordinary thoughts during the organ concert in Gdańsk. At least I did not crawl into his arms to pretend he was carrying me. I did show some restraint with this in mind. With a smirk, Dad took the picture. We have the same sense of mortality, the same sense of humor. Like the instigator that I am, others soon came to take pictures with the Pope. But none were as irreverent to give blessings of their own to the non-existent masses.

A quick stop at a wc lead to milling around, waiting for people to gather. Jozef Mazurkiewicz was wearing his nametag. He began to talk with a local man of the same age and another accompanying the local man. They were all in the war and spoke of some experiences. The local man was a member of the Polish army and his counterpart was from the Austrian military. Jozef Mazurkiewicz called for the Prorok Brothers to join the conversation. Joe Prorok was able to finally speak with a peer about his station in Poland during and immediately after the war. These five gentlemen were captivated with each other's stories and amazed with their serendipitous meeting. Before they left the local man told Jozef Mazurkiewicz that his last name was part of a slang expression from a popular Polish movie. When one is exasperated, or in disbelief, one would say, "ola boga, Mazurkiewicz!"

"Oh my god, Mazurkiewicz!" He loved this expression and for the remainder of the trip we used it frequently.

Immediately on board, Jozef Mazurkiewicz seized the microphone and conveyed the joke, not the war stories. Still with roaring laughter, Jozef Mazurkiewicz instructed all of us to use the expression as frequently as possible. It would be his signature expression, for any situation, from now on.

We called out numbers, sixteen, and headed for Old Town where our local guide was waiting. It was late in the day, about five o'clock; the schedule was delayed since Gniezno. Everyone was tired. Many were in need of rest. About half the group decided to stay on the bus instead of participating in the tour of Old Town, Mom and Dad were among them. Marie and I exited the bus for the final tour of the day, tired yet not willing to miss anything.

The jovial local guide truncated the tour based on time and the size of the group. He explained some of the facades as we walked towards Town Hall. Above this white building in either corner stood a statue of justice and a statue of war (with sword pointed down in peace). In the center below the statues was a clock, not highly embellished. When the clock strikes noon each day, goats break through the wooden gate and cause a delightful scene. We were much too late (or too early) to observe it, but we stared at the closed doors anyway. A redheaded college girl sitting on the edge of the adjacent fountain was staring at our group, maybe at me. Her slight features were draped in black leather, army green pants, and combat boots, striking a familiar contrast to shocking red hair. She was beautiful. The guide thought, perhaps, it would chime at six, only a short time away. We decided to have a half-hour of free time and then meet at the clock, to see if it would chime.

The grim reaper inhabited the central space between Town Hall and the fountain in the square. On his box he stood motionless while we examined his potential movement. He would not perform without a coin, thankfully. No one ventured to deposit one in his box. It was unnecessary. As Marie and I walked by closing shops, the girl started yelling across the square, "you, you, you!" By the last "you" she was screeching.

I looked at Marie and she at me, repeating in whisper almost in song, "you, you, you." She could not have been yelling for me. Who would yell across Town Square for me?

Not me…maybe me?

We kept on walking. Marie never questioned, just attempted to shop while storefronts and kiosks were being closed around us. By the time we walked to the end of the lane, all shops were locked, tarps concealing wares.

I am "you," and I felt terrible for it, ashamed. I should have stopped to talk with her.

Do I blame it on being tired? Do I blame it on the miscommunication all day long with others? A simple hello was all that was necessary. In this instance of stupidity I have possibly become in the mind of that student what I absolutely hate, an ignorant American tourist. This moment is my only regret of the entire journey. This moment is the only one I would love to live over again to change for the better. There is a valuable lesson learned: interaction with others cannot solely be based on oneself projected into the world but being able to accept the terms that the world gives, and mutually create a positive experience. Yet this experience will plague my mind for the rest of the evening.

Only restaurants were open now. We walked by an ice cream parlor where a young boy was getting a cone from the storefront window. Antoni passed by and told me to talk with the local people, to talk with the young boy. I said hello but the ice cream was more interesting. No response, just a smile at the cone as he walked away with his mother, who I quietly greeted as well, she reciprocated a smile. My bungle was noticed by many in the square apparently. Marie and I chose to sit under a canopy for a drink, which I could surely use. Matthew was walking by with a group of people including the local guide. We hailed them to join us. While everyone ordered local beer (Hevelius or something similar), I drank a glass of white wine and felt better for it. Cheeks burned instantly.

For the remaining time, we listened as the local guide told stories of being a tour guide for twenty years, how the industry has changed, how the tour groups are different. We told him of the day's events, of the schedule of the complete tour. Time passed quickly; we went to meet the others. Passing one more time through the square, passing the grim reaper, I made a point to turn towards the fountain, a last chance. She sat in the same position. This moment she turned to face the opposite direction, addressing the boy she was with for the first noticeable time. Gesture taken and rightly so. The bells did not chime at six; the goats did not perform.

Turning toward our group, we retraced the path to the bus three city blocks. Antoni continued alone at the head of the group spread out by varying stamina. Slyly quickening my pace, I met his stride in friendly conversation. I mentioned that I admired the renovation and rebuilding of Poland. We discussed the differences between Polish and American stereotypical lifestyles. Poles value living at home, in the same town in which one is born, while Americans move constantly, Antoni explained. He asked if I valued a certain room in my apartment, since it was assumed that I relocate several times a year, as he presumed all Americans did. I would not confide in him as I did in Kasia. His preconceived notions were more rigid and pinned than the fjords of Norway. Kasia and I related as versatile gulls moving from shore to shore for new perspective and sustenance, crags as comfortable a home as lawns of beach. Would Antoni respond as Kasia did, if we sat for a while to converse on home and travel, culture and lifestyle?

I responded that I value my kitchen, as I use it as a stained glass studio. If one could consider a countertop, sink, and small square table a studio, so it was. The stained glass of Poland was incredible, both in reproduction and original work, I observed. The juxtaposition of color and form in the window, particularly the nature scenes, were astonishing. He grinned at the compliment as if I had extolled his personal achievements. Antoni mentioned that there is a world-renowned stained glass studio in Kraków that does most of the reproduction work in Poland. He did not divulge the name of the studio or the prominent artists within the studio. No matter, after that comment I was fixated on one day visiting Kraków, one day soon. We met the bus with exhausted enthusiasm.

Hotel 500 resides in the outskirts of Poznań, our first suburban experience. The posh hotel seemed in the middle of nowhere, yet located on the major highway connecting Berlin and Warsaw. An atrium guided us into the reception desk, then to the grand staircase of brass and black marble. This was a new hotel built with modern amenities to attract North American tourists. After Marie and I checked into our room, we immediately headed for the bar. Another glass of wine warmed me up before dinner. I could not drink anymore or else I would be under the dining room table sleeping instead of eating. Marie enjoyed the red wine so much that she bought two bottles to bring home for a special occasion. It was a German wine. I told her she could most likely buy it at home.

"But that would defeat the point of the memory brought to the occasion," she elucidated. Conciliatory, I ushered her into the dining room with opened door and sway of free hand.

Dinner included a buffet of Polish specialties. A line had formed around the buffet tables before we entered the dining hall. A table of soups and salads was perpendicular to a table of fish and meats. The last connecting table held desserts and beverages. To start, a bowl of vegetable soup was taken to table by all four of us: Mom, Dad, Marie and I. We spoke of the long day and impressions thereof. Biskupin exhausted Mom and Marie. Young adults, not weathered senior citizens, best tended throngs of children they thought. Changing the tone of the conversation, Dad pronounced his thrill in seeing the monument and resting place of his favorite uncle's namesake. Seeing the statue of Boleslaw Chrobry was poignant, as if Uncle Brownie was somehow represented. Do famous figures gather the souls baring their names, like patron saints, Dad mused.

Soup over, we retraced steps to survey the other tables. Surprisingly most of the main dishes were gone. Hungry people piled plates high on first pass, leaving fragments for the rest of us. Someone asked if they might bring out more food from the kitchen. The waiter explained that the kitchen was closed for the evening. In Poland, the large meal is eaten at lunch, and dinner is a small snack. Not realizing the amount hungry Americans eat for dinner, the cooking staff prepared just enough food for a small Polish dinner. Dad found the last piece of baked fish and a stray gołabki. I enjoyed buttered golden potatoes with parsley and tossed salad, which were plentiful. Mom and Marie found enough to satiate appetites.

One last trip to the buffet produced coffee and a sweet roll, kulich. The spice of the sweet roll mingled on the palate with the sugar of the raisins and icing in balanced proportion. Once again my mind wandered and praised in the simple delights of Polish dessert. The darkness of the coffee, bordering on espresso, pulled all flavors together with vigor. Marie would go back to fight for another sweet roll. Just in time for dessert, Antoni joined us. He was seated with Kathy Jo and Doris for dinner. They discovered that the hotel had an Internet service and wanted to send messages home as well as surf the web for news. Not one to want to eat alone, he requested to sit with us. With an easy step he would cache from his adjacent table to ours.

Finally I was able to show someone the encyclopedia page on Wincenty. Although I knew the contents of the page, Antoni read it in modern Polish and sat for a moment thoughtfully, before speaking of his interpretation in English. Antoni explained that Wincenty wrote about a fellow doctor, Orlowski, who has a psychiatric hospital named after him in Warsaw. Orlowski was a pioneer in his own right, in psychology. There was a list of figures of which Wincenty wrote biographies. None of the names were familiar yet. Wincenty also painted a famous writer, Jan Kochanowski, and his beloved daughter, Urszułka. This fact stunned Antoni because Kochanowski prized Urszułka so much so that he would not allow her to be painted or drawn. For someone to win that honor means instant accomplishment and unusual talent, and possibly a friendship, he stated.

Antoni was interested by our heritage and Wincenty's repertoire, empathizing with an artistic family. He was the son of a soprano, and was raised traveling around Poland and Europe for her concerts with various orchestras. Love of music was a prerequisite for any future career. He plays piano, composes and teaches, guiding tours in the summer and early fall for extra income. His brother is a musician with the Warsaw Philharmonic along with his wife. All arts commingle. Dad began to tell Antoni of my brother, The Toy Inventor, my sister in Washington, D. C., The Artist, and not to forget about my brother, The Architect. There were six of us to brag about, going down the list, and then me, the seventh, the youngest, the floundering. Getting the conversation back on a genealogical track, I asked Antoni about procedures and protocol of a Polish library, in specific The National Library.

Antoni's explanation of library research in Poland illuminated and prepared thoughts for further gathering of information. Very similar to the methods of researching in archives or in prominent institutions, in Poland one must request to view certain material and wait in a reading room for that material to be delivered by a librarian or aid. It is preferable to call in advance to make an appointment for research. No roaming the stacks in the National Library of Poland. Materials must be kept in the reading room as well, most likely no copy machines for easy duplication. There would be no computers accessible to the public; no computerized card catalogue but a regular catalogue on index cards for author, title and subject searches. Notes must be written by hand and well enough to be understood at a later date to further research. There is no clock in the library, it may take hours for a librarian to retrieve desired materials. Time and abounding interest are necessary. All this information I gratefully absorbed for future use.

What interesting characters are in my family to influence my nature, Antoni wondered. He spoke of a bureau the Polish government has where any citizen could pay forty zlata, ten dollars, and receive a catalogue of every person related to oneself in recorded Polish history. That is why a group of tourists researching their genealogy is freakish here; there is no need to research, if you want to know, you pay and it is done for you.

"However very few people take advantage of this service," Antoni pointed out, "most Poles do not care for the past but look to the future, a future of strong economy and jobs for everyone."

I found that last statement difficult to believe. If they did not care for the past then why would they refurbish it? The Royal Palace would still be an exposed foundation if that statement were true. Marie was falling asleep in her coffee. I excused myself before Antoni's brash statements could upset me, using Marie as an easy alibi. The coffee offset the wine so I was able to carry myself to my room without assistance.

In private I broached a delicate topic for Marie, now slightly revived. Many people were upset with bench changing each day. Aggravation culminated today with Peg and Don being deposed. I begged her to retain the same bench from now on, not because of view but because it is best to keep peace and order among a group that requires peace and order. After several rounds of debates and brewing comments on stagnation, she agreed to keep the fourth bench for the duration of the trip, not for her satisfaction but to comply with the covert rules of our group. Thanking her, complimenting her as peacemaker, I was glad for unnecessary tremors within our group to flatten to stable ground. The troubles we could solve, we should. There was more to worry about beyond control than there was in clashing characters. Marie acquiesced, on all accounts flexible.

The soft bed cradled me instantly, sensing the need for renewal. Yet Marie beat me, as she always does, while I scribble she sleeps. Fading, fading fast, I am. The night draws in anticipation through windows held open for change.

ember 20, 2

SEPTEMBER 20, 2001

"For example..."
—ANTONI, ILLUSTRATING POINTS, WOULD ALWAYS SAY.

POZNAŃ—HOTEL 500

THE DAY BEGAN later than usual: the alarm clock never rang, the resulting scurry led us to be one of the last to have luggage ready by the door and to eat breakfast. All of the hurry was of no consequence because departure was delayed; some did not return keys to the front desk promptly. Kathy Jo and I made a quick run to the gas station on the corner while arrangements were being straightened. Keys located and replaced.

Fencing, orange brick towers at corners encircled the acre of parking lot. This forced us to shuffle through the diameter of the parking lot, through the only security gate, then, finally, to the street, fields, and woods. There were no mushroom harvesters along the road this morning; however, it was early.

She told me all about Doris tipping the man carrying her luggage. The round, middle-aged concierge then gave her a smile, a wink. Doris giggled and followed the luggage from room to the lobby. A handshake with another wink, a royal bow sealed the interaction with a romantic

181

air. Doris giggled. The suited concierge asked for her home address. Doris, flattered, thanked him for his assistance and would not give the address. Yet she was happy to have a story of flirtation to tell.

Laughter pushed open the glass doors of the gas station. The two attendants stood behind the counter glaring at us, not sure if we were laughing at them. Gathering our senses, we trampled frivolity and greeted the attendants with a polite hello. No response. We bought PL bumper stickers and issued a Polish thank you that provoked smiles from behind the counter. A backward smile pushed the glass doors in opposite direction.

Kathy Jo repeated the story again, the most pressing item on her mind in the moment. Laughter did not ensue a second time, circling back toward the bus, through turrets and gate. The black pavement stretched as storytelling turned to silence. The main topic resumed with a statement: there is little harm in exchanging address from across the world; the worst that could befall is a letter. Kathy Jo lapsed into assertions of principle, guise, and distrust.

"You are too trusting, too romantic," the accusation aroused.

I pondered. Silence buzzed as insects in hive. We approached the bus full with occupants ready for the next event. A grin bloomed across my face, freshly pollinated. She noticed yet would not discuss. We climbed aboard noiselessly and parted ways towards personal seats: hers with Doris in front, mine with Marie midway.

WROCŁAW—ART HOTEL

What was to come next I could not have imagined wildly. A new journey was born. The group met its next appointment at Kórnik Castle, a neo-Gothic residence of the eighteenth century built on medieval ruins. At the gates our group waited for entrance and local guide. While we were milling around the tree dappled and cobblestone courtyard, I decided to approach Matthew for his advice on researching Wincenty when we return to Warsaw.

Matthew was zealous. This search was extraordinary. Anything that stole attention from usual tours excited his interests. For he had conducted tours many times before and always reveled in the new aspects of old. He knew that there was a library in Kórnik Castle, which I did not know. With no prodding, he quickly and beautifully took reign. He asked the front security guard about the library; it was open and we were invited to use it. Speaking to every guard and docent, every student and librarian along the way in Polish, Matthew made friends at each turn as well as commanded the scene. His diplomatic nature of retired ambassador (during the Regan years) crowned itself. We climbed the grand staircase to the parquet third floor.

At the entrance of the library, Matthew whispered to me that we would begin in English, as that would draw attention. And it certainly did. A helpful, older lady with a gentility that pervaded her demeanor approached us; then left to get another who spoke better English as she explained. She returned with Jacek, a lanky young librarian who took one look at us and refused to speak English, unsure that he could speak English well. His professionalism and intelligence shown in every movement, each glided wave of hand, each poised gesture of refined information. The lady was surprised and told him that he spoke English very well. Nonetheless, he would be glad to help us while speaking Polish. Matthew understood and lapsed into a Polish explanation of our search. I gave Jacek the encyclopedia page on Wincenty. He understood. His soulful eyes bridged the gap across centuries.

Feeling the urge to explore, Matthew led Jacek and me through doors to an office room then into the adjoining room of rare manuscripts and an interior private office. Only with Matthew could I have browsed the stacks of a Polish library. His presence firmly requests the authority of privilege. Matthew explained to the astonish curator and his three appalled secretaries that he only wished to scan the holdings within the office and note the organization. The curator stood defending his office with polite but firm gestures. With an official bow and Polish salutation, Matthew diplomatically retreated after inspecting the premises to his full expectation.

Like a tethered child, I followed wide-eyed in sheer amazement. Jacek led me to the card catalogue where he opened the drawers with the tenderness of an affectionate grandfather, edges polished with respect. One entry, one index card, was found on Wincenty Smokowski. In a half-hour to forty minutes he would have the book in the reading room for us. I thanked him in Polish. Matthew spoke with him in Polish before allowing him to slip through the hallway to rooms of the strictest privacy, rooms I could only dream the contents and configuration.

We returned to the tour but I could not concentrate. I hunted for my parents in the crowd and told Mom what was happening. Dad was in front of the tour guide with metered attention for the slightly hard of hearing. Not willing to disrupt to attract Dad's attention I told only Mom, who would convey these happenings at the first convenient moment with Dad. Within an hour I would be holding a book, an original edition from 1843, that Wincenty illustrated. Stunned excitement thrilled every nerve. I could not control myself, my enthusiasm, my spirited mind wandering though thoughts it could not fully comprehend. Many years of wondering, daydreaming, were coming to fruition. Wincenty was here, not a figment across an ocean, but here, living in these historic ramparts. And I was here too, modern energy longing to hold the past. Matthew understood. After only twenty minutes, he grabbed my arm and once more we climbed the stairs, greeted the older, jovial lady at the top of the stairs and entered the reading room.

The book was not retrieved yet. Jacek was in the reading room minding the librarian's desk. Matthew and I browsed contemporary Polish encyclopedias and found an entry on Wincenty. It had a picture of one of his woodcuts representing his work, at least his work in wood. This contemporary information also listed where various works were stored. Boldly I asked Matthew to ask Jacek for a copy of this entry. Jacek agreed good-naturedly and left the room with the encyclopedia, his finger as bookmark noting the page. We sat for a few minutes at a long cherry wood table, exhilarated to find information as well as an illustrated manuscript.

The long glossy table recalled photographs of kin: Nana running a press as she coyly bats eye lashes over shoulder at the dashing, muscular figure of Teddy, who is standing at a cherry wood table with a huge roll of paper. Thaddeus (affectionately Teddy), my father's father, was a printer. John, Teddy's father, established *The Hercules Press* when he emigrated from Poland, which printed brochures, letterhead, invitations, an assortment of fine stationery. They would print anything as long as it was done well. It was a family business: Teddy, his older brother Edmund, and his younger sister Helen ran the machinery. John died of toxicity in 1930, chemicals and dyes from the press accumulated in his body. Printing, in those days, was not a job or even a career, but a life and a death. Edmund inherited the press in the wake of John. Nana, a young Polish woman with striking blue-gray eyes and self-assured disposition, worked as a typesetter at *Hercules Press*. Teddy was instantly impressed by her beauty and stubbornness. Everything Nana touched must be perfect; she demanded it of her craft, of herself. After Teddy and Nana married, Nana still worked at *Hercules Press* but now as part of the family until Teddy succumbed to advanced stages of tuberculosis in 1936. Dad was two years old.

Dad was raised in the murmur of the press, sitting at a long table and entertaining himself by flipping page after page of a dictionary. This was no ordinary dictionary, but a mammoth encyclopedic dictionary ten inches thick, resembling a medieval bible. Dictionary bigger than child, Dad would have to climb on chair to hover over the book, wings spread, over the table. Fascinated, he studied the binding and gilt edge more than the print and content. As he grew, so did the use of the dictionary, tool for homework and acquiring the English language. This print shop daycare is embossed in Dad's memory as the happiest times of childhood.

It was The Depression. Nana was a strong woman. She began to work two jobs: a daytime job at *Sailing Niagara*, a large corporation printing everything from posters to price tags, in the puzzle department, and her usual job at *Hercules Press* as well as any other odd jobs that were in need of completion. Now she brought home rejected prints with which Dad would play. Pictures of fuzzy, electric purple horses riding to an orange Camelot lined Dad's drawers. Prints of African animals on safari vertically streaked in blue and black covered school textbooks from potential damage. Mountains splotched yellow; blue and green were perfect scrap paper for homework. The haphazard rejects of puzzle art must have dislocated Dad's interests in art towards science. He would become a physicist. Yet the dictionary remained Dad's favorite.

In the 1950's Edmund sold *Hercules Press* to retire to comfortable estates. It was more than an amicable ending, as the family was warned about printing "liberal brochures," and so aided their contemplation of retirement. Nana still worked, but now sewing custom-made curtains. As a teenager, Dad walked through the press once before the keys were given to new owners. The dictionary was still there on its cherry table. An impulse to take the dictionary overcame him, but was suppressed at last moment. It would go to new owners with building, business and machinery. Every time I would complain of an unknown phrase in a reading assignment, or my brother would require the etymology of a word for Latin class, Dad would lament the loss of the dictionary on the cherry wood table. As children we thought that that volume held magical knowledge, elusive and precious. *Hercules Press* still exists today. I wonder if the dictionary does?

Settled at the cherry wood table, I daydreamt of Dad's dictionary: the most beautiful and comprehensive one in existence, leather bound and thumb indexed. Would Wincenty's book encompass the table as Dad's dictionary did? The time-space continuum lapsed to present day as Matthew tapped my shoulder.

Jacek had not returned yet. Matthew was in need of physical motion, roaming. We entertained ourselves by browsing new periodicals; Matthew interpreted headlines. Newsweek was just introduced the first week of September in Poland. It was everywhere. The tragedy of the attacks occurred after only one issue of it. The library held all three issues produced thus far in Poland: the initial issue, the issue of the attacks, and the special issue on all the events of September 11. We scanned them but did not dwell on them, yet continued to search through literary and historic journals. We were pulled into the past, into shelves of ancestral accomplishment, which would not be convoluted by thoughts of the present. Sifting through several literary journals, Czeslaw Milosz grinned through the stack. A close portrait of his face graced the cover of a journal, which contained an interview on his works and awards. The unrestrained eyebrows shielded the dark orbs of his enlightened gaze. His hair was a softer version on Einstein's unkempt look, combs unpopular with geniuses. I surveyed Matthew's person with Milosz in raised hand. They could have been related. Jokingly I told Matthew that he purposefully was trying to look like Milosz's wild brother. He rolled his eyes at me and replaced the journal on its proper shelf. Progressing to the next perpendicular wall, Matthew wanted to browse through the card catalogue on music. His interests were in classical music by Polish composers throughout history. Most particularly he searched for any selections on Leonard Bernstein. None were located at this library--not surprising since the focus of this library is history and science.

Jacek was still away. It was now over thirty minutes. I began to worry that the tour was over and we were delaying the group from the next scheduled tour. Matthew had not a care, for this was much more interesting to him. He, after all, is the leader, the coordinator, the grand master; every event on the scheduled tour waits for him. He had done all the tours before, knowing them sometimes better than the local guides. I was very grateful for his attention. Once more, we transposed our focus to the back of the reading room where the bound indexes and encyclopedias were stored.

Jacek entered the room with an armload of material: the encyclopedia and copy, dark and thin like a mimeograph, and Wincenty's book. After many thanks, we steadied ourselves at the table again, ready. The leather binding felt the weight of its age. I gingerly handled the book, turning pages with gentle caution. One page after another revealed a treasure: a woodcut of a medieval family by a tree followed one of jousting knights and coats of armor. These were incredible line drawings, intricate and delicate in composition yet powerful in depicting scenes of various aspects of medieval life and Teutonic Knighthood. This printing technique requires fastidious attention, as it must be carved in reverse image to be pressed into pages in correct form, an ancestor of lithography and the rubber stamp. I was in awe.

Although the woodcut technique was invented in Italy in the fourteenth century, its personal history resides in Poland. Beginning as folk art in Poland in the fifteenth and sixteenth centuries, woodcuts carved on wooden blocks were not durable for more than a few printings. Original woodcuts lost detail with each inky transposition. Wincenty invented a cylindrical woodcut, resembling a barrel with images carved into it. By rolling the cylinder over the stark paper the image is transposed as intended and the extended life of the barrel over flat boards allows for a greater number of prints to be made. This important invention was one step along the path of woodcuts becoming high art in Poland in the nineteenth century.

Immediately, Matthew wrote down salient details of each illustration and page number. I was holding history, a major contribution from my relative to Poland and Polish heritage. The scope of this accomplishment impressed me with a sense of pride and of emulation; to try to be as sincerely productive became a goal in this moment. How do I contribute to the community in which I live? How could I contribute to the world as I have been given so much from the world? The purpose of creativity, of art, means little without a feeling of contribution to beauty, to community, to Wisdom at some level.

My mind began to translate images into stained glass. These woodcuts could be interpreted in glass with little difficulty. With a reduction of lines to essentials only, these could be beautiful windows. What an incredible undertaking that would be! Who would be interested in such windows, however? Each member of my family will have one in their home. This could in no way emulate a global contribution, but it is a start: a new beginning in personal history. This is the inspiration of which I have been longing. Wincenty was there, in the room, guiding my hand, my heart, to finally find what he has known for centuries. Having streets named after you, being immortalized in bronze statue is not the fate that matters. Self-promotion is over inflated compared to adding a fiber to the shawl of the universe. Perhaps this is a Polish trait as well, a reason to rebuild, to contribute to the culture, for example. Contributing to a larger goal, a greater community, a culture while being whole in oneself is the point. Wincenty will be here forever, quietly and resoundingly marking the pages of history with bold new technique for his time. No other success could be more meaningful.

The pages turned and flipped on winged release. An illustration of an angel fluttered. We stopped, and Matthew noted the page and artwork with regularity. The angel in flight paused, feathered wings beating to hover while parchment-colored robes curl and wave. Immediately I knew her, Wincenty's wife the poetess. There was no information obtained on her or her work. Yet her influence as muse perched in gilded frame. Will she tell her story if I strain to hear the hushed voice? Eventually I will, with persistence. She glides into cream clouds of history, pages turn.

Still I hold the book and stare at woodcuts in awe with greedy vision hungry for more. This relic of the past I have permission to touch. This opportunity will not be given away hastily. Gilt tipped paper lingers in hand, illustrations untouched for sake of preservation. Staring hard and long, I do not know the next time I will see this book again. Binding, spine clutched a last time before approaching Jacek at the front desk. I handed the book to Jacek, which he placed on his desk with the usual care.

Matthew rigorously shook Jacek's hand in thanks and offered him ten złoty for his time and courtesy. Fervently Jacek denied the offer, strongly shaking his hands downwards, as if repelling an offensive physical object. Matthew told him that he would make a donation to the library with the money offered. Jacek agreed that was a suitable gesture. With soft handshake and simple "thank you" in Polish, I thanked Jacek for his efforts and kindness. He wrote the address and e-mail address of the library on a piece of paper and gave it to me. If I had any problems locating information or manuscripts in Warsaw or in the States, I may contact him at the library for further assistance. He was glad to help. A bright, earnest smile launched across my face and reached him in no time with more thanks and good wishes. He understood and reciprocated in quiet gentility reserved.

The tour was not over; but Matthew and I chose to tour the castle on our own, since we missed viewing the major galleries. Through the history museum connected to the library we roamed. Armor of many varieties stood in rows. Shields and other medieval weapons hung on the walls. The most impressive of these artifacts was the full-dress armor with wings attached. Huge white-gray feathers hung aloft from metal frame. How do wings help in battle or joust? It must have been presentation armor for royal occasions. We left the museum and descended a last time to the museum of the living quarters.

The drawing room flowed into the dining room, each filled with seventeenth to nineteenth-century furniture mainly produced in Gdansk. The ceiling of the dining room was vaulted. Every square housed a crest of a royal family, appropriately displayed in the dining hall where guests from these families or from other European lands would be welcome to dine. A short hallway led to a personal study with hunting theme. A bureau of historic guns designed the far wall while trophies of the hunt hang on other walls. We exited that room rather quickly.

Returning to the main entrance, we signed the guest registry and exited the castle to find our group on the drawbridge, just completing the tour themselves. I bounced up to Mom and Dad and explained the whole story in detail in single breath. The excitement could not have been controlled under any means. They were very pleased and proud.

Dad and I entered the small gift shop and purchased a book on Kórnik, and a few other souvenir pins and such.

The gardens of Kórnik Castle were part of a horticultural school. Pointed slats of a wrought iron gate blocked the path into the gardens. A separate entry fee was required for the garden walk with or without a guide. As with any other museums, there was a fee for photographing and a larger fee for video taping any of the grounds or museum interiors. Tall, old growth trees strained the view into the garden, not even a peak could be seen for free. We did not have the time to tour the gardens, sadly. The next town beckoned, we would be late.

Matthew requested us to call numbers, roll call. Sixteen, I said excitedly.

"Who is sixteen?" Edward beseeched Antoni.

"Sixteen is fascinating, with ideas and interests I cannot foresee." Antoni replied slyly so Matthew would not hear enough to notice the remark.

On the bus Matthew asked me to talk about our experience on the tour guide's microphone. I walked to the front of the bus and sat in the first seat, stumbling over words on how to begin. Briefly I spoke of family history and at length I spoke of the library and the history book in hand, the woodcuts and my first impressions of them. It was a great birthplace of new experience and new goals. And with new goals brought new friendship, an educated friendship with knowledgeable Jacek. With an ovation my story ended. This experience was a fine example of the merits of genealogical research, David noted energetically.

Brendon ruminated in aggravated silence over the fact that he had been researching for many years and had not made such a discovery in his family line. He would scheme to remedy this situation at all costs; his ego demanded so.

I teetered back to my seat where Charlotte, a spitfire girl in pin curls and a neatly casual suit, turned around and addressed me. Jean was in the bench with her, amused by my story and Charlotte's foreseen remarks.

"How does it feel to be royalty, Your Grace?" Charlotte asked with metered pomp and a glint in her eye.

My reply was simple: I know nothing of royalty, but I do know that there is no greater experience than interacting with a work of art that an ancestor contributed to history. The book itself was magnificent, its contents magical. Inspiration. It does not get any better than that. As for grace, I am, and always will be Grace. The upper tips of a grin, at this response, held Charlotte's large gray tinted glasses. Charlotte peered at Jean and they smiled at each other privately as if they knew secrets they were unwilling to tell, a conspiracy of elders.

Settling down for a long ride, I basked in the scenery passing. My mind was reeling. Wincenty's paintings are in the National Gallery, his sketchbooks and other writings and illustrations in the National Library in Warsaw. Tentative plans were scheduled in hazy vision: I could skip the last day of tours and take a cab to the library hoping some personnel speak English, or I could try to enlist someone to go with me, but I am interested in the places scheduled in the tour. What do I miss for the sake of the other? There is not enough time for every-thing. I need another week.

Dad would like me to research as much as possible. There is no way to predict or surmise the scope of information of which I would have access on one afternoon of research, giving no normal warning to these institutions that I would be attending. Yet Dad has lost confidence in his Polish speaking abilities; people speak too fast for him to under-stand completely what they are saying. The incident with the teenage waiter remained in the forefront of his memory, impeding any Polish communication. His hearing problems do not help this matter either. He would prefer to take the tours on our last day as well, but would like me to go to the library alone. Mom leaves the decision entirely in my hands with no pressure to do any one more than the other.

For entertainment Matthew begins another game of guess the translation by calling out obscure Polish words. Of course I know none. The people who are fluent find joy and humor in this game while I try to remember some of the words. By the end of the day I have forgotten most of them.

The countryside on this chilly, clear day relaxes the spirit to the point of slumber. Several people, including Dad, have a nap in the cozy green light in the fields of afternoon. I am comforted but not asleep. Marie is sleeping in the seat next to mine. I took out the book on Kórnik Castle, just purchased. At first review, the pictures are inviting and well framed the most treasured artifact at the focal point of each photograph. I started to read, but the movement on the bus jogged my concentration. It gave me a headache.

We stopped at a rest area for soup in the attached quaint restaurant...white borscht and a roll, excellent. Mom and I sat with Kathy Jo and Doris since Marie and Dad did not want a large lunch, staying outside. I asked about the castle tour, about what I missed. What did they learn? What did they see? The ladies had nothing to say other than it was pretty. Mom mentioned the Teutonic Knights' museum and the crests of heritage where many people may trace their family line. She mentioned a ghost story: a lady in white formal gown, cousin of the owner, who haunts the castle waiting for someone (her husband, her love). Intrigued, I thought of this elegant lady in white haunting a castle, her home. If one must haunt, home is the best place, especially if it is a castle. In a steady place, later in the hotel, I will read the book for more information.

The bus rolled on past field and forest. I imagined Wincenty walking this land with sketchbook in hand, studying the details, every mushroom a treasure, every tree an adventure, every tree feller a model. Could genetics explain so much: why do I run to the mountains of Newfoundland or consider it essential to hike the Grand Canyon? Is natural history exciting because it has interested others in our family line? The nature/nurture dichotomy will not be solved this afternoon. The rest of the ride into Wrocław ran quickly by, daydreaming of forests and ghosts.

Immediately upon arrival we met our local guide and began a tour of a small island, not a mile in diameter, called the Island of Cathedrals. Nine churches reside on this land. From the street we toured the oldest and smallest church at the tip of the island. It was not opened for tours of the interior, yet it greeted us as an introduction to what lies ahead in grander scale.

A Gothic cathedral stood at waters' edge, the front covered in scaffolding for maintenance of the entryway arches and towers. As we entered this cathedral, I do not recall its name, the assembly was bathed in red light: the dwindling afternoon sunshine spilt through the rose glass windows. Most of the windows were tonal studies in crimson; stylized roses and Mary in red finery were themes for most of these. The main body of the cathedral was gated, no admittance; three long narrow slits of stained glass windows led the altar to a heavenly spire. From afar these slits fractured into visually jagged patterns of burgundy and blue elongated figures, the whole indecipherable as an icon. The local guide paraded us into a side room, usually an altar. This room was being decorated as children's Christmas room. A gentle, elderly deaf man spent two months preparing the room for Advent. Trains sets streamed around islands of figurines and little trees. Mickey Mouse stood by dolls in traditional Polish dress with statues of the saints. On the opposite side of the room, a miniature pulpit housed a figure of the Pope who appeared every minute or so to wave and then recede. A village of trees and figures surrounded the pulpit as well. I have not seen more activity in the Macy's parade or in toy store displays. The room was only half decorated, as every inch will be covered by November. But the man was just beginning to create this Christmas festival, impressive to American adults and Polish children.

Reentering the red body of the cathedral, I fixed my attention one last time on the source of the atmospheric lighting: a blooming rose accented in black, tips pointing to multicolored background; stem and field abstract, fading into blocks of green and yellow. Its unusual beauty held my attention for as long as possible before our group once again assembled for the continuing tour outdoors.

Through the cobblestone streets and across a bridge of fanned brickwork and steel wings, we scampered. Many young people passed us and greeted us with smiles and quiet hellos. "Ha-lo" in Polish received an English "hell-o" as reply. The bridge led to a square called the Monument of Three Crosses. St. Joseph clutched a small, personal gold cross while from his stone pedestal he surveyed two crosses on the ground, one on each corner of the grassy square. He protected the Island of Cathedrals as well as welcomed its visitors, an ethereal host with crown of gilt stars. Into and out of another cathedral we went, too fast to observe any detail. Marie and Stella paused for the WC and to light a candle. For these two represented essentials of our group: to maintain basic needs with flexibility and to change what we could through hope and an exchange of good will with all we meet.

The group processed down the street without Marie and Stella; until the guides realized that some were missing. The fractured group stood waiting along the flying buttresses of the cathedral, across the street from a swinging arched colonnade that connected two more churches. Finally someone went to shepard the ladies back to the fold. As a whole, we paraded under the arch and through the path meandering by church and brick building, gardens and skeletal foundations of new building. There was interest in the garden path, but we had no time left. We were already terribly late for the second tour of Wrocław.

The bus was home to the weary travelers in our group once more, as we drove to Old Town to tour the square. Our hotel, ART Hotel, was on a street very close to the square. Checking into the hotel before the final tour, many chose to settle into their rooms instead of walking another tour, not me of course. Mom was visibly tired, as well as Dad. The smaller group congregated in the lobby and then proceeded up the block and over one to Old Town. The intoxicating aroma of fresh brewed coffee poured out of the doorway of a café. In the courtyard of a medieval church, spires gripping sky as wing tips and eagle talons, at the head of the street, there was a modern sculpture: a faceless curvilinear form, arm buds extended, ball of head bent in what could be interpreted as prayer. Striking contrast. This square was one of the largest in Poland, certainly the largest we toured. The gothic facades stretched for city blocks. In the center, a fountain melded cobblestone base with flowing waves of modern glass ice blue. Wrocław is a town fashioning old and new, living with the past to invite the future. Around the square the local guide pointed out buildings of significance: the Town Hall with clock tower, the medieval market center, and many other facts about many other buildings I did not absorb. Pigeons lined the angle of the doorframe to Town Hall, nesting for the evening.

The sun was setting, the stores closing. Marie and Jean broke away from the group to shop quickly. I was not in the mood to shop, but wanted to see what I could. I chose to stay with the group. We retraced our steps around the great square to the fountain. At the edge of Old Town there were two bookstores and a library interconnected. Too late, all closed; lights off. The smell of coffee again played in the air, leading back to the hotel.

Every corner and expanse of wall in the ART Hotel was exhibition space. I must explore. Abstract value studies in monochrome hung on the landing of each stairwell, encouraging one to climb the stairs rather than take the elevator. One landing held a study in blues, another swirls of crimson. At the entry to every floor, across from the elevator, was a rococo-style sofa or two gothic-style chairs.

In the foremost corner of the main floor was a massive bronze door. The lattice and rivets formed a pattern of diamonds with dotted centers. A modest doorknocker rested in the palm of sculpted leaves, completing the effect of a viny garden fence. The door was inoperable, an entrance to nowhere. A small plaque noted that in times past it was an entry to a room, yet I cannot remember what type of room for what purpose. My imagination concocted stories for this room being used in medieval times to hide Teutonic indulgences. Or possibly, it was a storage area to keep exquisite morsels for the feast. Better yet, it was a secret meeting room to plot for independence. A door to nowhere was a door to everywhere, a lovely garden door.

In the corner of the second floor was an entrance to an outdoor garden. The skylight of the room below was the floor of the garden walk. Some metal chairs invite lounging in corners, however the clear glass door was locked, forbidding entrance. Climbing the rest of the way to the top floor, my room was a spectacular loft with a view of the square. Leaning over window ledge, I watched the sun set and streetlights rise. Corrugated terra cotta roofs cascaded in view as far as one could see. Every moment was beautiful, peaceful. The hotel room with slanted walls offered respite until dinner.

The group assembled in the lobby to walk together to Spiz, an acclaimed restaurant in Old Town Square. The streets were in the process of changing from the commerce of the day into the shady excitement of nightlife. Young people waited on corners for friends to join them. By the fountain a small empty stage stood. Behind the stage two poles braced flags hung at half-mast: one the flag of Poland, the other of the United States. A crowd of people milled between the flagpoles, lighting candles and placing them at the base of the poles, now a makeshift shrine of condolence. We had missed the ceremony on stage, but were just in time for the end of the candlelight vigil.

Teenagers approached us, in Polish asking us to wear yellow satin ribbons to show solidarity with America. We told them that we were Americans from New York State traveling when the tragedy occurred. They were awestruck, dumbfounded to interact with Americans at that service, not knowing what to say. They told us of the ceremony we just missed and helped some ladies pin yellow ribbons on their jackets. A sense of urgency and community encircled us. Thanking them for their efforts, their ribbons of unity, we bustled into the restaurant.

The cold dark wind had already stolen the ribbons away from some of the ladies. I had not received a pin, just a ribbon, too busy talking and watching young and old place candles, sign crosses, hug friends, whisper sentiments. These were new bonds of solidarity encircled in yellow satin. We could not have found a more precious souvenir in store, church or square. These participates have made a contribution to solidarity, to global community. I felt proud and fortunate to have witnessed the end of this service. Yellow ribbon cradled in palm I would not release to the wind, however forceful. In the still warmth of the restaurant, I slid my ribbon into the pocket of my handbag and zipped it securely.

The meal was exquisite: cream of asparagus soup first course, potato dumplings and steamed julienne vegetables in a light, sweet vinaigrette main course, cappuccino and cheesecake with raisins lining the bottom dessert course. Dad and Marie enjoyed a local beer brewed at the restaurant. Mom and I sipped Riesling. None of us could grasp the reality of this day, this day of scheduled surprise, of hectic rest, of chaotic solidarity. Just as we were leaving, a band was assembling instruments and stage for a concert in the banquet room of the restaurant. We did not stay to hear what kind of music they would play.

In the square the crowds had passed, empty stage and flagpoles now background for a memorial of lingering candles. The wind would not relent. A lady bent in earnestness, relighting candles the wind had extinguished. Constantly she moved from one candle to another, monitoring, relighting. She would not allow the wind to prevail. Mom and Marie walked to her side. They stood blocking the wind so that for a brief moment most candles would remain lit. They embraced and began to pray together in a whisper, then silently. The lady stood with them, solidarity in a moment of silence. The red, yellow and blue vigil candles cast enlightened eyes on the ground, blinking in the defused wind. I did not partake directly but kept Dad occupied while taking a picture of them with my zoom lens. The moment could not pass without acknowledgment, for example. Even from this distance, I felt with them embracing the whole experience. Soft Polish and English words passed between Mom, Marie and the lady. Their eyes reflected candle lit hopes. Mom and Marie left the shrine to join us; the lady, still diligent, resumed candle relighting.

Hustling through the narrow street, the ART Hotel beseeched us forward. It was getting late; no one was interested in a nightcap. Still enthralled with the solemnity of the candlelit moment, Marie and I chose to retire to our room. A gaze, through loft window at the yawning square, bid goodnight and safe rest to welcome travelers. Marie, sleeping instantly, mumbles in her dreams. Night light still guides my fading pen, not willing to forget this day without first marking.

SEPTEMBER 21, 2001

ember 21, 2(

"On the right, you see Renault, a French car manufacturer; on the left, you see cabbage."

--Antoni explaining roadside sights in the suburbs of Warsaw

ROUTE 8, BETWEEN WROCŁAW AND WARSAW

THE INSATIABLE WIND from yesterday invited storm clouds and rain to join its happy party. I woke to the cold whistle of the window being pulled slightly open by the prying wind. Marie was already awake and getting ready for the day. She wanted an early start so we could go out on our own before the group met for the day's scheduled events.

Breakfast, as usual, was crusty rolls, hard-boiled egg, and coffee. At the circular buffet table a row of petite containers exhibited jewel-toned delights, homemade preserves. Strawberry preserves sparkled ruby red next to the royal purple currant jam. I was in heaven, taking half a spoonful of each on my plate to sample.

My roll saturated every drop of cherry preserves and black currant preserves on the plate; I swept it thoroughly to make sure. The sweet tart preserve was unmistakably pure, a delicious remembrance.

We returned to the hotel room to pack a few untidy things and place our luggage outside the door for the attendant to transport to the lobby. Before leaving for our excursion, we checked out of the hotel. As we left I saw the concierge organize our group's luggage in the lobby, more luggage continually added as the work continued. Mom accompanied us. Marie was out of złoty and wanted to cash a traveler's check. The hotel would not accept traveler's checks. We headed for the Town Square where a bank was spotted the day before. Mom and I chose to wait outside, the bank full and Marie taking only a few minutes. Umbrella and rain jacket combined did not repel the driving rain from seeping into bone. The stage for the solidarity rally was dismantled, flags still at half-mast. The makeshift memorial held its stature in the rough elements. Mom and I walked around briefly, taking a few pictures under cover.

Neat stacks of books form pyramids in the windows; beautiful art books stand proudly on easels, independent. Silhouettes of long tables and a labyrinth of bookcases were barely visible through the storm pressed glass. The bookstores and library would not open until ten; we would be long gone by then. The jaunt across the Old Town square seemed decades, rain pinching through twill pants, ricochet from medieval slate. Standing outside the bank we waited. Marie was taking a very long time.

I entered what I thought was the bank. A security guard buzzed and a gate opened. I asked if this was the bank. He did not speak English, but pointed to next door. Embarrassed, I realized that I entered an office building by mistake. The bank was the next door, he explained with out-stretched arm indicating the adjacent doorway. If Mom accompanied me, she would have laughingly insisted I run away with the dashing security guard, marrying him at the nearest chapel first. I would have jokingly accepted sojourned without pressure of the instant marriage. I thanked him as he chuckled with giddy eyes dancing around the witless tourist, and I exited the building to march one door over to the bank entrance. Climbing the stairs and scurrying across a lobby of marble and skylights, I encountered Marie sitting at a long desk beside a row of office cubicles. I approached her. She was frustrated and said that the bank did not know how to handle a traveler's check. The manager had to look up the procedure for processing the check in a manual that looked as large as a medieval tome. Since this process was eating all our time for exploration, Marie told us to venture on our own; she would meet us at the hotel entrance as soon as this mess was settled. She would not leave the bank without zwata. She was determined.

Very little time remained before the nine o'clock meeting for departure. Mom was feeling the pressure of the weather in her joints. We slowly aimed our path for the hotel. Mom crossed herself as we passed the amebic supplicant sculpture in courtyard of the gothic cathedral. One last time we passed the delicious café, bags of coffee beans on shelves all jumping through the window at me. Down the street we saw that the group and luggage were already loaded onto bus. There was no time to stop for a cappuccino. I inhaled deeply, happy aroma in hospitable lungs.

On the bus we explained that Marie would be here as soon as possible. I told the story of her in the bank. Some people grunted, as Marie knew they had trouble cashing traveler's checks days earlier in small towns such as this. Why couldn't she wait until we were in Warsaw later today? I would not answer for her. Luckily other people were fussing over room keys and checking out of their hotel rooms, so Marie was not the only person arresting the progress of the schedule. With the precision of a clockmaker, Steven was continually frustrated by the tardiness of a few inhibiting the progression of our group to scheduled sights. Alma, consequently, offered condoling words to placate, unnoted by Steven. In this instance, tempers sharpened to pointed comments, as Marie should have known better and unreturned keys thwarted departures days earlier. Our group was not becoming more coordinated, only more accustomed to personalities and their chronic idiosyncrasies. Yet Steven and Alma always maintained a polite aura at these discombobulated times. Others were not as refined. Finally she came, triumphantly waving receipt for the exchange. Nothing gets the better of Marie. I marveled at her nervy persistence.

All business accounted, all group members called, Edward drove to the newer section of town for our first stop: the Raclawice Panorama. The building, a rotunda, looked as if concrete spider web was cast over picket fence. Entering the building, one must pass through an underground tunnel and spiral staircase to emerge into the bright light of Polish history. From this central vantage point one is captured by the Kosciuszko Insurrection in progress: armed civilians thwarting the Russian troops receding, Polish cavalry advancing against them, soldiers taken as prisoners while others are taken to farm turned hospital for treatment. Women, children and old men kneel at the roadside altar near the farm, prayers for all wounded souls. This famous battle had become part of myth and a testament to the strength and endurance of Poles. This was a united peoples' battle for freedom and independence, farmer and soldier side by side.

The seamless painting drew three-dimensional props into the scene so homogeneously that one could not discriminate between the two. From every point of view it felt if one were standing in the countryside: on hilltop with birch trees and brush bare in autumnal anticipation, the landscape explodes in clusters of evergreens, fields, forests, and distant mountain peaks. The clear skies contrast the white smoke of artillery. I admired the landscape and rural features of the painting in the round; yet the energy and gore of the battle stations in the forefront overwhelmed me. This painting is a masterpiece of emotion, extreme emotion born of extreme events: mourning faces at roadside altar, a distressed woman hovering over her husband's body, determined faces marching toward action, and stricken faces bereaved—in disbelief.

A recorded commentary guided the group's viewing of the painting for one half-hour. Then we sallied down the way we came to our world waiting in modern time. A short break allowed for shopping and a brief stretch around the hilly grounds. Brick paths wobbled through woods and lawns of unrestrained park. We followed one for as long as ten minutes could sustain. The overcast skies provided a blank canvas for the trees to exalt their true colors: deep green of pine and fur pronounced the fiery-tipped maple leaves bold. Plush mint green grasses implored bare feet to run through them, not today. Walking was enough. Exercise was necessary; we were to ride five hours to Warsaw.

After counting off roll call, "sixteen," and settling ourselves, there was much talk to begin the long ride: Matthew reviewed his thoughts of the Panorama and added some historical facts to enrich the experience. General Kosciuszko participated in the American Revolution, bringing the ideas and fervor back to Poland after America's success. Residually, Poland is the second country in the world to have a constitution establishing a free democratic society. Although Poland historically has struggled for sovereignty much more than America, there is a kinship between the two. Suppressed during various periods of time, this connection has remained for centuries.

Reverie sank into the heart of the group, silence or whispers sustained. Some took a noontime nap while chocolate farmland lolled by window. Others read books. Whispered conversation, tête-à-tête, joined bus wheels in musical hum, a soothing accompaniment. A few of us who were keeping journals began to write. As one began to make notes, I withdrew my journal from purse. As one finished and another began, I launched through window into warm rays of grass and field, ready to tickle bare ankles. I was free.

Matthew passed by only once, checking on the general countenance of our members. As he passed my seat, he said, "writing, writing." Then he sat with the Prorok Brothers in the back seat for a time. Half an hour later, he again reviewed our dispositions. Walking once again to the front, he still found me writing.

"Would you make a copy of that journal available for the group to read. It may not be accurate, but it would be an interesting addition to Don's documentation." Don was the group's official scribe. He noted events in his journal with a promise to relinquish it to Matthew who would copy it for all who showed interest in reading it.

"I might." I indicated as I closed my journal from wayward glances.

Marie asked me if I saw her luggage being packed into the bus cargo hold. I did not. Everything was packed by the time I returned to the hotel. Furled brow, she asked if I thought our luggage was all right. Of course it was. She did not believe me. She began to worry.

We passed a farmer driving a horse-drawn cart overflowing with potatoes. The cart had car wheels and four farm hands where weighing down the crop by sprawling across the top of the heap. Were they going to market, to town or to storage? Is it comfortable to nap on a moving heap of potatoes? The men looked happy.

Once again the interplay of farmland and forest pranced before vision, no fences binding either. Orchards and rape fields line the road as well. Rapeseeds were ready for harvest and processing into oil or mustard. Rape oil is a delicacy, a delicacy to be savored as purely European. Personal silence allowed the voice of the landscape to be heard. Noticing the whole while already in action, pen outlines context, transposed below:

> Field and stream introduce
> Roadside forest
> Where mushroom harvesters
> Peer through glade for natural treasures
> Extending
> Back through time
> Back through landscapes of mind
> We glide
>
> Green perceptions, naïve impressions
> Shape experiences
> To change
> To deeper forests
> Recessed
> In poplars
> And linden trees
> Implore discovery

For a while I put my journal away, content to watch the passing scenery as if watching a lyrical foreign film. If only there were subtitles for this film I would understand more.

Reverie was interrupted by a question. Marie leaned over to my ear and asked if I would like to be a farmer. Smiling I told her that it would depend on what was being planted. I would be a Christmas tree farmer, spruce, fur and pine canvassing the fields as far and wide as a forest preserve. There would be a cozy farmhouse with the main floor being a bakery and tearoom. People would come during the holidays to cut their own tree and then stay for scones and tarts. In the summer, people would rent a picnic basket filled with goodies: quiche, fruit salad, lemon squares, and a book of poetry, and wile away an afternoon among the trees. My farm would provide beautiful experiences for visi-

tors to remember; not just a quick loaf of bread tucked in crook of arm
for the race home. And I'd write stories about all that came to visit, collected volumes published regularly. Of course the farmhouse windows
would be stained glass, fine examples from which people could order.
Would my farm be in America or in Poland? Could I feel at home
in either? The Polish countryside is reminiscent of upstate New York
and southern Ontario. My dream world fluttered in the air for a long
while before dispersing into fragmented wishes, faded into the passing
marsh.

Wincenty had similar qualities: many interests pulling in various
directions. Only he knew how to make each bloom. He was doctor and
artist, botanist and writer, each a successful career in and of itself, fields
across a lifetime. These careers augmented each other: the attention of
a doctor to artistic details, the rhetoric and ease of writing about flora
and fauna with the precision of a scalpel. At this moment I would be
happy to have one of my interests become successful, profitable enough
to sustain a modest and comfortable lifestyle where bills are not a strain
to pay and travel does not depend on thrifty saving.

Drifting back to the passing world, marsh released countryside
and orchard. A few apple and pear trees highlight the roadside before
field and farm. Some trees were ready for harvest while others seemed
already attended. The scene calmed the mind to flow a sentimental
stream of preserved memory.

On Saturday afternoons Dad would pile all of us into the army
green station wagon and race to the farms: in autumn we picked apples
and peaches, in winter we cut Christmas trees, in spring we selected
bulbs for planting in the garden patch by the garage, in summer we
forested strawberries and raspberries to eat off the vine as many as we
took home. I would run between Dad and siblings, checking progress
before settling for my task at hand, which most often was assisting

others more proficient at the job. Slung over Dad's shoulder, stained fingertips and lips, I would surrender a nap to the hatch of the wagon using my sibling's (whoever was willing) lap as a pillow. The ride home was always faster than the farm ride.

Mom and Nana would receive our bounty with the appreciation of a mail clerk on Christmas Eve; they knew the job that befell them during the upcoming week. Bushels were hauled into basement where Nana's old enamel stove was lit with a fury of unrestrained gas. Huge enamel vats, bigger than lobster pots, were filled: some with water to boil for sterilizing mason jars and some with cleaned fruit, sugar, the beginnings of preserves. Their entire day was spent over the flaming, sweating stove. Stir the pots. Retrieve the mason jars with padded gripping scissors. Dry the jars but quick to fill them before they cool. My older siblings helped as I watched from under foot or on green step stool. I would line the jars of hot nectar in the cupboard, playing with the arrangement. Through all seasons we would have homemade rhubarb jam on toast, Concord grape jelly in sandwiches, applesauce with blintzes, stewed pears and whipped cream, peach preserves in cobbler, and blueberry preserves in tarts. The cupboard was never empty, and neither were our Saturday afternoons. The jams served this morning at the ART Hotel resembled the sweet product of our weekend excursions. No chemicals, no preservatives, just the natural sweetness of personal care. Would Edward stop the bus for me to jump into the field quickly and pick just one pear? Or many pears for all of us? Splitting the delicate skin of ripe daydreams, Marie questioned me again.

"Do you really think our luggage is in the cargo hold safely?"

Marie relentlessly pursued. I tried my best to reassure her, then I resolved to joke: we'll just have to hire a taxi to drive us back to Wrocław tomorrow to retrieve our luggage. Then I will run away with the bank security guard. She was not laughing. She hailed Antoni's attention and explained her concern. He attempted to calm her as well. Nothing would calm her but a promise to open the holds and sift through for her luggage, at the next convenient stop, of course.

The aches of a long journey in one position began to set in. Some stirred, ready for exercise to stretch craving muscles. We stopped for lunch at another roadside restaurant. Everyone had a bowl of soup, either bean or vegetable, and bread. Antoni commented, soup and bread is dinner for the army; we were ready to join the army now that we eat soup everyday for lunch. Some people ordered full chicken dinners. Matthew commented as he extended arm to direct attention to the girl serving the corner table, our waitress looks like Meryl Streep. Antoni explained to her in Polish that she resembled a fine American actress. Her cheeks glowed red, head shaking sideways, eyes pointed to the floor as she exited for the kitchen. For a large bowl of soup, two rolls, and a bottle of water, the bill was four zwata, one dollar. Astonished, each waitress was tipped one złota, fifty groszy for their exceptional service and good humor. Meryl Streep deserved a good tip for enduring embarrassment. Besides, a local restaurant (not a chain or franchise) could not exist charging a dollar a meal, not in America anyway. It is a pleasure to support independent entrepreneurs.

After lunch we walked the premises for a few minutes, farmland abutting rest area. A farmer driving a tractor was tilling his field. By the distant farmhouse, laundry undulated on clothesline. Across the street was a windmill, ancient and worn as if Don Quixote himself had engaged it in battle. Its encompassing farm looked equally as dilapidated, its occupancy questionable, its safety doubtful. Behind were the hills, always the hills, spiny treetops defined expansion.

While walking in the parking lot, Marie took the opportunity to ask the alternate bus driver to open the holds. Indignantly he opened the first hatch. Edward took over the job, in the kindest manner. All five holds were opened before we spotted Marie's luggage in the corner of the last bay. The alternate bus driver confronted me, swearing in Polish. I was around enough to know a few of the words. His laser eyes cut as his words did. Now he was an inch from my face, too close, still shouting. I jumped backwards, grabbed Marie's fleeing arm, and pushed her forward telling him to yell at her, the offending party. In Polish she apologized for not trusting that he would carefully load all belongings. Appeased, he walked toward Edward to commiserate. I scampered behind the bus, in need of fresh air.

The stretch felt good, for there were still a couple hours ride before signs of Warsaw. I was not in a rush. Warsaw meant the end, the final destination of the journey. These hours were needed to mentally prepare for the last day and the dangerous possibilities of trying to return home. No one knew what to expect. Many were already getting anxious, Dad at the top of that list. His anxiety set in days ago, in Torun after the e-mail from my brother. The message, meant to calm, stirred traveling nerves longing to be settled by the comforts of home. His uneasiness subsided briefly in Kornik and at the Panorama. Yet as the days passed, uneasiness spread like the flu among school children. Some of us vaccinated to this effect would not relent. Each moment still held new discoveries.

Today as on many other days, Antoni would read the news from papers and magazines. He would interpret some headlines and provide synopsis of longer articles. A new reading over the microphone kept us busy as we employed the road to Warsaw. The elections in Poland were as much in the forefront of the news as the happenings in America. Many Poles were frustrated by the slow economic growth in this new capitalist system. The socialist candidate for president was expected to win the elections, although many candidates from several political parties were running for senate seats as well as president. Would capitalism and economic growth slow further if socialists controlled government? How would the government change? In America, some airports were opening tentatively. Security at borders and airports was doubling and tripling departure time. Bin Ladin was fingered as being the source behind the terror, even though he would not admit it. Talk of war enveloped the news, coalitions forming. News over, silence prevailed. Some napped on full stomach, Dad included. Mom read a novel. Marie leaned forward to talk quietly with Charlotte. All I could do was watch the hills.

The corrugated view sometime held marshes; other times woods, still most times fields, always hills softly coaxing the vegetation to have its way. Walking through these hills would be peaceful, like the trail at Gorzno without a guide. Nature may guide. I strained to catch every detail, every glimpse that might unfold the secrets only whispered in private context. Was that a hopping rabbit, a sleeping cow in the field or a disturbed vision from a jostling pothole in the road? I wished to see more and more. I wished to know more as well.

The landscape outside Warsaw was a contrast of economy: fields and lush meadows juxtapose new shopping malls. Ikea stood beside small houses. A Renault dealership was across the street from a cabbage farm. Matthew mentioned that we were lucky to visit Poland before it was as commercial as America. Visit while there was still open countryside to see. Incredulous, I could not agree with him. There would not be a Wilga Nature Preserve at Gorzno without a concern to keep Poland intact. The same Polish spirit that rebuilt the Royal Palace and conserves artwork in cathedrals and town halls across the country would endure culturally. Capitalism is no match for the spirit of Poland. Capitalism is a way to thrive economically, not culturally.

The Forum Hotel was like home. We knew it from the beginning of the trip and welcomed the sight of it as if in the home of a relative.

Our group checked into our rooms. With an hour before dinner, a small group of us ran out to shop. There was no time to fritter. Cepalia was closing for the evening. Matthew gently pushed his way onto the threshold to entreat the sales lady to let us shop for a few minutes. She gladly obliged, locking the door behind us so no one else could enter. For twenty-five minutes we filled our arms with souvenirs: dolls, pottery, lace table clothes. We thanked the two ladies and slowly walked to the hotel.

Marie and I stopped in the hotel gift store. Mom was there, buying postcards to write friends during the rest before dinner. From the top corner shelf, the Pope called Mom with holy smirk. She hailed our attention to him. The blown glass Pope ornament hugged himself and glimmering robes in prayerful glee. Mom was entranced. Pulling herself away after a long moment, she shuttled to her room, postcards ready for lined sentiment. Stella entered the shop with a hairstyle and wave that suited an invitation to a grand ball. Marie complimented Stella who reveled in new elegance. The beauty parlor was still open and accepting appointments, Stella informed. Marie dashed to the salon to get a shampoo and style before it closed. I was left alone in the shop to purchase Marie's selection for her. A crystal murmur from the corner shelf set gaze to visit his holy reverence. The Pope was calling. He wished to be with Mom, a surprise remembrance. The accommodating sales girl wrapped him delicately in tissue, bubble and tied box. There he would rest until Christmas, if only I could convey him home without damage. Very pleased with myself, I darted to my room to arrange a quilted vault in backpack for his safe, yet covert, transport.

Marie returned to the room in regal splendor, feeling as if a queen descending to the masses for courtesy. I fawned with lovely compliments. She swam in each one. We would spend a little extra time preparing ourselves for dinner this evening. After all, the dress must coordinate with hairstyle.

In the banquet hall of the hotel we met the group for dinner. Other tour groups were there, eating the buffet as well. I sat next to Richard at a rectangular table roomy enough for eight people to dine. After speaking of family, Richard mentioned a night class he recently took on philosophy. Coincidentally, he attended the class at my alumae matur with a professor I knew well. We began to talk of the philosophy professors at the college and the courses they taught. One professor was trying to write a universal definition of love, encompassing all other Western definitions past and present, in book form. We walked to the dessert bar for coffee and cakes.

A slender lady was at the bar carefully pouring coffee. She offered to pour one for me since she was already in position. Setting the cup under spout, I thanked her. She spoke of her tour of Warsaw, just beginning, and asked of my trip. Richard went back to table, pleased with raisin crumb cake and coffee. I told her highlights of my itinerary and that we were New Yorkers. Her light-hearted tone changed to an imploring one. First she offered sincere condolences for the tragic attacks; then she began her story.

Ever since the war, the Second World War, she had felt that people scorned her for being German, as if being German meant she was Nazi. For decades she felt that she had to apologize to recompense for Nazi terror. Touching my arm in gentle earnest, she stressed her point. Never allow the extreme acts of one to prejudge a culture or all members of that culture. Do not harbor resentment towards all Muslims for the acts of extremists such as bin Ladin. She was just now, in her seventies, feeling respected as a German for the first time. With a pat on her forearm, I reassured her that I would not hold anyone accountable for terrorist actions besides the terrorists. Her eyes were still searching to confirm the sincerity of the statement. My eyes met hers with tender regard and understanding. I knew her point and she knew I understood.

Again we spoke of our tours, hers yet to commence. She commented that mine was unusual: most tour companies suggest trips through Northern Europe or Southern Europe, not both in one jaunt. I explained that each of us had an option of where to travel for four days before the tour of Poland. I chose Rome.

"Yours is a pilgrim's journey," she stated in reverent tease intended to be playful, cheerful. I smiled at her comment in recognition of this truth, although uncertain of its repercussions. Yet we have gathered more than scrapbook memories, more than indulgences.

What kind of pilgrim am I? A gap-toothed Wife of Bath? No… The thought ended in gentle laughter as our dessert plates were overfilled.

We shook hands; I wished her a pleasant journey, and we returned to our parties.

Richard had finished his dessert. I sat down beside him to my luke-warm coffee and we began where we left, a universal definition of love. It seems so simple. Love is respected connection. Be it filial love, erotic love, unrequited love, possessive love, societal love or any of myriad types of friendship, it is all the same root. Within and between that respected connection, there is a sense of love being more than the sum of its parts. Some may call this phenomena energy, karma, bodhisat-tva or real life. It is all love, what we get from loving, who we become from loving, and what is done for others through love. One could meet another only once in life and have loved. Friendships made across a lifetime and friendships made within the hour hold the same respected connection. And in this connection we gain wisdom. Love is the glass through which one views universal truth.

The complexities of love and friendship vary from person to person, relationship to relationship. Those specifics are not for anyone to define besides those in love or friendship. In the whole of love we are one and in each one we are whole. Both cannot exist without the other. Love cannot be dissected for objective scrutiny, only manifestations of love may be scrutinized, the root still concealed. My apologies to Socrates, Decartes and C. S. Lewis; my definition more closely aligns with the Dahli Lama and Joseph Campbell. Richard excused himself from table to meet with friends at their hotel room. With a friendly smile, I wished him good night. Richard bowed slightly and left the conversation with lovely ideas bathing his countenance, invigorated.

Matthew flagged me to join him. This was opposite of me calling him in the same banquet room one week earlier. Now he was hailing me, the flirt. As I approached he invited me to take a walk with him and a few others. I accepted the invitation. Succinctly he offered advice on tomorrow's events: take the scheduled tours to learn about the people and history of Poland, and he would go to some bookstores and try to find a volume of or on Wincenty for me. I knew he was right. For my first journey to Poland I had found more information on Wincenty than I thought I would. It is more important to go on the tours and learn about the history and culture to which he was expressing than to search for his specific works. I could always write to the National Library and Gallery for information. With the plan for tomorrow settled, we ventured forth to seize the cold autumn night by the meaty hand.

It was after ten o'clock on a Friday night. The streets were filled with young people, some waiting for others or for a train, others milling around in clusters entertaining themselves. Five of us (Matthew and his lady friends, Stella and Fran, Richard and myself) walked down the street and into the pedestrian underpass. We had no aim. First we came above ground to find ourselves at an isolated train station disconnected from other thoroughfares. There was one exceptionally tall man at the train station. Matthew approached him and asked in Polish directions to get back on the street heading towards the central train terminal. We were surprised when he answered in perfect English, so we began to talk, introducing ourselves. His name was Casper and he was from Edmonton, Alberta. Teaching English at Berlitz, he had been living in Warsaw for a couple months. Pointing in various directions he explained the major train line in Warsaw and offered his help. Matthew and I spoke with him about our tour just before his train arrived. Still talking he offered once more to help. We did not want him to miss his train and plans. With a round of thanks and handshakes we bid farewell as he entered the train and we descended the stairs of the underpass. One last glance showed Casper peering out the train window watching us. I smiled at him before the descending concrete stair wall blocked the view.

Exiting at the correct gate, we emerged at the Hotel Metropol where we stayed the first night in Warsaw. Further, we passed the empty market square, vacant stalls forming a makeshift wall. Some drug stores were still open. Matthew had not shaved in days and Stella prodded him to buy a razor. For the sake of the group, she barbed. Succumbing to the pressure, he did buy a razor at a street side kiosk. Then we entered the Merriott, as some were interested in seeing it. Chandeliers hung in the vestibule leading to the marble floors of the lobby. An ensemble tucked in corner was playing chamber music. The music was beautiful yet I was uneasy in this opulence, as if crashing a royal ball or as if sneaking into the theatre without tickets in jeans and tee shirt. We poked around the newsstand adjacent to the musicians. Once around gift shop and lobby was enough to satisfy curiosity. There was more to see outdoors.

We crossed the street to enter the central train terminal. The small shops were closed, glass doors locked. Florescent lighting guided us towards the main artery of the station. It was busy. Natives familiar with the station sped past. The ladies in our small group changed their minds: they were not interested in getting trampled in order to get a flavor of how natives live in Warsaw. A young lanky man sitting on the concrete floor was playing guitar, instrument case open to catch spare change. The beat was contemporary. The ladies decided this was enough. Matthew was put off; he would have jumped in the crowd, talking with whom he thought interesting and observing the rest. I had no opinion to impose on this small group (however I would have ventured forth with Matthew if we were alone); I was along for the ride whatever that may be.

After a moment's hesitation, Matthew joined the ladies to retrace our path to the hotel. He walked on the outside, protecting me from the crowd as if my father, a sweet gesture. The street performer finished his song before we left the central terminal, but we were too far away, almost one city block, for me to give him monetary thanks or shrill verbal compliment.

The others walked quickly, but Matthew and I took our time. Matthew translated advertisements and store signs for me. I told him of the excellent bakery I discovered the first day in Warsaw, only two blocks away now. When we again were in front of our hotel, Matthew asked everyone to stop. Behind several groups of milling people, he noticed a monument. A small, dark wall abutting the wall of the building sheltered a row of potted chrysanthemums. We stood in front of a stone plaque giving honor and memory to those who lost their lives at this wall during the war, the exact day and time listed. On closer inspection, bullet marks blistered the stone. Matthew wiped his hand over stone face. Feeling this an invitation, I pressed my right hand to one cratered brick, cold and smooth. A bullet hole fell under my palm;

air accentuated it, vacuous. Shiver traveled from palm through arm to chest. What soul am I touching?

We stood for a moment in contemplative silence; the people must have thought we were crazy. On a Friday near midnight where youth runs city streets, we were a group of five mixed in age giving respect to an overshadowed war monument. A small votive light casts a hopeful ray on ground and flickering plant leaves, green, yellow, white.

Entering the hotel, Matthew postulated that similar monuments are everywhere. These are working monuments that have become integral cornerstones of buildings of daily function. Monuments are key to understanding the culture as much as talking to people in the train station or going on guided tours. We bid each other good night.

I unlocked my room to find the television blaring white light onto a sleeping Marie.

SEPTEMBER 22, 2001

"For Faith, For Justice, For Nation"
—MOTTO ON THE CREST AT THE ROYAL PALACE

WARSAW, AGAIN

THE CLOUDLESS SKY heralded the new day, marvelous. The sun's brilliant rays were in agreement. It would be a spectacular day. There was no choice in the matter.

Many people chose to use this last full day in Warsaw in various ways, splintering the group: several went to the Saturday open air market behind the train station, some went to bookstores and libraries to do research, many decided to go shopping in Old Town and other areas. About twenty of us chose to participate in the scheduled tours.

The congestion of city and suburban sprawl lessened as we proceeded northwest toward Zelazowa Wola, the birthplace of Chopin. Everyone knew of Chopin, as everyone knows something of Mozart and Beethoven: figures so engrained in history that children learn of them in school as geniuses of their era, even if their music is not presented. Or, we know the music dislocated from the composer or even the title. Bugs Bunny cartoons show the ease of play: one cute bunny could play a composition while munching a carrot or answering a telephone or swatting a mouse. Antoni gave a detailed account of Chopin's life and music on the bus ride to Zelazowa Wola. Antoni related as pianist and composer as well as tour guide, repeating the complexities of Chopin's various compositions.

Our American English overcame us at last. Poles pronounce Chopin as "chopping," an action verb. Many in the group then followed suit, but on this I could not relent. In my best English with French accent (a butchered mimic of French pronunciation learned in high school) I would sing Chopin as "show pan," with a schow and a short a-sound in pan. Show Pan. I pictured Chopin as a whimsical fairy, demigod character as Pan. To make matters worse, no one could pronounce the village of his birth, Zelazowa Wola. Poles say it so quickly that our repetition of it always became "Zela-blah-blah-blah-blah." Not to further embarrass ourselves, we would just refer to it as His Birthplace. Are we chopping blah blah yet? A moment of levity before we enter the gardens.

The gatehouse is in the style of a Prussian farmhouse, although relatively new in comparison. The estate is surrounded by red brick wall and entrance gate of wrought iron spires. The paved walk leads to another farmhouse on the left, a shop, and park benches on the right before it tapers into a brick path in two directions or a dirt path more obscure in divergent direction. Paths are rivulets and tributaries flowing to and from the source, Chopin's house. We follow the first brick path through maples, pines, and chestnut trees into a smaller circular path in front of His Birthplace. In the epicenter there is a towering statue of Chopin, arms wrapping around his torso, eyes cast on the ground in reflective embrace. Antoni draws our attention to a chestnut tree beside the path. The farm was destroyed in one of the wars; only the small servants' home in which Chopin's family lived would remain. Consequently, the farmland was designed as a garden with multiple paths. The chestnut tree, the thickness would take two people to completely fence, is the only tree in the garden surviving from Chopin's time. Autumn breezes bring chestnuts and leaves tumbling to ground. Gold and orange are beginning to creep into the tree leaves. The group walks on. I bend to quickly snatch a chestnut from the paved way, cradling it in palm. If everyone who visited here in autumn picked up debris from the ground the gardeners would be grateful to do less cleaning. For the rest of the visit the chestnut is in hand, velvet touch supple to accept anything.

The white house with wooden roof tiles is simple and elegant in form: thick columns ensconce entryway topped in pediment, house expansion on either side. A private concert is in session. We are not allowed admittance. Quietly, Antoni lead us to the far end of the house where an outdoor seating area of long backless benches occupied. We sit to listen. Butterflies flicker sunlit wings in a patch of daisy, hawthorn, and giant crocus along the wall of the house near the doors, a symphony of colors. Through open windows and closed French doors we hear Chopin's music: notes tickling emotion into patriotic revolution or contemplative tenderness. The chestnut wriggles. I unveil the warm midday.

Nana would tend to her garden on beautiful days such as this: picking ripe raspberries from the bushes, watering the rhubarb before investigating the greenery, but always doting over her rose bushes. Whether from a friend's garden or a rare gift of fresh cut roses from a florist, Nana would choose a rose that caught her fancy. The long stem, with at least five buds, was rooted in a mason jar. At any given time Nana would have one rooting on the window ledge. At precisely the right time, of which I could never quite comprehend, she would plant the rose. On the small hill in the backyard, she would not line the bushes geometrically but plant them where she thought they needed to

be. Inverted mason jars protected the transplants from storm and butterfly, until Nana deemed them ready for the world. Like gazing balls,
these rosy mason jars shone and reflected dots of light around the yard,
creating the illusion of a greater space. Rose bushes were her pride, and
they blossomed for only her continuously, under her meticulous care.
The purple and yellow crocus, the pure white daisies under butterfly
dances are inverted mason jars protecting the bloom of present day
memory.

In a ghost-like silence we remain still, uninvited guests relegated to
the corners as children before an adult reception. It is covert. Birds fly
overhead, chasing between trees. Paths trickle from the house in many
directions. The music follows these waves, released from private audience into the world. I would rather be a covert attendant than private
guest; there is more to see out here. The music stops, dramatically.
Resolute. The end. We cannot remain silent, but offer applause for a
concert beautifully played. With a few moments' hesitation, the last
notes resound through tree and flower.

The dignitaries are ushered to where they need to be before we
enter the house. A small group of tourists join the end of our group
for the advantage of a guided tour. The forier is simple and leads to the
parlor on the right. The parlor, beams exposed and painted with tendril
fruits and flowers, holds a piano and many period chairs and sofas.
Sheer, bustled curtains filter light from the windows and French doors.
The effect is soft elegance from hardwood floor to ceiling, fitting the
romantic portrait of Chopin on the opposite wall. Now I understand a
concert experience indoors: Chopin is always in attendance among his
beautiful relics, in his time preserved.

Moving through the dining room, one could observe the family
portraits among the accommodating furnishings. I could picture the
Chopin children rushing and playing in this room: sharing poetry, mu-

sical verse, and charcoal sketches. At dinner they would tell stories of the day's lessons and adventures. Along the far wall a narrow room is corded off. An enormous goblet vase holds an arrangement of lovely and exotic flowers in fall colors of which I could only identify a few. This perpetual fresh arrangement honors Fryderyk Chopin's mother in the room where he was born. These two adjacent rooms run together as the children did.

Retiring to the front of the house, a smaller study keeps desk and upright piano. On the walls hang examples of Chopin's childhood work: a draft of a polonaise, a copied script of verse, and a sketch of village landscape. His father must be proud to have taught his receptive children well-rounded curricula. When one art is mastered, others follow at will. Chopin drew a fine picture of rural nineteenth century life: children playing in front of a castle while a farmer carries a tree limb up a road leading to a cluster of village cottages with bridge and a dome of church in the background.

A small receiving parlor connects to the forier, completing the floor plan. The room looks onto the circular garden with Chopin's maudlin statue and the chestnut tree off to the right-hand side. The chestnut gleams filtered light from inside the house, welcome. Sparsely furnished, this parlor creates a space of anticipation before being ushered into or out of the home. We are preparing to exit. One look by the corner window scans a correspondence Chopin wrote in youth. Even his handwriting is beautiful: curving and swooping script as if each letter a bird's flight.

When we leave the house, the extra tour group splits from our path onto their own. We are led to the bridge and the garden walk along the river Utrata. On the bridge we meander, observing the still water and noontime sun. A group picture was taken on the bridge; planks and spaces in the rail resemble a piano keyboard. Sunlight is dramatic today. Ambling along the path, the light asked to be photographed. The understanding chestnut drops into pocket as I take out my camera. It is the perfect autumn day in these lush gardens: ivy covered maple trees invite smaller trees and brush to riverside; white light shines leaves yellow, green, and red. We stop at the obelisk along the far boundary wall of the estate. A bronze profile of Chopin marks the obelisk with the date of his birth. For a moment we stand to absorb the sight and the view from the monument. The path curves, changing direction towards the entrance. The path ends where it began.

In a patch of ivy and grasses, a pine tree looms tall and bare except for its crown. I am photographing it as daylight causes brief contrast in environment: vertical starkness of trunk opposing the vibrant greens, many shades of green, from grass to crown. Joining the group with a quick step, Mom tells me we have ten minutes to shop. Ten minutes. We climb the stairs of the red paneled gift shop and to the jewelry case on the side porch. In need of a second opinion, Mom asks my advice on an amber ring for my sister. After affirming the choice, I tell her that I will meet her in a few minutes by the gate. Seven minutes.

Swimming again on the main rivulet, I veer to the extreme left onto a dirt path. At the first bend in this tributary there is an enormous linden tree. Water droplet leaves reflect yellow-green. In its shadow I settle myself, withdraw journal from purse, and begin to transform the ebb and flow of the experience into meandering expression. This is the eternal moment. The one that will last until it chooses to finish. I am alone yet never alone in this birthplace of creativity.

Footsteps draw near, faintly perceived. Mind busy reeling from other stimuli. Footsteps recede to their origin. I am left undisturbed, perhaps unnoticeable in silent repose, thankfully. Tranquilly I write, embracing what comes at its unmeasured pace.

Theme and Variation

Rhythms of treed sunshine
Play on back and shoulders
Polonaise
To choreograph
A butterfly dance
In azalea and impatience.

Country dogs bark
And light traffic rides
With faint perception;
Gardens stand aloof today.

Chopin
Musician, composer, poet
Be housed in circumstance
Profound, complete
In tendrils of history
Sad yet strong—
Farmhouse ruins crunch
Under soldiers streaming
March
Trace of field serenade
In patriotic memory
Of what was and should be.

Resilient
Tree flourishes
To house breezy
Crescendos of poetry
Inspiration
For all who know to listen.

Foreign heart with native heritage
Finds refuge—
Indigenous topography
Of Soul always home.

Elated from this waft of creativity I tread from the path, always in memory as my path, my tree evermore, to the gatehouse. Some are still shopping while others exit. Dad and Antoni converse until I approach, then they both venture to garner the group, Dad just looking for Mom. Frank and Rosemary sit at the café table on the lawn in front of the gift shop. Romantically they hold hands across the table, looking at the gardens across the way. Chopin inspired them as well. Their worked hands and weathered faces could not wither the love in their eyes. Greeting them and complimenting their tenderness, I burst forth and ask to take their photograph. Pleased, enthusiastically, they agree. Timeless love in this moment preserved for others to see. Through the gates we travel.

Along the street to the parking lot, kiosks welcome tourists with an assembly of goods: ornate wooden trinket boxes, carved wooden eggs and religious or historic figures, statues of Chopin and dolls in folk dress. We could not resist. Many continued to shop while others bought ice cream or bottled water at a small cafeteria. A dog, a mutt patched in brown and gray, wandered through the adjacent parking area. I petted him but he maneuvered away since I had no food. Jozef Mazurkiewicz was finishing a chocolate cone and gave the last bite, the tip, to the dog. As if it found treasure, the dog bolted to a remote corner of the paved lot and languorously ate the cone. Laughing, Jozef watched the dog until it had licked every spot the cone tip touched. Before the dog proceeded begging, Jozef met the bus.

Even though Matthew was not present, indeed half the group was missing, Antoni instructed us to call numbers. Sixteen, I said.

"Who is sixteen?" Edward asked of Antoni.

"Sixteen is wonderful." Antoni replied.

All aboard, a content murmur of light conversation filled the air. Happy for a respite yet energized, the bus passed farm and manufacturing plant and shopping mall to return to Warsaw with a crew ready for the next experience. The road led to Old Town. Our group became smaller as a few left to shop in the square. Our remaining fifteen huddled in the Great Courtyard of the Royal Palace. The expansion of courtyard swallowed the group as crumbs on a dinner plate. Antoni had difficulty obtaining admission tickets: since the group was half the size as originally quoted the rate fluctuated. He haggled to fix a new price in our favor, which took time. We had all day; ten minutes to negotiate meant more time to bask in the reflective light of history from the bulbous spire of the Baroque towers. Time stood still inside the palace, the rush of the weekend lay outside its walls. We were ushered into the basement.

This original substructure of red brick columns and vaults was the prison cellar, now cloak room, bookstore, and reconstruction exhibit. Giant mounted photographs lined the walls documenting the destruction of the Royal Palace during the war. One floor of the tower and one section of foundation remained standing after many bombardments. As many artifacts and works of art as possible were rescued and hidden before the final explosion: every few feet holes were drilled in walls in which explosives crammed, with an easy ignition the building was a pile of dust, shards of former glory. Immediately the people wanted to reconstruct, but politics and economy did not allow it until the 1970's when the Polish people at home and abroad contributed to the project themselves.

Our docent was an older lady, small and round and pleasant in a grandmotherly way. She carried a Japanese paper fan with her, using it as a pointer. She led us from the basement, up the winding stairs to the great rooms and the King's Apartment. While walking up the stairs or between rooms, she would study her fan: notes on each room in tight script were written on each panel of her fan. If a question was asked, she repeated her script hoping that a reiteration would clear away any inquiries. Quickly we learned questioning led to a disruption in the pattern of the tour, which took several moments to recuperate. For the rest of the tour we would respectfully nod and smile as she presented information.

Each room was grand. One could tell if looking closely that original pieces were used in rebuilding whenever possible: in the corner of the ceiling border a piece of molding with gold leaf, no bigger than a six inch block, is slightly darker in color than the rest of the room's molding. Yet it has the complete motif of curvilinear leaves and vines intact. Beautifully relics and reproductions mesh into one whole, bountiful and seamless.

The reception hall flowed into the thrown room. The wonders of paintings, sculpture and furnishings were framed by a room of red and gold detailing, luxurious. Portraits hovering over thresholds surveyed the passing tours with cunning vision. Bacciarelli painted some of those portraits as well as the magnificent, mythological ceiling of the dining hall. Horses and gods ran from the Roman ceiling into the room in a rush of waves, water or lit sky. Who would eat in this room? I would sit and stare with open mouth, as now I stand and do the same. This reproduction is inspiring; one could not tell the difference. The king's bedroom changed mood to regal green, dark tones. The short bed with canopy of damask was a child-size surprise. Medically, it was considered healthy to sleep upright, the bed constructed only to accommodate resting legs and erect body.

In a smaller room, almost a corridor, two great mirrors perched opposite each other above mantles. Framed in the richness of gold, each wall-size mirror stood as a testament of itself. A chandelier in the center of the room glittered crystal refracted light. When standing under the chandelier peering into one mirror one could see myriad reflections bouncing between mirrors in unending play. It felt as if I was inside a diamond, space bending with colored light and image. The most impressive room was still to come.

In eggshell and gold stucco, paintings were ensconced in panels tailored for each one. From eye-level to ceiling, salon style, the room pronounced the name of one great artist: Canaletto. Each meticulous painting depicted a scene from the streets of Warsaw in his time. Studying one at a time was as if leaping into the scene with both feet thrust forward: open thoroughfares carrying the eye to the majesty of the Royal Palace (only half as wide and a third story taller at the time), or to the sprawling opulence of the Palace of Wilanow. Nature and people blended into the busy cityscapes as the structures were bathed in the dramatic light of sunrise or sunset. Awe struck. One Canaletto would have been enough to highlight the experience, yet a roomful was too rich to behold in a few passing moments. These exacting paintings were examined to verify plans for reconstruction of the palace. My eyes shot on each, careful not to miss a single one. His story intrigues: commissioned to paint, he traveled from Italy to Warsaw for a three-day visit; he stayed for the rest of his life. A connection between Italy and Poland matured as great artists traveled for projects. The number of works by Bacciarelli and Canaletto in one museum amazed. One room competed with the next in splendor and artistry, a friendly competition. By the end of the hour we reached saturation point; memory could not hold all one wished it would.

A brief stop in the bookstore entertained until Antoni returned for us. In the square, we were given half an hour to have lunch before our next excursion. The only restaurant in sight was a Pizza Hut, half full. When the first few of our group entered the restaurant all the tables were occupied. Mom, Dad and I chose to walk the square instead of eating lunch. A festival was in progress. We could not identify the reason for the festival. Children ran through the cobbled square in groups on a treasure hunt. One group of children ran past us to get a ribbon from a festival worker, with colorful tee shirt. Once they obtained the ribbon, they checked a list and ran to another point in the square. It was fun to watch the children enjoying the activities. After the hunt, there was a karate demonstration on stage where two men lunged at each other in different ways while a commentator shouted out the names of the moves. The children were captivated.

A street vendor planted his cart on the corner of the square and an Old Town street. His banner read "American Hot-Dogi." Enjoying the mixture of Poland and America, a couple from our group tried the hot-dogi… they thought it as good as any street vendor in American big cities. I could not keep from chuckling at the juxtaposition. Perceptions of American culture were seeping into Poland along with capitalism. Does he make good money, I wonder?

Walking back to the entrance of the Royal Palace, we waited for the group to reassemble. City Hall was half way up the block. I could see a car decorated with ribbons and bows. A bridal party exited the car and processed into City Hall, very simple. It was Saturday, wedding day again. Everyone came together. Processing through the square and to the bus we passed a church with another wedding party at its feet. A small group of attendants were throwing coins at the newlyweds. Laughingly they collected the money from the ground. The afternoon haze smiled on them as we cached around the outskirts of the party, wishing them well. The hospitable day was waiting at our next destination.

On the way to Lazienki Park, Mom's arthritis grew from mild to moderate. She decided to stay on the bus with a good book rather than go to tour the Summer Palace. The rest of us strolled through the park: wedding parties gathered in picturesque frames on a garden path, near the reflecting pool, outside the palace. We stride by them all. A young mother with twin toddlers allowed them to make natural discoveries of grass and leaf in the cul-de-sac at the entrance of a smaller mansion. The Prorok Brothers, although nine years apart in age, could pass as twins. They approached the mother and asked in Polish to have their picture taken with the twins, fibbing that they were twins. She gladly rustled the children into one spot. Marie, homesick for her twin grandsons, quickly jumped into the scene and sat on the grass by the twins. The blonde boys did not know what to make of this crazy woman at their side and old men behind their backs. They looked perplexed, not scared, and ignored everyone to turn from searching for grass to the discovery of pebbles, fascinating. I took two pictures, hoping one would turn out nicely, and we thanked the mother for her consideration.

Far behind, we hustled to meet the group on the foyer steps only to find them waiting for the palace guide who was late. Wonderful, now we have a few moments to enjoy the scenery: boats masked as swans take joyful tourists on rides in the lake, a fountain to the right of the palace entrance provides a soothing water music to the events in the park, two wedding groups pose in a heavily wooded area to the left. The palace guide did not disappoint. She was a statuesque redhead in jeans and white oxford, speaking proper English with a gentile accent. I knew immediately this would be a fantastic tour.

Before entering, everyone must wear cloth galoshes over shoes to protect the parquet and marble floors. There was only one size of galoshes: a man's extra huge. I put them on and knew instantly they would not stay on my freakishly small lady's feet. To accommodate, I shuffled through the vestibule as if ice skating, feet never leaving the floor. With just a little wax, I could have buffed the floors for them, complimentarily.

The foyer emptied into a room of fountains where Roman gods bathed with sirens. This room would cool any king from midsummer heat, our guide imagined with zeal. Passing through concert hall and drawing rooms, marble and fresco gods commiserated with royal portraits. The gallery in the back of the palace faced the gardens where waist-high labyrinths confused the eye, each twisting route ending in flower patch or fountain. Room after room our guide explained the details, symbolism and history of the palace and its artworks. I cannot remember everything but recall her sincere admiration and understanding, rediscovering her nation's past and culture with every tour. Her gentle earnestness led us upstairs to the king's private chambers.

The galoshes flopped. I tucked the long, sagging elastic into my shoe. That worked for a step or two. Then I bent over and pulled the elastic taut, as if my feet were puppets to master. My back ached from that stance, as I looked like an ape or a cartoon character, best yet an ape cartoon. Being at the end of the group, I finally reached the second floor with little notice or commotion.

The receiving room introduced the king's study, both designed in cool hues. A hunting theme united the décor as still life paintings of fresh game and fruit offset the landscape frescos of the hunt itself. The king's desk viewed the courtyard, lake, and woods. The adjacent room was called the Rafael Room, however there were none in it because all were lost in the war. Laura in dejected contemplation explained the plunder: transient victors, Nazis or Allies, claimed priceless artwork as souvenirs never to be recovered. I could understand Hitler absconding with one or two Rafael's then destroying everything on his hateful agenda, but the latter implications confounded me. To lose national treasures representing an era is heartbreaking. Laura in sweet dismay hoped that one day at least some are rediscovered and returned in reasonable condition. One work of art that was pilfered during the war was purchased by a Polish American businessman and given back, not a Rafael though.

A narrow passageway skirted around the dome of the room below, creating an interesting space of flat ceiling and curving vaults of wall. The view disoriented: looking down on the marble floor and crowns of statues as if part of the dome, yet being separate from the dome in a hall of white walls instead of arching frescos. We prowled through the hall as if cats on a fence. This led to the Room of Virtues.

The creamy walls contrasted the oversize photographs hanging on them. The Room of Virtues documented the Nazi occupation of the Summer Palace. Hitler planned to destroy the palace and ordered holes drilled every few feet. Fortunately before the holes could be filled with explosives, the war ended. Directly after the war, the holes were filled with concrete, or possibly some other building material, to reestablish the structure of the palace walls and foundation. In the photographs distinct polka-dotted walls span the palatial horizon, not noticed on first glance outside today. Our attention was drawn to the four oval portraits living in the cathedral ceiling above the exhibit. Laura said that they were the four virtues each king must acquire in order to rule benevolently, intelligently: justice, wisdom, grace and faith.

These renaissance muses conquered the room and the palace collection, forthright women that they are. My eyes immediately shot towards Grace, with flowing amber hair and soft demeanor. In a moment, I noticed I was watched as I studied my namesake. Red-faced, my embarrassed glance averted to the floor. Check vanity. Move on to Wisdom: hair the blue black of midnight fell on eggshell robes and encircled an even temper, thoughtful stare. Anyone who would befriend these virtues may live a marvelous life. The group was leaving; wistfully, one last time, I bid them farewell.

One might think descending stairs should be easier to maneuver with flopping galoshes. That assumption is wrong. The sliding, ice skating technique I used thus far cannot manage stairs. I tried. The stairs were too short; galoshes flew freely, wildly before haphazardly perching on the step below. I stumbled. Only the sudden grasp of the handrail kept me from rolling down the flight of stairs. That was enough. Dirt cleans easier than blood. I flicked off the galoshes and carried them the rest of the way, for the first time assuming a somewhat dignified stance. On the bottom landing I replaced the galoshes and skated for the remainder of the tour, as it was only a few moments longer.

Laura extended her best regards to our group, and we thanked her for the insightful, heartfelt guidance. Turning to the path on which we came, new wedding couples now occupied the benches lining the lake before the woods. Another wedding couple was boarding a swan boat for pictures on the lake. The late afternoon sunlight dramatically burst through tree trunks illuminating the lake in spotlights and trees in yellow halos. Laura strode into the woods on the far side of the lake, following a golden walkway speckled with reds and oranges of fallen leaves. As we passed the thick of the woods, light grew dimmer, colder, only to emerge in triumphant encore at street side. On the bus ride, Dad, Marie and I told Mom of the park and palace. This conversation drove us to the hotel where we had an hour to dress for a farewell dinner party.

Although all of our clothes were worn many times the past couple weeks, I chose the best to wear for this special occasion. Marie did as well, her salon hairstyle still lovely from yesterday. As I folded my pants, the chestnut leapt and rolled from view. Bouncing once…twice…then rolling to a dark spot…out of sight. Crawling on the floor I scoured for it until the chestnut revealed its hiding place under the chair by the window. Still affable, the chestnut lolled in hand. It found a new home in the zipped pocket of my purse, with the yellow ribbon as housemate. Primping and fussing for forty minutes produced a special effect. We would at least attempt to be fancy, nothing "too bright" but the elegant black of Wisdom.

In the lobby the group met. Mom wrote postcard greetings when on the bus and wished to mail them. Venturing onto the sidewalk I attempted to point out the mailbox, but Mom received help from a porter. When I noticed his assistance, I thanked him in Polish. He smiled, joined the security guard at the door and said to the guard, "She is individual."

With that overheard comment I could have leapt into his arms. Appearances do not shape individuality; molding of a framework of understanding does. Through education and experience one creates personal philosophy, strength of character. Individuality inhabits and extends. By knowing oneself, there is a welcoming to know others, thereby further creating oneself through this discourse. If I were to sit for a few moments with the porter to relate to him as an individual, I would learn of his beliefs, culture, values, and experiences. One connects with another in similarity and difference. This was the kindest compliment and the biggest challenge of my life.

I am individual. I am American.

American is being one and accepted within society without having to be the same—a single strip of glass in a mosaic window of the cathedral of freedom. As one we shine—eagle in flight, tree in bloom, light through patterned window—yet without the individual pieces the picture shattered, void released, hole gaping to be filled.

As we processed through the exit, I smiled at him as he continued to speak with the security guard, now speaking in Polish.

The restaurant occupied a corner of a large building partially on a hill. Through winding patios, unoccupied in the dark cool breeze

of autumn twilight, we hiked to the entrance. The romance of the
intimate patio tables magnified indoors: dreamy light from Chinese
lanterns slept on each table; wicker chairs with scrolling arms and large
red cushions surround. Asian prints and abstract paintings decorate the
red walls. As the first course of white borsch was served, a three-piece
ensemble began to play wafts of classical music. The atmosphere was
ideal romance.

   This did not prevent my companions from being morose. While
shopping this afternoon, Kathy Jo stopped in a flower boutique. A
young man bought a bouquet stunning in color and composition. She
complimented the bouquet. He said that he was on his way to the
American Embassy to add the bouquet to the memorial wall in honor
of his friends. With welling eyes he explained that his three friends
were sent to New York City for company training. They worked in the
World Trade Center and had completed all training required. They
were scheduled to return home, to come back to Poland. Now they
are lost. He broke into tears. Kathy Jo embraced him and began to
cry. Both stood lost in the comfort of each other's sorrows. For one
long moment their muffled embrace closed shop to usual market noise.
Everyone fell silent. The young man tightly held her hand, and with
whispered parting words of empathy released it and departed.

   Upon hearing the story, I was almost at tears, unable to speak.
Kathy Jo and Doris filled the heavy air with complaints. They were
ready to go home ever since Gdańsk, feeling dragged and prodded by
our group to continue the tour. I mentioned some cherished events I
was thankful for experiencing. They agreed with each other that if they
knew the world events that did happen beforehand, they would never
have ventured on the plane. I would not agree with them. For some
reason we were on a plane when the attacks occurred, and in Saint
Peter's square for the Pope's moving speech. Equally, there is a reason

for our witnessing the American Embassy of flowers and prayers and longing for home while still cherishing the journey. They would not have had solace with the young man or anyone else. The main course was served: bigos and potatoes, pure hunter's stew. Many were happy with this authentic cuisine, yet the gloomy atmosphere at our table would not dissipate.

Doris and Kathy Jo commiserated; all worldly travels and adventures they would readily exchange for one more day with their husbands. My sensibilities would fathom a love so dear to rescind all others. Conversely, I could not consider a husband that would deny these experiences that would refuse the journey. My thoughts were kept to themselves boiling with teetering lid.

Matthew scuttled by, trying to be sly, and offered me the opportunity to present gratitude and monetary token to Antoni. The offer I could not refuse: the oldest member of the group was presenting the gift to Edward and I the youngest needed to present to Antoni. Matthew suggested I compose a short speech of thanks and remembrance. As soon as he left I began to think of various ways to express appreciation while conversing at table, not justifying either strain of thought.

Brendon called for attention; he had a special announcement. While researching his multiple family lines this afternoon, he discovered over fifty surnames that were related to his. In one of those lines, a famous poet was born. He took credit for, therefore, being directly related to creative genius. To quiet him, we clapped. I was stunned, could not remember the name of the poet the instant he pronounced it. Brendon sat and began to list all fifty surnames on a cocktail napkin. David stood from his seat across from Brendon and excused himself for a moment.

David approached every table to photograph; ours was the last as his digital camera consumed its battery. The ladies urged him to add a chair to our table and eat dessert with us. Thankfully he obliged, and the conversation finally changed tune. Confused and amazed by the digital camera, the ladies questioned David on all functions of the camera leading into exposition on technology and his career as a computer programmer. Fascinated, the ladies lifted their spirits for the first today. Compliments rolled through air like smoke in a tobacco shop, leaving a coating on all it touched.

Switching trains of thought, David expressed his frustration with Brendon. "He is obsessed," David noted, obsessed with his heritage being incomparable to all else in his mind. Since Kornik, he needed to trace an artist in one line or else he would go mad. All of David's spare time had been spent in libraries and cemeteries searching for ancestors. He lamented momentarily. There would be another trip; he was young and prosperous.

Suddenly, Matthew lapsed into grand marshall-of-ceremony mode. I was asked to perform, ill prepared. In the center of the floor, I stood and explained what I was asked to do. Some hecklers yelled that I should say the speech in Polish, to which I simply shook my head no in reply. With light heart and sincere demeanor I thanked him: "From the rainy streets of Gdańsk through the bright gardens of Chopin, you guided us. For this we are truly thankful and give this token of our appreciation."

Antoni was still eating dessert, in his private world of sweetness. Surprised, he stood to accept the envelope with a gentle handshake. He embraced me with all the kindness and kinship I felt throughout the journey: in the words of the Pope, in the gray eyes of the grandmother in the Gdańsk cafeteria, in the midnight conversation with Kasia, in Jacek's extraordinary research assistance, in the curious peaking through cover of renovation. A lovelier gesture could not have ended this journey. I gave him a brilliant smile of gratitude and we parted warmly.

Someone said in a half-whisper that Antoni and I would make a cute couple, out of my earshot. Matthew bellowed with the conviction of a wronged priest, "one is married and one is single!"

The comment was out of context for most of the room, only Matthew's table knew the original comment to incite his anger. No one knew how to react to his brash statement. All conversation ceased. Flushed, I sat in embarrassment, abashed. Jokes of elopement with European strangers I take sportingly but not with married men, however attractive. This comment was not a joke; I took offense accordingly.

Jean, as the oldest member of our group although not the oldest looking, presented thanks to Edward now. In contrast, she said a few words in Polish, in personal quiet. He kissed her hand and cheek in gratitude and affection. My dismay subsided, as their exchange was proportionate to Antoni's and mine.

It was Jean's eightieth birthday. She did not want a fuss, therefore Matthew shouted birthday greetings and required the ensemble to play "Happy Birthday" and we all sang to her, first in English then in Polish. "Happy Birthday" in Polish I knew from childhood. She was happily embarrassed. Subtly changing mood, the ensemble played my song, "Amazing Grace." I was transfixed.

Encouraged, Mom, Marie and I, along with a few others, sang. The words flew, as they always do, with peaceful stirring of dove's wings for distant lands. "We've no less days to sing God's praise then when we first begun." I gazed at Mom who winked at me. Drawing near their table, Dad said he was proud of me and of our journey together. My sentimental moment was extinguished by din over anthem.

A rousing version of "God Bless America" pulled everyone from chairs to nearly shout the verses. Tranquilly, I sang too. Energy consumed by ringing patriotism, we filed through the maze of tables to the doors. The ensemble now a reception line at the exit, everyone in turn thanked and complimented their efforts. The night wind called through the patio umbrellas. Satisfied we returned to our cordial hotel to organize for tomorrow's flight.

Kicking off my shoes, I needed a drink to face the task ahead. The nectar of half a glass of wine would placate mounting anxieties. Lou was passing by and offered a glass of Italian white wine in her room. Gladly, I accompanied her. She displayed on her bed the day's treasures procured at the market. We sipped the last of her wine from the vineyards of Tivoli and surveyed the lovely figurines, lace napkins and table clothes, crystal wine goblets and street artist's portrait of her. The most prized object was carefully arranged in box and cotton wrap: a pewter statuette of the Pope with hand-painted detailing of robes and peaceful expression. Lou was proud of all of her souvenirs, already knowing the spaces in her home where she would display these treasures of the journey. Thoughtfully, she found a special place for each in satchel and carpetbag. Configuring her luggage, I thanked her for the nightcap and wondered down the hall toward my room in stocking feet.

Matthew came out of the elevator with a wheelchair full of alcohol and soda. This loot would never be accepted as carry-on luggage in the plane tomorrow, he explained in jest and jibe. He invited me to a party in his room, which I accepted. The jovial group already had at least one nightcap each. We were all slightly tipsy. David just purchased a book of the origins of names. Gleefully, Matthew interpreted the Polish text in the way only a tipsy old man with a raw sense of humor could. It was a free interpretation, as each person had one's name reviewed for its eschewed, ribald meaning. We laughed and drank. Shot of Chopin vodka became warm in my hand as it was sipped over half an hour. Each exposure lit lips and throat aflame. Instantly, Matthew pushed shot of Gold Vassar into my hand, seeing Chopin vodka finally imbibed. I had had more than enough. As this merry group teased and prodded each other, the bathroom sink guzzled my shot of Gold Vassar undetected. I know my limitations.

While the others still tippled and roared with humor, I meandered through hallway to elevator, stocking feet cold.

Once again, I found myself knocking on the hotel room door late at night, waking Marie. Tonight she was in a better state of mind, and did not reprimand but fell into bed with resolution. Instantly I accepted the posh warmth of pierzina and poduszka, and, after scribbling, slept the dreamless, careless sleep of a drunken sailor.

"Do you have the maps? Make sure you have the maps."
— MARIE IN HER SLEEP.

WARSAW, AT LAST SIGHT

EARLY, I WOKE melancholy and grew darker as the day progressed. Lying in my supple bed anticipating the day and waxing nostalgic already, I listened to Marie's garbled talk. She too was concerned for the journey home; only she would not allow worry to overcome any moment of pleasure. Sleep colors worries daylight bleaches. Marie woke like a clock, 6:30, immediately beginning her morning rituals. I double-checked my packing: both ribbon and chestnut were placed in the zippered inner pocket of my tote, everything accounted. We prepared to meet church-going members of the group in the lobby to attend 8:00 a.m. mass at the Church of the Sacred Heart. There was no internal struggle of participation this week; I wanted to see the resting-place of Chopin's heart. Edward was kind enough to take us there so early, after a late night.

On the sidewalk in front of the church a young man in a wheelchair sat facing the street. One leg ended at mid-thigh. He held a sign, saying in Polish that he was injured in an accident and needed money for a prosthetic leg. Some gave him coins as we ascended the massive whitewashed stone staircase to the entry.

The church was packed to capacity. Our group split into smaller units to sit wherever two or three empty seats permitted. Marie went to sit in the second row, while Mom, Dad and I sat in the first available section, five pews from the back. The pews were narrow and at an inverted angle, forcing one to sit straight or slide to the edge of the seat. Good posture brings attention. Our seats were diagonally across from Chopin's heart, very close. Ornate gold script on pure white billowing column heralded the resting-place. The column resembled a cumulus cloud reaching toward the heavenly vaulted ceiling. The mass began. In Polish, I understood little, which gave me leave the marvel in my surroundings for an hour.

The sweeping arches of the white ceiling cradled streaks of blue with gold stars. Small altars and statues hid along either side. Every view led to and from Chopin's heart, a glorious eternal home. The many manifestations of God strike awe into spirit. God inspires reverence of the heart of a beautiful, complex musician. God strengthens reserve to conserve and rebuild churches, palaces and communities from wartime destruction. Yet the same God is excuse to terrorize and kill. The only way we overcome this dichotomy is to accept the god in others, acknowledge the buddhisatva in everyone. Personal altars of heart preserved could manifest the goodness each one has given to the world. How would my personal altar be inscribed? Rhythmic prayers in Polish inspire meditation in ways only the music of language could produce.

The ushers holding baskets for offerings circulated, beginning in the front. Dad was nervous; he usually donates and had no money left. I sifted through my purse and gave him my second last bill. The last was reserved to buy lunch for the three of us. Dad winked at me, accepting the bill.

As the usher approached, Dad relinquished the money in a stately manner. The usher looked at me. I bowed my head to him.

He said, "Bóg Zaptać." I smiled at him. He continued.

I turned to Dad for translation, which he whispered, into my ear. "God bless you."

A papal blessing could not mean more. Maybe I am less doomed now.

At the sign of peace, Dad and I shook hands; I kissed Mom's cheek. We offered handshakes to those around welcoming the gesture. I offered a half-smile and soft bow to others near who did not handshake. This gesture was received with a smile by most. If they were amused or appreciative of the gesture I do not know, probably both. The organ burst forth in glorious song, calling attention to the main altar.

After mass, Matthew called our group members to assembly. He wished to give a brief tour of Church of the Sacred Heart on our own. Crowds were gathering to form tours awaiting guides. Parishioners were departing and entering for the next service. Worrying about adhering to the stricked schedule of today, a couple people went directly to the bus. We participated in Matthew's tour, just beginning at the tomb of Chopin's heart. Interrupting, two came to retrieve us, as most were on the bus ready to go. Leaving the marble and fresco of the brilliant church, we descended the stairs to see once more the handicapped young man. Matthew stopped to speak with him.

The young man told his story, however briefly, of an accident claiming his leg. With monetary donations, he is saving for a prosthetic leg so he could rejoin society as a working, capable person. Several from our group gave him money and words of encouragement. With hearts filled with the satisfaction of a good deed done, everyone entered the bus to return to the hotel for breakfast and luggage.

In our hotel room, Marie and I double-checked our packing, ensuring that every item was secure and in its place, knowing that airport security will go through everything thoroughly. To remember our trip together, Marie gave me krakupani, a doll dressed in traditional folk garb. It was a sweet and sentimental gift that simultaneously evoked feelings of gladness, joy and bitter anticipation of the end. I embraced her with thanks.

Breakfast was eaten with the relish of peasants indulging in Christmas dinner. Dad went to the buffet twice for herring. I nibbled my hard-boiled brown egg and popover. Most of all, the red currant juice was savored and drained from table. Now, we were truly ready for the day.

The Sunday morning streets were empty as we rode to Wilanówie Palace. Edward parked one block away, so we strolled by shops secured for the day off until we reached the park and lawns leading to Sobieski's tomb and the gate to Wilanówie Palace. Sobieski built the palace for his wife, for he truly loved his wife, rare in a king. Initially trees along the path hid the tomb from view until in the center of the park. Then, expanse burst forth in open lawns and to the left, the gothic spires and mythological scenes carved into the stonewalls stole the view. The life-size stone likenesses of king and queen lie together, side by side, across the scenes on the base and staring at the infinite scrollwork of the canopy. Remaining on the path, we gaped at the sight before pausing at the gates, not yet open. The god of war spied our movements from the left pillar, cannon at the ready, while the god of justice peered from the right pillar, shield lolling at her side unused on a lazy Sunday morning. There was little for these gods to survey, for we were the only ones in the autumn-colored park.

As the admission booth opened, a lady joined our group for the tour. She spoke in Polish to Antoni and Matthew. The gods were just in protecting this palace as fortress walls and fountains ensconced the circular courtyard. The lawns alone sprawled a city block. The palace would not end: Corinthian columns introduced doorways and arched windows of each wing; baroque towers pronounced both corners where one wing met another. Wilanowie Palace was comparable in size and magnificence to the Royal Palace. Yet, it did not suffer physical ravages of the war, structure and contents entact. All aspects of this palace were original seventeenth century inspiration.

Our tour guide was waiting for us, a kind older lady with a tight perm and firm voice. Her knowledge was apparent instantly with the great details she explained upon entering the first basement room. The palace was primarily an art museum now, holding original furnishings and using every section of wall space industriously to display as much artwork as possible. Beyond salon style is opulence. Every nook and panel exhibited a treasure, offering itself for exploration. Can one open eyes wide enough to see it all? As the tour continued, I focused on works that captured interest rather than works our guide was pointing out. Landscape paintings, romantic portraits, moldings, frames and curious views demanded attention. I could not attend to all of them; it was impossible at the speed of the tour. I wondered if Wincenty created any of these works. The structure of the tour inhibited my asking. Yet, the probability was favorable that at least one he sponsored.

Four gentlemen from Sudan, touring the palace independently, joined our group for the guided tour. They followed directly behind the guide, so I did not have the opportunity to interact with them. Matthew had consumed the breaks in between lectures with conversation.

Through the imperials halls of state business and banquets we traveled into the once private wing of the palace. In the king's dressing room a white border encompassed the aqua walls: rich ribbon circled and swayed to shields of crest, one centered on each wall. Lions and spears protected each crest from the retreating ribbons. On one curious wall panel the pattern was altered, a man's head with handlebar mustache was impaled on a spear. I Moved through the group to Matthew and asked him whose likeness that is, expecting a historical answer. Matthew replied it was Brendon after dinner last night, and raced to reclaim his position at the head of the group.

The anteroom to the children's bedroom was sky blue. Cherubs in clouds lounged and played across the ceiling, however the border to this fresco contained the most telling element of the palace: a cat, ready to pounce hiding half behind a sconce, while two bluebirds cavort. One bird is about to take flight staring at the cherubs, while the other sits looking ahead oblivious of danger. Which bird will the cat strike? Very witty. A pleasant and unexpected juxtaposition with the ornate renaissance scene of the heavens, this inconspicuous hunt must have been enjoyed by the youthful residents. Are pouncing cats in heaven? These artists had a wonderful sense of humor.

Another corridor revealed another wing, this one formal and stately. Portraits filled all useable space, room upon room, until one portrait in gentle beseachment grabbed undivided attention. She was nestled by the French doors, content with the view of the gardens and Roman bath. She was a peasant girl, a farmer's daughter in field of green and blue. Although she would not tell me her name, I knew what she was doing, the laundry, or another outdoor chore. Yet she is thinking beyond her work and swings a shawl in front of her. Her black curly hair hung wildly across her back as the wind furls her shawl. Her eyes glisten in pure amusement, imploring me to join her. Her dancing arms and waving shawl create a circle, or more an infinity symbol. She is infinite. In joy she is infinite. I turn to attend to the guided facts, but her vision will not release me. She has been twirling, swirling in the natural elation of life. I want to dance with her. And in her telling vision I know I already am a whirl of grateful, joyful spirit. She elicits that response. She is beautiful, this peasant girl of infinite vision. For her introduction alone the tour was worthwhile. Unwillingly I follow the group into the adjacent room. It is unnecessary to say farewell to her.

The tour looped and ended at the entrance. Peering through shop windows, it was Sunday, stores closed. A museum clerk opened one store selling crystal. A line formed as a new group commenced the tour with shopping. The store selling books remained closed, so I was not tempted to spend my last lunch money.

The noontime sun shone dimly through the foreboding clouds. The courtyard filled with other tourists. A few street vendors lined the park thoroughfare now. At the edge of the courtyard by the gates of war and justice, it was suggested that we take a last group picture. The quiet Polish lady who had toured with us was invited into the group along with the gentlemen from Sudan. As we congregated, Don composing the shot, Matthew loudly introduced these gentlemen and two of the four men chose not to be photographed. After the round of pictures, several must be taken so that one may actually turn out well; I approached the two men standing to the side observing and thanked them for joining us. Their journey had just begun. I offered best wishes for a wonderful trip. As they meandered through the garden, we exited the gate into the park. The Polish lady had quickly departed with private farewell to few.

Swarming around the vendor's kiosks, some relished another shopping opportunity. I browsed knowing I would not buy. A few items did tempt me, but they were more than I had. The tomb of Sobieski called for exploration. Dad and I answered the call. Four lions holding crests guarded the corners of the tomb, yet they were not fierce but domesticated. They would wag their tails for a scratch behind the ears. Dad explored the perimeter as I ascended the steps to study the intricate sculpture scenes in four panels at the base. Angels blessed carvings of artist and muses. Were they mythological or representations of Sobieski and his beloved wife? Their effigies would not tell the secret. These panels repeated themselves on each side of the base, an important theme.

Descending, I introduced myself to a friendly lion holding a crest with front paws. We instantly created rapport. Dad posed the camera from below and I hugged the lion. My new friend welcomed the quixotic affection on this chilly afternoon. On the ground, I met Dad for a last walk around the perimeter before finding the group. The panels marked the activity with precision: the artist sculpting a bust in view of the muses; the central muses notes a document with artist's pallet, and the far right muse holds an embossed document while glancing at the artist.

The group dispersed. Some gathered at street side waiting for the bus to arrive. They were the most anxious about the flight. Dad went to this group to join Mom. I found Marie still shopping at a kiosk. Several people, including Matthew, relaxed on park benches, watching the last couple people shop. Matthew then stood to gather the remainder and everyone fell into line. Antoni mentioned that the bus was to meet us one block eas:, not at the entrance where half the group was loitering. I jogged and wrangled the small excitable group and led them to the correct area. Walking with Mom and Dad, we passed a church next to the park. The church was overflowing with parishioners. People congregated outside to hear the mass on loudspeaker, no more room inside. In times of stress people become faithful, Mom commented. Yet in our experiences, Poles seem faithful overall, enduring.

Edward met us, and boarding quietly, we rode to the airport. For the last time, Matthew required us to call roll. Sixteen, I said monotonously.

"Who is sixteen?" Edward gently questioned Antoni.

"Sixteen is swimming in melancholy; she is unapproachable." Antoni responded.

"No," Edward retorted, "She is overwhelmed, sentimental, thinking too much of experiences." Antoni raised eyebrow and sat in silence.

Again, the American Embassy was noticed: the retaining wall memorial, flanked by guards in militia gear, grew in candlelight, flowers, prayers and banners. Across the street Lazienski Park rested with few occupants leisurely strolling. Lazienski Park was our last scheduled tour, but the palace tour ran long and the airport security is now requiring at least four hours to inspect before flight. Edward stopped the bus and we were able to look into the park. A meditative Chopin was seated under a breezy willow tree. The statue was as lively and elegant as his music.

The green tree lined boulevard of our arrival was now apple, pumpkin and corn-colored in the thick of autumn. The traffic became dense. Edward fought for curbside parking. He ensured that everyone had all belongings before a handshake and wave goodbye. We were hurried into a line and asked to produce plane ticket and passport to army guards before entering the building. I did not hear Edward pull away.

Antoni guided us to the line for international screening; he would stay with us until our group was past this checkpoint to ensure we were together and secure. Everyone completed a form declaring any electronic devices or any potentially dangerous tools. Kathy Jo and Doris were ahead of Marie and me, with Mom and Dad at the end of the line. After scanning their bags, security opened every compartment of their bags and unpacked everything, scrutinizing as they proceeded. I knew I was next. I braced for the impeding by unlocking zippers and declaring every electrical item (hairdryer and CD player) and every pointed object (pen) in my possession. It was my turn. The guard in army camouflage took my report and questioned me in Polish. I asked if he spoke English. He smiled and shook his head, no. I proceeded to explain that our group toured Poland for two weeks and we were already here when the attack occurred; I had nothing extraordinary to declare, however welcomed him to search my luggage. A lady scanned my bags. The guard approached her, handing her my declaration. Then the guard spoke to the guard watching the scanner and the girl, they laughed. I thought they would begin to tear apart my bags. The guard waved me through the checkpoint, not one thing neither opened nor disturbed. I thanked him, smiling, and continued to baggage check. From then on, no one questioned my carry-on backpack or me. Marie had her bags searched, dismantled. Mom did not. Dad's luggage was thoroughly examined. He was forced to surrender his disposable razor; we did not understand why.

Once baggage and passports were checked, we were free to roam through the corridors for two hours before flight time. Our group converged on a small café with a dozen tables and quickly took over the scene. Dad was too nervous to eat. We decided to have bottled water and muffins for lunch, which left me with five złoty. We pooled our pocket change together and found enough money to purchase a box of Chopin chocolates. These would be saved for a special occasion at home, Christmas dessert.

The uncertainty that I flew into was overwhelming: going home to no job, wondering what to do next. Do I go back to teaching? Will my struggling new catering business succeed or fail in this recession and possible war? Should I go back to school to become a professor? What will end and what will begin anew? These are many possibilities with no one easy answer. Solutions still eluded my consciousness.

My parents knew enough of my anxiety to give me space, thankfully. Marie also knew but has a heart that tries to sympathize. She attempted jokes and banal conversation. Nothing much worked until we entered the passport gates and began to shop. Looking through shops of Polish treasures reminded us of the extraordinary journey we have collectively experienced: krukuvienke dolls swing through the arms of their partners as they dance as we dine the first night of European experience; showcases of amber jewelry harkens seagulls and fisherman on the Sopot Pier, an empty cruise ship to Hel; cabinets of crystal goblets and decanters whisper royal memories of an amalgam of palace salons, castle halls.

A huge, unorganized line formed at the gate for the last checkpoint. There was still an hour before flight time. Mom, Marie and I rustled through gift shops to view Polish essentials one last time: amber jewelry, hand painted eggs, crystal and gold Vassar. Then we realized that the haphazard line was filtering all international flights, Paris, London and Toronto, and we needed to be in that line. An hour to spare transformed into a rush as Mom, Dad and Marie, along with every other person in line, had their carry on bags disassembled.

My backpack and purse proceeded intact. I glided through with a respectful smile. Chestnut and yellow ribbon secure in the zipped compartment of my purse lining. The Pope was nestled in backpack. Dharma beads were ensconced in the bottom of backpack, next to the Pope.

Security questioned the authenticity of Mom's prescription medication. They were being extraordinarily thorough. Our plane was boarding. Although I was clear to pass, I waited for them. Mom's sewing scissors and nail file were confiscated along with Marie's Swiss army knife. They did not care as long as they were able to get on the plane. Dad relinquished the right to any personal privacy, nearly dumping his toiletry bag as he unfastened it wide.

Amazingly Marie's leaves from Gorzno were not confiscated, nor even harmed, but neatly wrapped in napkins in the lining of her cosmetic bag. Once more, Peg's dried rose from Rome proceeded through security without detection. Her sweet remembrance was still fragrant. Alma too, had the luck of a pilgrim: her father's bark meshed into jewelry boxes it was nestled within and was never questioned. All of our sentimental contraband remained protected and protective.

We were the last to board the plane, glad to be allowed aboard. Mom and Dad settled into seats quickly, nervously, and then reassembled their bags. Marie, frazzled, would not sit until her disheveled bags were in acceptable order. In frenzied thought, I would not have minded time to go to the gallery, park and library, or explore for a few leisurely days. Not to mention that Krakow and Wilne were waiting for me.

Ends are much more difficult than beginnings.

Following the sun and pushing forward the time zones, I did not feel the need to be home until the mysterious blue-gray Atlantic floated underneath us. I had not said goodbye to Antoni or to Edward. I am horrible with good-byes; they always induce tears and kicked puppy expressions. Sadness begins when activity and expressions of life transform into glimpses of memory already vague and idealized. When life cannot return to its previous state, that is a true journey. I have traveled far.

We flew into the light, never really having the opportunity to rest. A stewardess spilled hot water for tea down Matthew's front. He had burn marks on his chest and abdomen and was required to file an accident report with the airline. The plane landed in darkness and we readied for a long wait on the Peace Bridge. Those arches that heralded a peaceful journey were now black in starless midnight. This was the last hurtle, the new strict and fearful guidelines we would live by.

Fortunately, there were short lines. Only a short line of commercial trucks was stalled. The inspector instructed us to park at the depot for an elaborate search of all luggage and identification. The patrol guards within the depot, after seeing the exhausted expressions on our faces and understanding that we were Americans coming home, recalled the demand and did not inspect luggage. As each of our passports was checked, we received a soft "welcome back" from the desk clerk. Relieved, we boarded the bus for our last destination as a group, as our group, Saint Barbara's Church parking lot.

The fifteen minutes between The Peace Bridge and Saint Barbara's Church was enough time for me to finally fall asleep. My head nodded and bobbed meaninglessly as Marie loudly prattled about topics I could not comprehend in slumber. Her keen voice was comforting though. My eyes flickered, attempting to remain awake for these last few moments of the journey. But I could not.

Saint Barbara's Church sat blankly on the ridge. We pulled into the parking lot where the streetlights remained lit, anticipating our arrival. Many relatives were there waiting to see us disembark, to be the first of family to embrace us. We were home now.

James was waiting in the parking lot for us, as tall and lean as Saint Barbara's turret. I knew he would be here for us no matter the time of day or night. Exhaustion would not overtake concern for all to have the comfort and safety of their luggage, their welcoming family member and ride home. A round of hugs and kisses welcomed James and said goodbye to each member of our group no longer banded by circumstance, our touring company, our new friends.

Travel makes home foreign, reviving the senses, precepts discarded.

LACKAWANNA, NEW YORK, UNITED STATES–HOME

THE MOROSE EMOTIONS have subsided into nostalgia. My heart and mind are filled with new ideas and experiences: Michelangelo's candy wrapper, the ancient seated tree of Villa D'Este gardens, holding Wincenty's book, viewing Grace and Wisdom in the Summer Palace. For these, I am truly thankful.

I love to travel, to explore the world and learn the lessons it must teach. Then I love to return home to the safety of acceptance and familiarity where no explanation is necessary. Home is enhanced by journeying away; details come alive with the newness of appreciation. Home is a medicine bag in need of gems and herbs of experience to progress.

During the tour I acquired some fine habits I wish to sustain: healthy, regular eating patterns of fresh food; walking to explore and exercise mind and body; writing without fail or reservation. I have eaten better than I do at home, varying fruits, vegetables and grains rather than eating quick pasta or fast food. Exercise outside of work is vital.

Just walking activates body and mind. I feel healthier now than when I departed for the journey. Most importantly, I am inspired. Writing everyday without reservation, without fail, and without criticism allows ideas to mature, the metamorphosis of experience into wisdom. Also, ideas for stained glass windows dance in mind, another inspiration. Miniature representations of some of the windows I studied will be a wonderful start. Attempting to translate Wincenty's woodcuts into glass is another inspired challenge. I shall try to nurture these new habits in a new lifestyle.

Some people, some habits do not change. As Dad was emptying his luggage this afternoon I shuttered. He had scavenged and pilfered, as I did not know. Spoons and plastic cups from the airplane were in his toiletry bag; a small pitcher he received at room service in Rome was among his clothes; soaps and shampoos from every hotel were in chronological order of acquisition on his dresser. With all this he had successfully absconded without notice. I am appalled. I am amused. What is the difference between finding value in a leaf or a chestnut and finding value in a plastic cup or travel size shampoo? Dad always surprises me.

I think of digging graves now: of contacting relatives formerly unreachable, of outlining family history, not to revel in a romantic idealism of past eras but to learn why and how it speaks to the future. The idea of rummaging through church documents and state notices to trace lineage that I once found dull is now intriguing. Brendon, although lacking in decorum, was right: the bonds of lineage are stronger when they are known in detail. Mom's lineage also has lessons to tell. With a beheaded saint in her family line, she entices me to research her family as well. With this in mind I tease her with tentative plans for a journey to Alsace, France, the Nicaise family origin. In turn, Mom should bask in the immortal sunshine of heritage while Dad holds the supportive hand. However, this is for another time of its own, another set of lessons and family folklore, another book to be written.

Traveling under stressful world events, the terrorist attacks, reflects the brightest qualities of the people we encountered—illuminating kindness, morality and depth of sympathy of peoples around the world. The artist in Fountain Plaza of Rome expressed condolence. With Kasia of Gorzno, we joked and laughed to banish worry. With Antoni, always curious, we peaked at the restoration work behind curtains of diligence at Saint Adalbert's Cathedral in Gnieznie. The German lady at dinner in Warsaw cautioned against residual prejudice. Terror has not broken the capitalist systems of the world, but has united people of varying religions and races who cherish freedom, who cherish the right to be one's self while being tolerant of other selves. Without retaliation, the free world has overcome terrorism with ubiquitous love, respected connection. And with this, Americans may begin to rebuild our sacred edifices and our spirits.

In war tomorrow is vague. Plans are tentative. Senses heighten as if each glimpse and emotion would be the last. Maybe this was good—a way to view the world with utmost appreciation, utmost tenderness. With this state of being we tread and will remember all that was lost on September 11th and all that is experienced forthwith.

New friendships have begun. With any hope, these fledgling friendships born in peace and discovery will grow. And if they fade, we have made impressions. With every encounter we leave impressions of being American, of being young or old, of being a tourist, of being individual, of being thoughtful. However slight or great, these impressions will last and may change perspective.

I am awed by this journey. It will be carried with me until dawn closes day, and even then, thankfully reside within. My Polish American heart is full, continually replenishing itself in the hope of old things to come.

So to my new friends and supportive relations, to those I have affected and who have affected me, I end and begin with a poem.

The sky is clear blue.
Refreshing times flow gently
Where I last saw you.

ACKNOWLEDGMENTS

The writing process brought many people to my aid that I wish to thank many times over. Special thanks to David Newman who helped insure that all of the Polish language within the book was correct. Many thanks go to my Polish Language teacher Wanda Chomiska for her enthusiasm about the project. Also, special thanks go to Marcella Corallo and Gianna Daddi for insight into the Italian way of life and language. There were many people who read various editions of the book in order to come to a final version: Mary Mach, James Smokowski, Daniel Kij, Frances Smokowski and David Newman. Most importantly, many, many thanks to Brian McKenzie without whose love, support and encouragement I would not have had the tenacity to publish this book.

Printed in the United States
64385LVS00006B/61-78